ERP &
Data Warehousing in Organizations: Issues and Challenges

Gerald Grant
Carleton University, Canada

IRM Press
Publisher of innovative scholarly and professional
information technology titles in the cyberage

Hershey • London • Melbourne • Singapore • Beijing

Acquisitions Editor: Mehdi Khosrow-Pour
Senior Managing Editor: Jan Travers
Managing Editor: Amanda Appicello
Development Editor: Michele Rossi
Copy Editor: Ingrid Widitz
Typesetter: Amanda Appicello
Cover Design: Michelle Waters
Printed at: Integrated Book Technology

Published in the United States of America by
        IRM Press (an imprint of Idea Group Inc.)
        1331 E. Chocolate Avenue, Suite 200
        Hershey PA 17033-1117
        Tel: 717-533-8845
        Fax: 717-533-8661
        E-mail: cust@idea-group.com
        Web site: http://www.irm-press.com

and in the United Kingdom by
        IRM Press (an imprint of Idea Group Inc.)
        3 Henrietta Street
        Covent Garden
        London WC2E 8LU
        Tel: 44 20 7240 0856
        Fax: 44 20 7379 3313
        Web site: http://www.eurospan.co.uk

Library of Congress Cataloging-in-Publication Data

Grant, Gerald G.
   ERP & data warehousing in organizations : issues and challenges /
Gerald Grant.
        p. cm.
Also available in electronic form.
   ISBN 1-931777-49-7 (soft-cover) -- ISBN 1-931777-65-9 (e-book)
   1. Management information systems. 2. Data warehousing. I. Title:
ERP and data warehousing in organizations. II. Title.
   HD30.213.G73 2003
   658.4'012--dc21

                                                    2002156235

British Cataloguing in Publication Data
A Cataloguing in Publication record for this book is available from the British Library.

New Releases from IRM Press

- **Multimedia and Interactive Digital TV: Managing the Opportunities Created by Digital Convergence**/Margherita Pagani
  ISBN: 1-931777-38-1; eISBN: 1-931777-54-3 / US$59.95 / © 2003
- **Virtual Education: Cases in Learning & Teaching Technologies**/ Fawzi Albalooshi (Ed.), ISBN: 1-931777-39-X; eISBN: 1-931777-55-1 / US$59.95 / © 2003
- **Managing IT in Government, Business & Communities**/Gerry Gingrich (Ed.)
  ISBN: 1-931777-40-3; eISBN: 1-931777-56-X / US$59.95 / © 2003
- **Information Management: Support Systems & Multimedia Technology**/ George Ditsa (Ed.), ISBN: 1-931777-41-1; eISBN: 1-931777-57-8 / US$59.95 / © 2003
- **Managing Globally with Information Technology**/Sherif Kamel (Ed.)
  ISBN: 42-X; eISBN: 1-931777-58-6 / US$59.95 / © 2003
- **Current Security Management & Ethical Issues of Information Technology**/Rasool Azari (Ed.), ISBN: 1-931777-43-8; eISBN: 1-931777-59-4 / US$59.95 / © 2003
- **UML and the Unified Process**/Liliana Favre (Ed.)
  ISBN: 1-931777-44-6; eISBN: 1-931777-60-8 / US$59.95 / © 2003
- **Business Strategies for Information Technology Management**/Kalle Kangas (Ed.)
  ISBN: 1-931777-45-4; eISBN: 1-931777-61-6 / US$59.95 / © 2003
- **Managing E-Commerce and Mobile Computing Technologies**/Julie Mariga (Ed.)
  ISBN: 1-931777-46-2; eISBN: 1-931777-62-4 / US$59.95 / © 2003
- **Effective Databases for Text & Document Management**/Shirley A. Becker (Ed.)
  ISBN: 1-931777-47-0; eISBN: 1-931777-63-2 / US$59.95 / © 2003
- **Technologies & Methodologies for Evaluating Information Technology in Business**/ Charles K. Davis (Ed.), ISBN: 1-931777-48-9; eISBN: 1-931777-64-0 / US$59.95 / © 2003
- **ERP & Data Warehousing in Organizations: Issues and Challenges**/Gerald Grant (Ed.), ISBN: 1-931777-49-7; eISBN: 1-931777-65-9 / US$59.95 / © 2003
- **Practicing Software Engineering in the 21ˢᵗ Century**/Joan Peckham (Ed.)
  ISBN: 1-931777-50-0; eISBN: 1-931777-66-7 / US$59.95 / © 2003
- **Knowledge Management: Current Issues and Challenges**/Elayne Coakes (Ed.)
  ISBN: 1-931777-51-9; eISBN: 1-931777-67-5 / US$59.95 / © 2003
- **Computing Information Technology: The Human Side**/Steven Gordon (Ed.)
  ISBN: 1-931777-52-7; eISBN: 1-931777-68-3 / US$59.95 / © 2003
- **Current Issues in IT Education**/Tanya McGill (Ed.)
  ISBN: 1-931777-53-5; eISBN: 1-931777-69-1 / US$59.95 / © 2003

Excellent additions to your institution's library!
Recommend these titles to your Librarian!

To receive a copy of the IRM Press catalog, please contact
1/717-533-8845 ext. 10, fax 1/717-533-8661,
or visit the IRM Press Online Bookstore at: [http://www.irm-press.com]!

Note: All IRM Press books are also available as ebooks on netlibrary.com as well as other ebook sources. Contact Ms. Carrie Skovrinskie at [cskovrinskie@idea-group.com] to receive a complete list of sources where you can obtain ebook information or
IRM Press titles.

ERP & Data Warehousing in Organizations: Issues and Challenges

Table of Contents

Preface

In an increasingly complex business operating environment, organizations around the world face the twin challenge of creating and deploying information technology application infrastructure for information capture and sharing, and for making effective use of the information in decision making. Two categories of IT applications, enterprise resource planning (ERP) and data warehousing (DW), encapsulate the attempts by organizations to make more effective and proactive uses of organizational information to support strategic and tactical decision making.

ENTERPRISE RESOURCE PLANNING

Since the mid-1990s, companies worldwide have invested heavily in a variety of ERP systems from companies such as SAP_AG, Oracle, and Peoplesoft. Partly in a bid to renew IT infrastructure, and spurred to a large extent by the Y2K crisis, companies, using these commercial off-the-shelf software (COTS) packages, are attempting to create "seamless" integrated information environments that provide the agility and flexibility needed to pursue and support current and future growth. The deployment of these systems promises to end the information anarchy typically found in both private and public sector organizations. ERPs, like other enterprise systems, are designed to streamline data flows within and between organizations, providing management and other organizational members with direct access to real-time operating information (Davenport, 1998). When implemented effectively, these systems can provide a variety of strategic, organizational, operational, and technological opportunities (Ali, 2000; Markus & Tanis, 2000).

The ERP implementation experience has been and continues to be mixed. While there have been many notables successes (Kalakota & Robinson,1999; Davenport, 2000; Brown & Vessey, 2001), there have been a significant number of failures (Stedman, 1999; Schneider, 2000; Stedman, 2000a; Scott & Vessey, 2002). According to Markus et al. (2000), many of these failures seem to occur during the "shakedown" phase of the ERP implementation. Many organizations adopting ERP systems seem to be somewhat naïve about the risks faced in deploying such systems and are prone to panic when they run into trouble. Implementing an ERP system can be a tremendous business risk, and, as such, executives need to be cognizant of the risks faced and address them appropriately (Scott & Vessey, 2002).

Early generation ERP systems almost entirely focused on infrastructure renewal and creating efficiencies in back office operations around key functional areas such as finance and production management. These systems, while useful, did not address the mission critical issues such as supply chain management (SCM), customer relationship management (CRM), and knowledge management (KM). New generation systems have sought to address these shortcomings in a variety of ways. Also, while early generation ERP systems were found mainly in large organizations, newer systems are now being targeted at small and medium enterprises as means of expanding the ERP market.

The purported benefits of deploying ERP systems have been widely discussed. However, it is not entirely clear how these benefits can be realized in practice. To what extent does ERP implementation contribute to overall organizational effectiveness? What has been the impact of deploying ERP systems on organizations, their structures, their jobs, and their employees? How can they be used to facilitate collaborative work and information sharing? These and other issues will be addressed in the first seven chapters of the book.

DATA WAREHOUSING

Even when data is efficiently captured and stored, it may remain relatively useless for reporting and decision making purposes. Transaction and other data often need to be combined in order to provide useful information for those requiring it, be it senior decision makers or individual employees doing their assigned jobs. Data warehouses provide a mechanism for storing and combining data from a large number of sources for the purpose of querying, reporting and decision-making. Data warehouses are different from online transaction processing databases. They are "subject-oriented, integrated, time-variant, non-volatile collection of data" used to support decision making (Gray & Watson, 1998, p. 89).

Data warehousing was initially viewed as a way to solve the problems associated with independently maintained legacy data. Legacy data systems were originally developed to support functional activities such as accounting, sales and human resources. They often contained duplicate, dissimilar, or inaccurate information about the same entity. For example, three databases may have different renderings of the address of the same company. However, creating a single data warehouse to address the problems associated with non-integrated legacy data has itself proved to be difficult and problematic. Some of the difficulties relate to the nature of the data in a data warehouse, the cost and complexity of building and maintaining it, and the challenges associated with using the data contained in the warehouse.

Since single, large-scale data warehouses are proving to be too difficult to build and maintain, there is a move to develop distributed data warehouses. Distributed data warehouses, especially those built around Internet technology, hold the promise for increased functionality and usability, as well as reduced deployment costs (Hsieh & Lin, 2003).

Once a data warehouse is built, a number of issues related to obtaining useful information out of the warehouse arise. These include data quality, techniques for mining the data, and the correctness and relevance of the data. Chapters 8-14 of this book address these issues.

ORGANIZATION OF THE BOOK

This book is divided into two parts. The first seven chapters of the book focus on issues related to ERP systems and enterprise integration. The second part contains seven chapters addressing issues related to data warehousing and data utilization.

Part 1:   ERP Systems and Enterprise Integration

In Chapter 1, Hedman and Borell use an artifact evaluation approach to address the issue of ERP implementation and its impact on organizational effectiveness. Adopting the Competing Values Model (Quinn & Rohrbaugh, 1981; Rohrbaugh, 1981), they conducted an organizational level analysis of the impact of SAP R/3 enterprise system on the effectiveness of adopting organizations. Their evaluation suggests that there are both strengths and weaknesses associated with the ERP system as it relates to four organizational models. ERP systems are strong as they relate to internal process (IP) and their rational goal (RG) models of organization. ERPs have significant shortcomings in relation to human relations (HR) and open systems (OS) models.

Berlak and Deifel, in Chapter 2, propose a cybernetic model of order management to address the challenge of flexibility and responsiveness of order management systems (OMS) to variations in the business operating environment.

The decision process surrounding the selection of an ERP package is critical to the eventual success of the system deployment and use. Deciding on which ERP package to acquire is not a single decision but involves multiple iterative activities geared towards evaluating factors such as functionality, price, training requirements, and post-implementation maintenance of the acquired system. In Chapter 3, Bernroider and Koch propose a rational process model for ERP software acquisition. He uses empirical data obtained from a survey of Austrian organizations to investigate five hypotheses and every stage of the process acquisition model proposed. The findings suggest that smaller organizations adopt less complex approaches to ERP software acquisition and tend to expend less effort during all stages of the decision making process.

The first wave of ERP implementations focused primarily on IT infrastructure renewal in large organizations. With the market for large-scale ERP implementations slowing, software vendors such as SAP have begun to target small and medium enterprises with scaled-down versions of their products. The vendors have also turned their attention to developing software that provides extended functionality for interacting with customers, suppliers, and partners. Stein and Hawking provide insight into the penetration of SAP into the Australasian market. Using data supplied by SAP Asia-Pacific as well as three mini case studies, they trace the development and growth of the Australasian market for ERP software. They highlight the fact that as mature users of ERP seek to benefit from their previous investments they are more open to adopting software with additional functionality.

In Chapter 5, Schelp and Rowohl address the issue of enterprise application integration. They highlight the fact that because organizations operate in dynamic and heterogeneous environments; there is a growing and pervasive need for integrating applications across functions and processes. These needs cannot possibly be met by any single application such as an ERP system. However, solutions provided by either software vendors or scientists address only some portions of the complex problems associated with enterprise application integration. They call for an integrated approach and suggest some topics that an approach should address.

As organizations undertake the deployment of integrated ERP systems, concerns are growing about its impact on people occupying jobs and roles in those organizations. Grant and Uruthirapathy set out to assess the impact of ERP implementation on job characteristics. Using the Hackman and Oldham job characteristics model as a basis, the study assesses how ERP affected work redesign and job satisfaction of people working in several Canadian federal government organizations.

ERPs provide a collaborative environment where people perform a variety of tasks in their assigned roles. The effectiveness with which those tasks are performed is dependent on the level of awareness each actor has of the role as it exists in an ERP process map. In Chapter 7, Daneshgar introduces a conceptual object-oriented framework based on the notion of process awareness to assist in the analysis and design of ERP systems for virtual communities (VC).

Part II: Data Warehousing and Data Utilization

In the second part of the book, chapters addressing issues around data warehousing and data utilization are presented.

In the chapter, *Distributed Data Warehouse for Geo-spatial Services*, Sikder and Gangopadhyay address the issues and challenges involved with decision making using spatially distributed data and data models. Focusing on the specific area of geo-spatial data, they advance ideas for addressing the lack of standardization for re-use specification of existing spatial models, emphasizing the need to take a user or decision maker view. They present a prototype system, GEO-ELCA, to illustrate collaborative access to data and model for supporting spatial decision-making.

In Chapter 9, Lee, Otondo, Kim, Prasarnphanich and Nichols examine the use of data mining tools to address data mining for business process reengineering. While most data mining problems are solved using set-theoretic approaches, business process reengineering problems require graph-theoretic approaches to find a solution. Using the case of Poplar County Criminal Justice System (PCCJS), the researchers applied two different data mining technologies in an attempt to generate meaningful hypotheses for business process reengineering. They were successful in this effort even though they had to switch data mining technologies during the research.

In Chapter 10, Borchers discusses intrinsic and contextual data quality and the effects of media and personal involvement on these. Using a controlled experiment, the author tests four hypotheses about perceptions of data quality in information about cancer. The results of the experiment suggest that media is not a significant factor in perceptions of data quality. Limited support was found for the notion that people become more discriminating of data quality for topics they are personally involved with.

The next three chapters address issues concerning the effective use of healthcare information. In Chapter 11, Kraft, Desouza and Androwich provide a detailed discussion of the concept of healthcare information, particularly from a nursing perspective. They define core constructs such as healthcare informatics as well as address key issues related to healthcare records and databases. Through a data mining exploration of the Veteran's Health Administration (VHA) Spinal Cord Injury (SCI) clinical database, the researchers sought to discover if there were patterns of patient needs, nursing diagnoses, nursing interventions, and patient outcomes.

Gorla and Bennon demonstrate the use of data mining techniques, particularly clustering algorithms, to address the problem of duplicate patient information in healthcare information repositories. Duplicate data, arising from a number of sources, is a significant issue faced by health service providers because of the potential for misleading healthcare workers in making diagnoses or other interventions. The researchers used hierarchical, partitioned, and hybrid clustering algorithms to determine which approach produced the best results. Hybrid clustering methods appeared to be best.

In Chapter 13, Schuring and Spil introduce the notion of relevance and micro-relevance as precursors to actual information technology use in organizations. Based on their case studies of general practitioners' use of an electronic prescription system in the Netherlands, they assert that the sub-optimal use of IT systems will persist if there continues to be a mismatch between what is relevant to the user as opposed to the creators and owners of the system.

In the last chapter, Baim presents a proposal to create interactive websites in support of community policing programs. Data collected from residents in three communities highlighted varying degrees of readiness for use of interactive websites.

CONCLUSION

Addressing two very substantial subjects in one book is not only challenging but is destined to be inadequate. This book is not intended to provide definitive coverage of all the issues concerning either ERP or data warehousing. What it attempts to do is to provide insight into current thinking and research about two very important information management topics.

REFERENCES

Ali, M. K. (2000). Issues in implementing enterprise resource planning (ERP): A management perspective, MMS Research Project, School of Business, Carleton University.

Brown, C. V. & Vessey, I. (2001). Nibco's "Big Bang". *Communications of the AIS*, 5(1), January.

Davenport, T. (2000). Does ERP build a better business? *CIO Magazine*, (February 15, 2000), Accessed at http://www.cio.com/archive/021500_excerpt_ content.html.

Davenport, T. H. (1998). Putting the enterprise into the enterprise system. *Harvard Business Review*, (July-August), pp. 121-131.

Gray, P. & Watson, H. J. (1998). Present and future directions in data warehousing, *The Data Base for Advances in Information Systems*, Summer, pp. 83-90.

Hsieh, C. & Lin, B. (2003). Web-based data warehousing: current status and perspective, *Journal of Computer Information Systems*, Winter, pp. 1-8.

Markus, M. L. & Tanis, C. (2000). The enterprise system experience: From adoption to success. In Zmud, R. W. (Ed.), *Framing the Domains of IT Management: Projecting the Future through the Past*, Pinaflex Educational Resources, Inc., pp. 173-207.

Markus, M. L., Axline, S., Petrie, D. & Tanis, C. (2000). Learning from adopters' experiences with ERP: Problems encountered and success achieved, *Journal of Information Technology*, 15, pp. 245-265.

Schneider, P. (2000). Another trip to hell: Lessons learned. *CIO Magazine*, February 12, 2000, Accessed on June 27, 200 at: http://www2.cio.com/archive/021500_hell_content.html.

Scott, J. E. & Vessey, I. (2002). Managing the risks of enterprise systems implementations, *Communications of the ACM*, 45(4), April, pp. 74-81.

Stedman, C. (1999). Update: failed ERP gamble hurts Hershey, *ComputerWorld*, October, Accessed April 3, 2000 at http://www.computerworld.com/home/news.nsf/all/9910295hershey.

Stedman, C. (2000). ERP problems put the brakes on Volkswagen parts shipment, *ComputerWorld*, March, Accessed April 3, 2000 at: http://www.computerworld.com/home/print.nsf/all/000103D7AA.

Acknowledgments

This book would not have been possible without the help of a large number of people. I would like to acknowledge those who were involved in collating the book and assisting with the review of the chapters. The authors who provided the chapters deserve particular mention. Thank you for the insights provided by your chapters and the contributions you've made to our understanding of two very important subjects.

Ultimately, the success of this book is possible mainly because of the professional support provided by Mehdi Khosrow-Pour and the Idea Group team. Special thanks to Amanda Appicello and other staff members at Idea Group, Inc. who guided this whole process. Thanks for their patience in working with me as editor.

Finally, I would like to thank Joan, my wife, and my sons, Julian and Jeremy, for their love and patient support while I spent time on this project.

Gerald Grant
Carleton University, Canada
March 4, 2003

Part I

ERP Systems and Enterprise Integration

Chapter I

ERP Systems Impact on Organizations

Jonas Hedman
Lund University, Sweden

Andreas Borell
Tetra Pak Information Management, Sweden

ABSTRACT

Enterprise Resource Planning (ERP) systems are in most cases implemented to improve organizational effectiveness. Current research makes it difficult to conclude how organizations may be affected by implementing ERP systems. This chapter addresses this issue by presenting an artifact evaluation of ERP systems. The evaluation is based on the Competing Values Model (Quinn & Rohrbaugh, 1981; Rohrbaugh, 1981). The evaluation shows that ERP systems support effectiveness criteria, related to internal and rational goals of organizations. The evaluation also points out weaknesses in ERP systems, especially in areas related to human resource management and organizational flexibility. The result of the evaluation is used to discuss the impact of ERP systems on organizations and is presented as a series of hypotheses.

INTRODUCTION

Enterprise Resource Planning (ERP) systems have had an enormous impact on businesses and organizations around the world (Howcroft & Truex, 2001; Swanson, 2000). ERP systems are in most cases implemented with the goal to improve some aspect of the organization, e.g., strategic, organizational, business, management, operational, or IT-infrastructure (Hedman & Borell, 2002).

Studies show improvements, such as business process improvement, increased productivity and improved integration between business units (Davenport, 2000; Hedman & Borell, 2002; Hitt, Wu, & Zhou, 2002; Howcroft & Truex, 2002; Masini, 2001; Murphy & Simon, 2001; Poston & Grabski, 2001; Shang & Seddon, 2000). In order to achieve these benefits, organizational changes are required (Van der Zee & De Jong, 1999). Thereby, ERP systems are often assumed to be a deterministic technology, since organizations have to align their organizational structure, business process and workflow to the embedded logic of the ERP system (Glass, 1998). However, the casual relationship between ERP systems and organizational change has been questioned (Boudreau & Robey, 1999). The impact and benefit of ERP systems is unclear (Andersson & Nilsson, 1996). The only thing we know for certain is that the implementations are very resource consuming (Davenport, 1998).

The ability to determine or to appraise the impact of ERP systems would be of great importance from both theoretical and practical perspective. However, this is difficult for several reasons: First, it is not possible to draw explicit conclusions from IS benefit research (DeLone & McLean, 1992) on ERP systems. Second, there are inconsistent and contradictory findings from research on information technology and organizational change (Robey & Boudreau, 1999). Third, the interdependency between ERP system and organization requires interpretive and holistic evaluation methods (Borell & Hedman, 2001). Fourth, the measurement of organizational effectiveness is an elusive, complex and socially constructed construct (Campbell, 1977). Fifth, there is a lack of theorizing regarding the IT-artifact (Orlikowski & Iacono, 2001).

The purpose of this chapter is to evaluate the market leading ERP system, i.e., SAP R/3 Enterprise, in order to increase the understanding of how ERP systems may affect organizations and organizational effectiveness. The next section argues for conducting and evaluation of ERP systems with IS research as a frame of reference. The subsequent sections present an artifact-evaluation approach, an evaluation framework based on the Competing Values Model (Quinn & Rohrbaugh, 1981; Rohrbaugh, 1981), and the ERP system in question. In the final section, the results are summarized and presented as a series of hypotheses speculating how ERP system might affect organizations and organizational effectiveness. Future research directions are also suggested.

BACKGROUND

Requirements specification is a problematic area in most IS implementations (Jackson, 1995), since *"...we have a tendency to focus on the solution, in large part because it is easier to notice a pattern in the systems that we build than it is to see the pattern in the problems we are solving that lead to the patterns in our solutions to them"* (R. Johnson in Jackson, 1995, p. 2). This applies in particular to the implementation of ERP systems (Borell & Hedman, 2000; Rolland, 2000). One of the reasons for this is the difference between implementations based on traditional information system development methods and the process of selecting and implementing ERP systems. It no longer appears meaningful to speak about analysis and design in a traditional fashion, because there is no analysis and design process as such. Instead, an evaluation of the reference model and the functionality of the ERP system is made, followed by a selection process. For each ERP system (or part of a ERP system) considered, there are three basic options: accept, accept with changes, or reject - all with different organizational consequences. These options must be considered in light of the requirements specification, which in turn has to reflect this (Borell & Hedman, 2000). These differences are illustrated in *Figure 1*. This line of reasoning is equally applicable to implementation of upgrades and extensions.

Another reason for addressing evaluation of ERP system comes from the conceptual thinking of IS researchers, such as Rudy Hirschheim and Barbara Farbey. Hirschheim & Smithson (1998) conclude in their literature survey of IS evaluation that the focus on tools and techniques from a positivistic approach has provided the foundation for traditional IS evaluation. The result has been *"a more 'technical' interpretation of evaluation"* (p. 402) – partly because of the

Figure 1: Comparison of traditional information system development methods and the process of selecting and implementing ERP systems

Traditional	ERP system
User	Designer
Designer	System
System	Organization

widespread belief that IS are fundamentally technical systems. They argue that omitting the social domain makes it unlikely to produce a true or meaningful evaluative picture and that a more interpretive IS perspective seems to be the best vehicle for doing so.

Farbey, Land, & Targett (1995) propose a model known as The Benefits Evaluation Ladder, which they claim relates specifically to the need for evaluation. They argue that two of the most influential factors when selecting an evaluation method are application and objective (of change). A classification of *"the uses of information systems may therefore be of fundamental importance in selecting suitable evaluation methods"* (p. 41). Based on the perception that it is possible to classify IS applications associated with different types of organizational change. Their model consists of eight rungs, ranging from mandatory changes and automation to strategic systems and business transformation. Their classification is not rigid, but implies potential benefit as well as the uncertainty of outcome. Potential benefits and the level of uncertainty are both cumulative, thus systems classified on a certain stratum may have all the benefits (and accumulated uncertainty) from any or all of the strata below. They conclude that for the implementation of systems on the eighth rung *"...benefits stem from the transformation as a whole. IT provides only one component of what is often a complex series of changes. It is not possible to attribute a portion of the benefits gained to any one factor"* (p. 49). We conclude that in the taxonomy of Farbey et al. (1995), ERP systems are on the eighth rung and that they have the possible benefits and accumulated uncertainty of all the strata below. Therefore, it is highly unlikely that any two implementations will have identical requirements or consequences, even if they are based on the same generic software packages. While the potential benefits might be articulated, determination of the actual benefits from implementing an ERP system is difficult to foresee.

McKeen, Smith & Parent (1999) proposed a "supra-framework labeled Organizational Economics." They propose that their model *"...can apply to all sorts of projects and organizational forms"* (p. 13) and suggest that IT investments can be considered as part of a chain of events: a senior management decision ('IT Governance') has to be made that leads to a specific *investment* in IT which then needs to be *deployed* (selected and implemented) before it can be *used* by an organization to enhance its *performance*. In their first postulate, McKeen & Parent (1999) state that *"With the focus at the enterprise level, it should be possible to capture the effects of the total IT investment on the organization's performance provided that the performance measure is related to the usage of the technology"* (p. 15). The delimitation of level of analysis to an entire enterprise is based on the anticipated possibilities to obtain relevant measurements of cost and performance combined with a holistic perspective on the decision process. Investing in an ERP system is a top-management decision. It will have an impact on the culture, processes, structures and strategies of an organization (Davenport, 1998; Davison, 2002; Hanseth & Braa, 1998; Hanseth, Ciborra, & Braa, 2001; Kennerley & Neely, 2001), and therefore the only suitable level of analysis is the enterprise level, i.e., organizational.

ARTIFACT EVALUATION

Evaluation of the impact of ERP systems on organizational effectiveness is difficult (Murphy & Simon, 2001; Stefanou, 2001a, 2001b). Some of the problems that arise are the complexity and comprehensiveness of ERP systems, the lack of empirical research on the impact of ERP systems on organizational effectiveness (Hitt et al., 2002; Irani, 2002; Skok & Legge, 2001), and the shortcomings of traditional multivariate methods (such as factor analysis) for solving problems related to organizational effectiveness (Campbell, 1977). Following Hirschheim & Smithson (1998), we approached the problem in an interpretive way by applying an artifact-evaluation approach. This research approach belongs to a research stream stressing artifact utility, which can be broadly divided into artifact-building and artifact-evaluation approaches (Järvinen, 1999; Järvinen, 2000). Although critical, it is not well represented in IS research (Järvinen, 1999; Järvinen, 2000; Lee, 2000; March, Hevner, & Ram, 2000; March & Smith, 1995). An artifact can be a construct (concept), model, method, technique, instantiation of an information system or an ERP system. In artifact-building research, the focus is on questions such as: "Is it possible to build a certain artifact?; How should a certain artifact be defined?; and, How can we develop it?" In evaluation research, questions like "How effective and efficient is this artifact?" are posed and addressed.

To evaluate the effectiveness and efficiency of the artifact, both criteria and measurements are needed. To this end we chose the Competing Values Model (CVM). There were three main reasons for this choice: First, it is a well-established framework, empirically tested in organizational research (Buenger, Daft, Conlon, & Austin, 1996; Quinn & Cameron, 1983), management research (Hart & Quinn, 1993), and IS research (Carlsson & Widmeyer, 1994; McCartt & Rohrbaugh, 1995; Sääksjärvi & Talvinen, 1996) over a number of years. Second, it is related to the critical constructs of individual and organizational effectiveness. Third, it is addressing the organizational level of analysis. Later versions and extensions of CVM for assessing management competence (Quinn, 1989) and diagnosing organizational culture (Cameron & Quinn, 1999) were assessed, but they were not found to be appropriate for this evaluation due to their shortcomings regarding lower level efficiency.

Competing Values Model

Until the development of contingency theory, organizational effectiveness was perceived as an applied area, not a theoretical issue in organizational theory. Contingency theorists' addition to the development of organizational effectiveness as a theoretical issue were arguments that some organizational structures were more suitable than others to certain task, size, and environment, i.e., contingency factors (Scott, 1998). The question that followed was: "Suited in what sense?" The answer given to this question in most cases was in terms of effectiveness (Cameron, 1981; Campbell, 1977; Goodman & Pennings, 1977; Olerup, 1982; Scott, 1998).

Traditionally, organizational effectiveness was defined as meeting or surpassing organizational goals (Bedeian, 1987). The goal approach has dominated organizational effectiveness studies, despite criticisms (Hall, 1980) that organizations have multiple goals (Cameron, 1981) and that criteria for measuring effectiveness are ambiguous (Meyer, 1985). Alternative approaches to organizational effectiveness studies have emerged to deal with both these problems and others: e.g., the resource approach (Cunningham, 1978; Pfeffer & Salancik, 1978), the internal process approach (Ostroff & Schmitt, 1993), the stakeholder approach (Tusi, 1990), and the Competing Values Approach (Quinn, 1981; Quinn & Rohrbaugh, 1981; Rohrbaugh, 1981; Thompson, McGrath, & Whorton, 1981). Despite these efforts, it is still difficult and potentially controversial to quantify organizational effectiveness (Cameron & Whetten, 1983). Effectiveness criteria can be described in very general and broad terms, e.g., survival or profit, or in more narrow terms based on functions, e.g., hierarchical levels, roles, or processes in organizations based on the participants and constituents. The complexity of the concept of organizational effectiveness can be illustrated by Campbell's (Campbell, 1977) list of 30 different criteria for measuring organizational effectiveness, ranging from job satisfaction to growth and productivity. With regard to this, CVM is especially notable, since it combines diverse indicators of effectiveness and performance.

The Competing Values Model is based on the hypothesis that there is a tension between underlying value dimensions (Quinn, 1981; Quinn & Cameron, 1988; Quinn & McGrath, 1982). The first value dimension is focus - internal focus puts emphasis on the well being of the organization itself, while external focus is placed on the organization within its environment. Structure is the second value dimension – stability refers to the need for top management and control and flexibility refers to the need for adaptation and change in organizational structure. The third dimension relates to means and ends in different organizational effectiveness measures (Quinn & Rohrbaugh, 1981; Rohrbaugh, 1981). The measures that underlie the value dimensions reflect one of four organizational models: human relations model (HR), open systems model (OS), internal process model (IP), and rational goal model (RG). A critical point to note is that while different organizational models reflect different effectiveness criteria, they are not dichotomic. Effectiveness may require that organizations are both flexible and stable, as well as have a synchronous internal and external focus (Quinn & Cameron, 1988). The models reflect opposing views of organizational effectiveness simultaneously.

The HR model focuses on internal flexibility to develop employee cohesion and morale. It stresses human resource development, participation, empowerment, team building, trust building, conflict management, supporting, communication internally, developing individual development plans, feedback to individuals and groups, and developing management skills (Quinn, 1989).

The OS model focuses on external flexibility and suggests readiness and flexibility as the reason by which growth may be gained. Important issues are the acquisition of scarce resources, the support of interaction with the external environment, the identification of major trends, the development of business intelligence, the creation of mental models, facilitation of changes, dedication to research and development, the identification of problems, influences from the environment, and the maintenance of external legitimacy through a network of external contacts (Quinn, 1989).

The IP model focuses on internal stability and uses information management, information processing, and communication to develop stability and control. This is done by collecting data (mainly internal quantitative information used to check organizational performance), enhancing the understanding of activities, ensuring that standards, goals, and rules are met, maintaining organizational structure and workflow, coordinating activities, and collecting and distributing information internally (Quinn, 1989).

Figure 2: Competing Values Model based on Quinn (1981) and Rohrbaugh (1981)

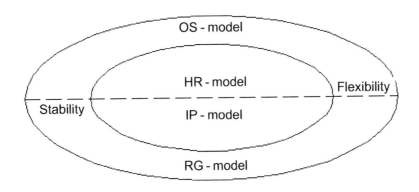

The RG model is characterized by a focus on external control and relies on planning and goal setting to gain productivity. This includes clarification of expectations, goals and purposes through planning and goal setting, definition of problems, generation and evaluation of alternatives, generation of rules and polices, evaluation of performance, decision support, quality control, motivation of organizational members to enhance productivity, sales support, and maximization of profit (Quinn, 1989).

A summary of the four organizational models (HR, OS, IP, and RG), the value dimensions, and related measures of organizational effectiveness is depicted in *Figure 2*. The value dimensions and the related organizational models should not be directly compared to the major organizational perspectives that exist in organizational theory: namely rational, natural, and open. Take for instance the open system perspective, which views organizations as open systems but also emphasizes information processing, which relates to the internal process model in CVM.

CVM is traditionally depicted as a grid or quadrant, as are many other models and frameworks, e.g., the balanced scorecard (Kaplan & Norton, 1996) or SWOT (Andrews, 1971). The quadratic way of representing organizations and information systems may not be the best approach. In information systems are organizations commonly represented through an ellipse. Therefore, we have chosen to depict CVM by using modeling techniques common in the information systems community.

ERP Systems – SAP R/3

For the evaluation of ERP systems, we chose SAP R/3 Enterprise, which was recently released during second half of year 2002. Enterprise has basically the same functionality as the previous SAP R/3 version 4.6b, but a new technological platform. The new R/3 architecture is built on the ideas of layered architecture and maintainability, where functionality and technology are separated to enable different release strategies for functionality and technology. This increases the system's portability of technical platform, as well as input and output devices, respectively. The technology in SAP R/3 Enterprise is based on SAP WEB Application Server, which has been in place for different mySAP.com components, such as the mySAP Business Information Warehouse (SAP's data warehouse).

The major implication of this change is that new releases of R/3 can either be of technical or functional nature, and each will have its own release strategy. Furthermore, the functionality, which is represented in the reference model, is divided into Enterprise Core and Enterprise Extensions processes. The first type of processes is internally oriented and contains the same functionality as version 4.6, but the process model has been optimized. For example, fixed asset accounting and payroll processing are two such Enterprise Core processes that are bounded to a firm from a practical and legal perspective. Enterprise Extensions processes include new functionalities, e.g., electronic bank account statements have been added to the financial model and mobile time management has enhanced the human resource model. The separation of Core and Extensions processes makes it easier for a customer to upgrade those parts of the system that are considered essential for them. (Details on SAP R/3 Enterprise are best found on SAP Service marketplace: http://service.sap.com/enterprise.)

One of the attractions of ERP systems is the value of integration. There are other perceived benefits associated to ERP systems including business process improvement, integration among business units, real-time access to data and information (Davenport, 2000), standardization of company processes, increased flexibility, increased productivity, increased customer satisfaction, optimized supply chain, business growth, improvement of order-to-cash time, competitive positioning ability, shared services, improved time to market cycles, and improved product quality (Cooke & Peterson, 1998). To summarize, ERP systems can support an organization in six main ways (Hedman & Borell, 2002):

- First, they support organizations by integrating information flows (such as customer information, financial and accounting information, human resources information, and supply chain information) and making it available to the entire organization (Davenport, 1998).

- Second, they integrate diverse primary business activities, functions, processes, tasks, and workflows (such as accounting, finance, and procurement) as well as secondary activities with primary activities (such as inventory management) (Davenport, 1998).

- Third, they serve as a common data repository (master data) for organizations (Scheer, 1998). The benefit of a data repository for an organization is that it may define the format of the data, which makes communication and interpretation easier.

- Fourth, they specify how organizations should conduct their business based on a best business practice reference model (Kumar & Hillegersberg, 2000).

- Fifth, they reduce the number of logical computer based information systems (Joseph & Swansson, 1998) and replace old legacy systems (Markus & Tanis, 2000).

- The last, and maybe the most obvious support, is that they deliver functionality per se, see below and Rashid, Hossain, & Patrick (2002). There are user administrative tools, data base administration tools, e-mail, appointment calendar, functionality for room reservations, ordering food, a software development workbench, telephone integration, workflow system, and an executive information system.

SAP R/3 Enterprise consists of functionality from three general business areas with different sub-areas. The first one is accounting and it deals with information flows concerning planning, controlling, and value representation of business processes, functions, and business units in an enterprise. Accounting is divided into external and internal accounting, in accordance with the target groups. External accounting (financial accounting) is structured according to legal requirements and the organization's openness to external parties, such as tax authorities and investors. Internal accounting, on the other hand, consists of cost and benefits accounting and is used to provide quantitative information to decision-makers within an enterprise.

The second part is logistics and includes all functionality for the design of material and information and production flow from the vendor, through production, to the consumer. Logistics is dived into three main areas: Sales and Distribution, Materials Management, and Production and Control. With the logistics module an enterprise can plan, control and coordinate logistical processes across department boundaries, based on the integration of existing data and functions. Logistics is similar to MRP II systems (Material Resource Planning systems).

Human resource management is the last part and is divided into two areas. The first area is Personal Planning and Development, which supports the strategic use of personal by giving the enterprise the functionality that makes it possible to manage personal systematically and qualitatively. Functions as organizational management, personnel development, workforce planning, training and recruitment are supported. Personal Administration and Payroll Accounting, which is the second part of human resource management, combines the administrative and operational tasks of human resources management. Here you can find functions for time management, incentive wages, payroll accounting, and travel expense.

In sum, ERP systems are large integrated computer software packages consisting of components, each with a given set of functions. All available functions operate on a shared set of data, thereby achieving integration. The idea of these systems is to support every single aspect of organizational storage, processing, retrieval, and distribution of data and information. This is supposedly done without regard to organizational scope, business, or comprehensiveness – at least that is what the vendors say. In that sense, an ERP system is a generic solution with different levels of adaptability, which makes every implementation unique in some sense since an organization must configure the system to its own specific requirements. In many cases, the system is customized to special requirements that are not supported by standard R/3.

Procedure

The evaluation of R/3 systems was performed in a three-step process. First, the functionality found in the system and reported benefits associated with ERP systems were listed. Then we categorized ERP capabilities with respect the value dimensions – internal vs. external and stable vs. flexible. The third step was to classify the functionality with regard to the value dimensions in CVM. The authors performed the evaluation and classification independently and the outcomes were then compared. There was substantial agreement, approximately 90%, between the evaluations (some functionalities were question-marked in the evaluations). Where disagreements existed, the functionality was reevaluated and a final classification and evaluation decision was made, which satisfied both authors. To some extent, we verified the classification from published articles on ERP systems benefits, but in most cases this was not possible. This is because most research on ERP systems does not describe the ERP functionality to such a detail that it is possible to verify the classification.

This approach has its limitations. For example, production planning is essential to manufacturing firms but is of little or no value to retail firms. In addition, there is the impact of the environment and technology of the user - some capabilities are more important than others depending on the environment and technology of the organization in question. An accountant does not need production planning functionality. Finally, the number of users of each function

*Figure 3: Mapping of ERP system capabilities into CVM. *Parentheses indicate functions within functionality*

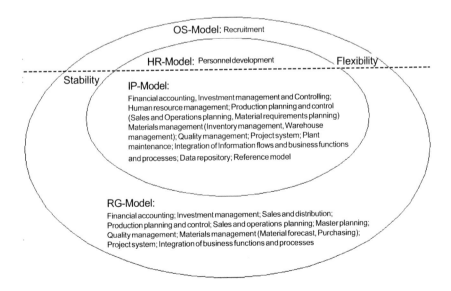

in an organization – it's likely to assume that some functionalities will have several users, e.g., a firm will have several sales persons.

Result

Most of the functionality and benefits map to either the IP model or the RG model; some of the functionality is interpretable as belonging to both models. This is because system functionality supports several organizational functions with different effectiveness metrics.

Accordingly, ERP systems and perceived benefits relate to IP-and RG-associated organizational goals and effectiveness metrics. Hence, ERP systems primarily support tasks related to control, efficiency, productivity, and stability by improving information management, coordination, and planning. The strong support of the IP model is natural since ERP systems (as are most IS, e.g., MIS, controlling systems, and inventory systems) are internal systems that are designed to support the internal processes and functions of organizations. Another important and critical functionality is the creation of master data records for customers and vendor. This functionality is used as a repository for data and makes it possible to communicate information through an organization. This is what makes integration of information and processes possible. However, the lack of support for HR and OS models was surprising. The outcome of the classification and evaluation of the functionality and benefits of ERP systems is presented in *Figure 3*.

DISCUSSION

The artifact evaluation of the functionality of SAP R/3 Enterprise shows the existence of an, in part, implicit shared framework with CVM. This, combined with research performed on CVM makes it possible for us to draw conclusions, which we present as a series of hypotheses that predict the impact of ERP system on organizations and organizational effectiveness.

The first conclusion regarding ERP systems such as R/3 is that there is a lack of support regarding HR and OS model effectiveness constructs, i.e., an unbalanced support of organizational effectiveness. Such a suggestion is based on the idea that well-balanced support is in generally beneficial, and that an organization must simultaneously attain several different, and possibly contradictory, goals to become effective (Campbell, 1977). Predictions about ERP systems impact on organizations form our first hypotheses.

- *Hypothesis 1a.* ERP systems will affect organizations and improve those areas that are tied to organizational effectiveness measures related to IP and RG models.

- *Hypothesis 1b.* An organization with certain organizational effectiveness requirements must seek capabilities in the corresponding quadrant, which requires an evaluation of the organizations effectiveness requirements.

- *Hypothesis 1c.* A successful implementation of ERP systems has to be followed by organizational change efforts that will improve organizational effectiveness associated to HR and OS models, i.e., human resource development, flexibility, and adaptability.

- *Hypothesis 1d.* Organizations with an identified effectiveness focus in the HR or OS models will become less effective if they implement an ERP system.

Studies within the CVM framework suggest that all effectiveness constructs are not equally important and critical at the same time. There are changes in the importance of the effectiveness constructs in relation to hierarchical levels and what stage of the life cycle a firm is in. Quinn and Cameron (1983) found, in relation to the CVM framework, four different stages a firm can be in: 1) entrepreneurial, 2) collectivity, 3) formalization and control, and 4) elaboration of structure stage. See *Figure 4.*

Figure 4: The four stages a firm can be in, in relation to the CVM framework

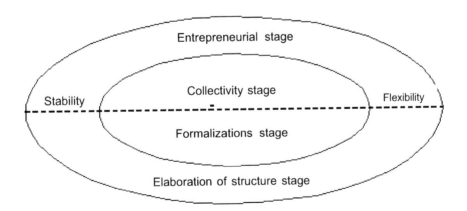

The critical effectiveness constructs of entrepreneurial stage lie in the OS model, while the critical effectiveness constructs of the collectivity stage lie in the HR model. In the formalization and control stage, the effectiveness constructs are based on the IP and RG models. The elaboration of structure stage has a more balanced emphasis upon the effectiveness constructs. The following hypotheses predicts the influence what stage in the life cycle a firm is in on the impact of ERP systems on organizations.

- *Hypothesis 2a.* For organizations in the entrepreneurial or collectivity stage, ERP systems are less beneficial, since they do not provide support for their critical effectiveness constructs, i.e., cohesion, morale, human resource development, innovation, adaptation, and growth.

- *Hypothesis 2b.* Organizations in the formalization and control stage, as well as the elaboration of structure stage, will be effectively supported by ERP systems since they give good support to those effectiveness constructs.

- *Hypothesis 2c.* Organizations that are in the process of moving from the collectivity stage to the formalization and control state could use an ERP system implementation to impose the structures and formalization needed in that stage.

- *Hypothesis 2d.* The probability of success of an ERP system implementation will differ depending on the current position of the organization in its life cycle. Most likely to achieve success are those organizations that are in the formalization and control stage.

In another study, it was found that there is also a difference in the importance of the effectiveness constructs in relation to hierarchical levels (Quinn 1989). The two major findings in the study were that: 1) there exists an equal emphasis for the IP and RG model - related effectiveness measurers, and 2) the importance of the OS models increases at higher hierarchical levels. In relation to our evaluation of ERP systems, these findings lead to the following hypotheses:

- *Hypothesis 3a.* ERP systems will provide support for middle- and lower-level managers.

- *Hypothesis 3b.* ERP systems do not provide sufficient support for top-level managers.

A question that arose regarding SAP R/3 was "is it effective or not?" This, of course, depends on various contextual factors, e.g., the stage of the life cycle and hierarchical level, which have to be addressed separately. However, it is obvious that R/3 Enterprise does not support top-level managers, expansion and growth of a firm, or the way a firm builds its corporate culture. That said, SAP has responded to some of these weaknesses. Lack of management support is addressed through Management Cockpit, a multi-dimensional executive information system, and drill-down possibilities have been provide in their Data Warehouse solution. The lack of flexibility and shortcomings regarding connections to the external environment is to some extent addressed by the Enterprise Portal. Increased compatibly is provided by BAPIs (Business Application Programming Interface) through predefined interfaces for communicating with other applications. One area, Human Resource Development, is currently not well supported by SAP's ERP system, and we are not aware of any major initiative by SAP to address this issue. This leads us to the final set of hypotheses related to ERP systems and organizations in general:

- *Hypothesis 4a.* Organizations cannot only rely on ERP systems for their information processing needs and have to seek alternative solutions for information processing related to HR model and OS model.

- *Hypothesis 4b.* ERP systems vendors have to develop alternative systems that address organizational flexibility and the relationship to the environment. For instance, CRM and SCM systems.

CONCLUSION

This chapter presents an artifact evaluation of an ERP system using an accepted framework of organizational effectiveness. The purpose of the evaluation was to improve the understanding of how ERP systems may or may not affect organizational effectiveness. The evaluation demonstrates both strengths and weaknesses of ERP systems. The strength of an ERP system is mostly related to IP model and RG model and the shortcomings are related to HR model and OS model.

In a real-case situation, our method must be complemented with both formal and informal methods and techniques. One such method or technique is the "competing values organizational effectiveness instrument" (Quinn, 1989) - the instrument measures perceptions of organizational performance. By applying said techniques and methods, it is possible to assess how different organizations perceive effectiveness constructs, as well as what they perceive as critical for that organization (Cameron & Quinn, 1999). Together these instruments and supplementary ways may be used to develop a recommendation for how competing values should be changed and how an ERP system can support different organizational effectiveness measurers.

Future research on ERP systems will include the development of instruments to diagnose organizations' effectiveness constructs and, in particular, this must include the development of computer-based support for this. This will enable us to determine the critical effectiveness constructs of an organization, which can be mapped to ERP systems. Future research will also include empirical studies addressing the relationship between ERP system use and support for organizational functions and processes, and how this is linked to individual and organizational performance. The result can improve our ability to design and configure ERP systems and prescribe how ERP systems can be used to improve organizational effectiveness.

ACKNOWLEDGMENT

We would like to thank Agneta Olerup, Sven Carlsson, Kevin Fissum and Jonas Larsson for their comments on earlier versions of this chapter.

REFERENCES

Andersson, R., & Nilsson, A. G. (1996). The standard application package market - An industry in transition? In M. Lundeberg & B. Sundgren (Eds.), *Advancing Your Business: People and Information Systems in Concert*. Stockholm: EFI and Stockholm School of Economics.

Andrews, K. R. (1971). *The concept of corporate strategy*. Homewood: Dow Jones-Irwin.

Bedeian, A. G. (1987). Organization theory: Current controversies, issues, and directions. In C. L. Cooper & I. T. Robertson (Eds.), *International review of industrial and organizational psychology, 1987* (pp. 1-33). Chichester: John Wiley & Sons.

Borell, A., & Hedman, J. (2000). *CVA-Based framework for ERP requirements specification*. Paper presented at the Information Systems Research in Scandinavia IRIS, University of Trollhättan, Uddevalla.

Borell, A., & Hedman, J. (2001). *Artifact evaluation of ES impact on organizational effectiveness*. Paper presented at the 2001 Americas Conference on Information Systems, Boston, MA.

Boudreau, M.C., & Robey, D. (1999). *Organizational transition to Enterprise Resource Planning Systems: Theoretical choices for process research*. Paper presented at the International Conference on Information Systems (ICIS).

Buenger, V., Daft, R. L., Conlon, E. J., & Austin, J. (1996). Competing values in organizations: Contextual influences and structural consequences. *Organization Science, 7* (5), 557-576.

Cameron, K. S. (1981). Domains of organizational effectiveness. *Academy of Management Journal, 24*, 25-47.

Cameron, K. S., & Quinn, R. E. (1999). *Diagnosing and changing organizational culture: Based on the competing values framework*. Reading, MA: Addison-Wesley.

Cameron, K. S., & Whetten, D. (Eds.). (1983). *Organizational effectiveness: A comparison of multiple models*. San Diego, CA: Academic Press.

Campbell, J. P. (1977). On the nature of organizational effectiveness. In P. S. Goodman & J. Pennings (Eds.), *New perspectives on organizational effectiveness (pp. 13-55)*. San Francisco: Jossey-Bass.

Carlsson, S. A., & Widmeyer, G. R. (1994). Conceptualization of executive support systems: A Competing Values Approach. *Decision Science, 3* (4), 339-358.

Cooke, D., & Peterson, W. J. (1998). *SAP implementation: Strategies and results* (R-1217-98-RR). New York: The Conference Board, Inc.

Cunningham, J. B. (1978). A systems resource approach for evaluating organizational effectiveness. *Human Relations, 31*, 631-656.

Davenport, T. H. (1998, July/August). Putting the Enterprise into the Enterprise System. *Harvard Business Review*, pp. 121-131.

Davenport, T. H. (2000). *Mission critical: Realizing the promise of Enterprise Systems*. Boston, MA: Harvard Business School Press.

Davison, R. (2002). Cultural complications of ERP. *Communications of the ACM, 45* (7), 109.

DeLone, W. H., & McLean, E. R. (1992). Information Systems success: The quest for the dependent variable. *Information Systems Research, 3* (1), 60-95.

Farbey, B., Land, F. F., & Targett, D. (1995). A taxonomy of Information Systems applications: The benefits' of Evaluation Ladder. *European Journal of Information Systems, 4* (1), 41-50.

Glass, R. L. (1998). Enterprise Resource Planning: Breakthrough and/or term problem. *The DATA BASE for Advances in Information Systems, 29* (2), 14-15.

Goodman, P. S., & Pennings, J. M. (Eds.). (1977). *New perspectives on organizational effectiveness*. San Francisco: Jossey-Bass.

Hall, R. (1980). Effectiveness theory and organizational effectiveness. *Journal of Applied Behavioral Science, 16,* 536-545.

Hanseth, O., & Braa, K. (1998, December 13-16). *Technology as traitor: Emergent SAP infrastructure in a global organization.* Paper presented at the International Conference on Information Systems, Helsinki, Finland.

Hanseth, O., Ciborra, C. U., & Braa, K. (2001). The control devolution: ERP and the side effects of globalization. *The DATA BASE for Advances in Information Systems, 32* (4), 34-46.

Hart, S. L., & Quinn, R. E. (1993). Roles executives play: CEOs, behavioral complexity, and firm performance. *Human Relations, 46* (5), 543-574.

Hedman, J., & Borell, A. (2002). The impact of Enterprise Resource Planning Systems on organizational effectiveness: An artifact evaluation. In L. Hossain, J. D. Patrick, & M. A. Rashid (Eds.), *Enterprise Resource Planning: Global opportunities & challenges* (pp. 78-96). Hershey, PA: Idea Group Publishing.

Hirschheim, R. A., & Smithson, S. (1998). Evaluation of Information Systems: A critical assessment. In L. Willcocks & S. Lester (Eds.), *Beyond the IT productivity paradox* (pp. 381-409). John Wiley & Son, Ltd.

Hitt, L. M., Wu, D. J., & Zhou, X. (2002). Investment in enterprise resource planning: Business impact and productivity measures. *Journal of Management Information Systems, 19* (1), 71-98.

Howcroft, D., & Truex, D. (2001). Critical analyses of ERP Systems: The macro level. *The DATA BASE for Advances in Information Systems, 31* (4), 13-18.

Howcroft, D., & Truex, D. (2002). Critical analyses of ERP Systems: The micro level. *The DATA BASE for Advances in Information Systems, 33* (1), 7-12.

Irani, Z. (2002). Developing a frame of reference for ex-ante IT/IS investment evaluation. *European Journal of Information Systems, 11* (1), 74.

Jackson, M. A. (1995). *Software requirements & specifications: A lexicon of practice, principles, and prejudices.* Wokingham: ACM Press.

Järvinen, P. (1999). *On research methods.* Tampere: University of Tampere.

Järvinen, P. H. (2000). *Research questions guiding selection of an appropriate research method.* Paper presented at the Proceedings of the Eighth European Conference on Information Systems, Vienna.

Joseph, T., & Swansson, E. B. (Eds.). (1998). *The package alternative in system replacement: Evidence for innovation convergence.* Hershey, PA: Idea Group Publishing.

Kaplan, R. S., & Norton, D. P. (1996). *The balanced scorecard : translating strategy into action.* Boston, Mass.: Harvard Business School Press.

Kennerley, M., & Neely, A. (2001). Enterprise Resource Planning: Analysing the impact. *Integrated Manufacturing Systems, 12* (2), 103-113.

Kumar, K., & Hillegersberg, J. V. (2000). ERP experience and evolution. *Communications of the ACM, 43* (4), 23-26.

Lee, A. S. (2000). The social and political context of doing relevant research. *MIS Quarterly, 24* (3), V.

March, S., Hevner, A., & Ram, S. (2000). Research commentary: An agenda for information technology research in heterogeneous and distributed environments. *Information Systems Research, 11* (4), 327-341.

March, S. T., & Smith, G.F. (1995). Design and natural science research on information technology. *Decision Support Systems, 15* (4), 251-266.

Markus, M. L., & Tanis, C. (2000). The Enterprise Systems experience: From adoption to success. In R. Zmud (Ed.), *Framing the domains of its management: projecting the future ... through the past.* Cincinnati, Ohio: Pinnaflex Educational Resources.

Masini, A. (2001). *The ERP paradox: Understanding the impact of enterprise resource planning systems on firm performance.* Paper presented at the Portland International Conference on Management of Engineering and Technology. PICMET '01.

McCartt, A. T., & Rohrbaugh, J. (1995). Managerial openness to change and the introduction of Gdss: Explaining initial success and failure in decision conferencing. *Organization Science, 6* (5), 569-584.

McKeen, J. D., Smith, H. A. & Parent, M. (1999). An integrative research approach to assess the business value of information technology. In M. A. Mahmood & E. J. Szewczak (Eds.), *Measuring Information Technology payoff: Contemporary approaches* (pp. 5-23). Hershey, PA: Idea Group Publishing.

Meyer, M. (1985). Limits to bureaucratic growth. Walter DeGruyter, Inc.

Murphy, K., & Simon, S. (2001). *Using cost benefit analysis for Enterprise Resource Planning project evaluation: A case for including intangibles.* Paper presented at the Hawaii International Conference on Systems Sciences.

Olerup, A. (1982). *A contextual framework for computerized Information Systems.* Copenhagen, Denmark: Erhversökonomiskt Förlag.

Orlikowski, W. J., & Iacono, C. S. (2001). Research commentary: Desperately seeking the "IT" in IT research - A call to theorizing the IT artifact. *Information Systems Research, 12* (2), 121-134.

Ostroff, C., & Schmitt, N. (1993). Configurations of organizational effectiveness and efficiency. *Academy of Management Journal, 36*, 1345-1361.

Pfeffer, J., & Salancik, G. R. (1978). *The external control of organizations: A resource dependence perspective.* New York: Harper & Row.

Poston, R., & Grabski, S. (2001). Financial impacts of Enterprise Resource Planning implementations. *International Journal of Accounting Information Systems, 2*, 271-294.

Quinn, R. E. (1981). A Competing Values Approach to organizational effectiveness. *Public Productivity Review, 5* (2), 122.

Quinn, R. E. (1989). *Beyond rational management: Mastering the paradoxes and competing demands of high performance*. San Francisco: Jossey-Bass Publishers.

Quinn, R. E., & Cameron, K. (1983). Organizational life cycles and shifting criteria of effectiveness: Some preliminary evidence. *Management Science, 29* (1), 33-51.

Quinn, R. E., & Cameron, K. S. (1988). Paradox and transformation. In R. E. Quinn & K. S. Cameron (Eds.), *Paradox and transformation: Toward a theory of change in organization and management*. Cambridge, MA: Ballinger Publishing Company.

Quinn, R. E., & McGrath, M. R. (1982). Moving beyond the single-solution perspective: The Competing Values Approach as a diagnostic tool. *The Journal of Applied Behavioral Science, 18* (4), 462-472.

Quinn, R. E., & Rohrbaugh, J. (1981). A Competing Values Approach to organizational effectiveness. *Public Productivity Review, 5* (2), 122-140.

Rashid, M. A., Hossain, L., & Patrick, J. D. (2002). The evolution of ERP Systems: A historical perspective. In L. Hossain, J. D. Patrick, & M. A. Rashid (Eds.), *Enterprise Resource Planning: Global opportunities & challenges* (pp. 1-16). Hershey, PA: Idea Group Publishing.

Robey, D., & Boudreau, M. C. (1999). Accounting for the contradictory organizational consequences of information technology: Theoretical directions and methodological implications. *Information Systems Research, 10* (2), 167-185.

Rohrbaugh, J. (1981). Operationalizing the Competing Values Approach: Measuring performance in the employment service. *Public Productivity Review, 5* (2), 141.

Rolland, C., & Prakash, N. (2000). Bridging the gap between organisational needs and ERP functionality. *Requirements Engineering, 5* (3), 180-193.

Sääksjärvi, M., & Talvinen, J. M. (1996). *Evaluation of organisational effectiveness of marketing information systems - The critical role of respondents*. Paper presented at the Proceedings of the Fourth European Conference on Information Systems, Lisbon, Portugal.

Scheer, A.W. (1998). *Business process engineering: reference models for industrial enterprises* (Study ed.). Berlin; New York: Springer.

Scott, W. R. (1998). *Organizations: Rational, natural, and open systems* (4th ed.). Upper Saddle River, NJ: Prentice Hall.

Shang, S., & Seddon, P. B. (2000). *A comprehensive framework for classifying the benefits of ERP Systems*. Paper presented at the Americas Conference on Information Systems.

Skok, W., & Legge, M. (2001). Evaluating Enterprise Resource Planning (ERP) Systems using an interpretive approach. *Knowledge and Process Management, 9* (2), 72-82.

Stefanou, C. J. (2001a). A framework for the ex-ante evaluation of ERP software. *European Journal of Information Systems, 10* (4), 204-215.

Swanson, E. B. (2000). *Innovating with packaged business software in the 1990s* (Working Paper). The Anderson School at UCLA.

Thompson, M. P., McGrath, M. R., & Whorton, J. (1981). The Competing Values Approach: Its application and utility. *Public Productivity Review, 5* (2), 188.

Tusi, A. S. (1990). A Multiple-Constituency Model of effectiveness: An empirical examination at the Human Resource Subunit level. *Administrative Science Quarterly, 35*, 458-483.

Van der Zee, J. T. M., & De Jong, B. (1999). Alignment is not enough: Integrating Business and Information Technology. *Journal of Management Information Systems, 16* (2), 137-158.

Chapter II

Challenging the Unpredictable: Changeable Order Management Systems

Joachim Berlak
Technische Universitaet Muenchen, Germany

Bernhard Deifel
Technische Universitaet Muenchen, Germany

ABSTRACT

This chapter deals with the changeability of order management systems (OMS). OMS are here referred to complex commercial off-the-shelf software (CCOTS) used, for example, for enterprise resource planning (ERP). Due to turbulent conditions in the business environment, a permanent need for change is the defining challenge for enterprises. However, far too often the rigidity of today's CCOTS-OMS does not allow users to implement the intended changes in the business organization. In order to deal with this challenge, a cybernetic model of order management is presented in this chapter. Additionally, a decision oriented software engineering and architectural design for CCOTS-OMS is sketched. The authors are convinced that these approaches enhance the changeability of the development and operation of CCOTS-OMS as well as their co-operation with a business organization.

INTRODUCTION

The inevitability of rapid change in the competitive environment of business is a commonly agreed fact (Das & Elango, 1995; Tetenbaum, 1998). The changing business environment, coupled with maturing sales and procurement markets, results in enormous pressures on enterprises in their efforts to be competitive (Vollmann, Berry, & Whybark, 1993). Hence, companies have to operate their businesses under increasingly complex, turbulent, uncertain and unpredictable conditions. Significantly, the dynamic features of this turbulent environment are not just the outcome of the interactions between enterprises (Chakravarthy, 1998; Reinhart et. al., 1999; Schreyoegg, 1999). Furthermore, this turbulence is generated by the business environment itself (Emery & Trist, 1965).

To cope with these conditions, a permanent need for change will be the defining feature in the future business landscape (Bower, 1994; Milberg, 1997). However, especially small and medium-sized enterprises (SMEs) are challenged by the turbulence on sales and procurement markets. According to the European Council (1996), these enterprises can be characterized by less than 250 employees and 40 million € sales volume per year. SMEs commonly produce parts, subassemblies, products and/or service for large-scale manufacturers (Hauser, 2001). Hence, SMEs are located at the lower levels of their encompassing supply chain (see *Figure 1*).

A supply chain starts from the origin of the raw material and ends once the product has been consumed by a customer (Fredenall & Hill, 2000). The so-called "bullwhip effect," which is presented in *Figure 1* and typical for supply chains, may be one explanation for the turbulent, uncertain and unpredictable conditions often perceived by SME suppliers (Forrester, 1961). This effect comprises unexpected changes in demand patterns that continue to escalate further down the supply chain (Chopra & Meindl, 2000). Due to distortions of

Figure 1: An exemplified supply chain and the bullwhip effect

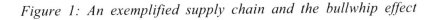

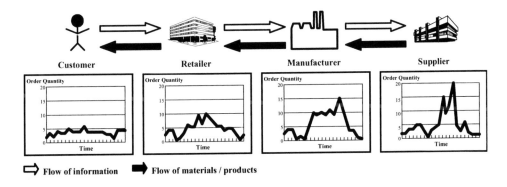

Figure 2: Need for organizational change vs. OMS rigidity (Berlak & Deifel, 2002)

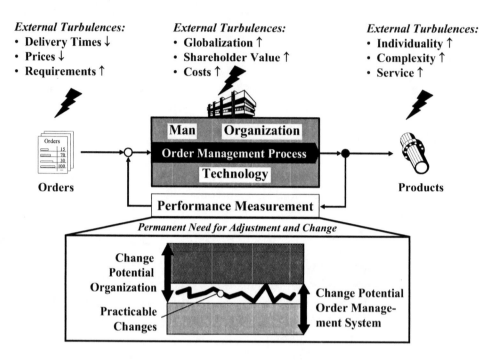

information flows and a minimal communication between the participating companies, a small wave in the middle of the ocean (steady customer demand) ends up as a tidal wave near the shore (fuzzy demand appreciated by suppliers). In addition, other factors like the ongoing globalization of competition and the growing pressure on costs and shareholder value, as well as an increasing individualization of products, causes external turbulences for SME suppliers (see *Figure 2*).

As mentioned before, SMEs deliver products and/or services by the transformation of orders from their encompassing supply chain and/or an internal sales plan. Accordingly, this so-called order management process is formed by the interaction of man and the structural and process organization, as well as the used technology (e.g., an OMS). In order to stay competitive, an enterprise acts like a closed feedback system using performance measurement to evaluate the effectiveness and efficiency of the order management process. In case of deviations due to external turbulences or internal insufficiency, essential changes are initiated.

However, far too often these changes in the business organization and/or processes can not be implemented as intended. The lack of ability of today's order management systems (OMS) to support necessary organizational changes

Figure 3: Results of an empirical investigation of Suisse SMEs (Hafen et. al., 1999)

Does the rigidity of the existing OMS obstruct the organizational change ?

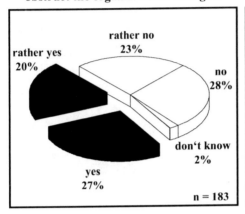

Does the existing OMS completely cover the changing functional requirements ?

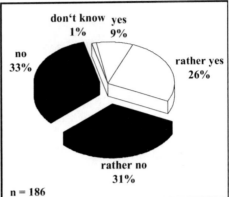

is a substantial cause for this problem. An empirical investigation regarding Suisse SMEs revealed that almost 47% confirmed the interference of their existing OMS with organizational changes. Furthermore, only 35% deployed an OMS with suitable functionality to cover their changing requirements (see *Figure 3*).

Reasons for the rigidity of OMS are various will be described later on. As a consequence, research is challenged to develop changeable OMS, which adequately support business changes. Furthermore, the entire co-operation between a business organization and the OMS must be tailored towards changeability.

The research project CHANGESYS of the Research Consortium for Software Engineering (FORSOFT), which is funded by the Bavarian Research Fund, focuses on this challenge.

In this applied science research project, an interdisciplinary team of researchers in the field of industrial management, mechanical and software engineering is working closely together with different companies like Rohde and Schwarz (an OMS user) and OCE Printing Systems (an OMS user and manufacturer), as well as ADICOM (an OMS manufacturer). The main research objective is to get a comprehensive understanding of the correlation of organizations and OMS in the case of changes (see *Figure 4*). In addition, concepts to enhance the changeability of OMS, organizations and the co-operation between both are developed.

Figure 4: Structure of the research project CHANGESYS

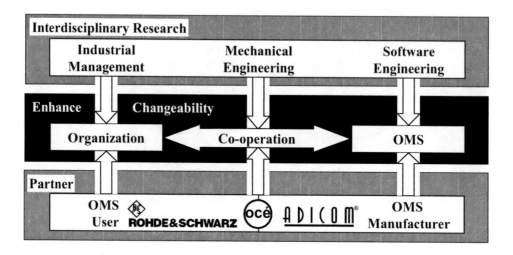

In this chapter, corresponding research results are presented. First, a cybernetic model of order management is developed. This approach communicates a mutual understanding of the interdisciplinary synergy of an organization and the OMS. Furthermore, a decision-oriented approach, which allows a systematic derivation of an architectural design for such kind of software, is sketched. Additionally, decision orientation is applied for the first steps of architectural CCOTS-OMS design. Finally, a conclusion and an outlook for future research are presented.

BASIC TERMS AND DEFINITIONS

In this chapter, basic terms and definitions are introduced.

Order Management

The term order management denotes, in general, the value creation process initiated by certain customers and/or sales plan, covering all planning and execution tasks from the order receipt to the final delivery of the manufactured product (Anderson & Pine, 1997). However, this term is widely defined and used in literature and practice (Darr, 1992). In order to declare the term order management, the following model is applied (*Figure 5*).

Figure 5: Order management (Berlak, 2001)

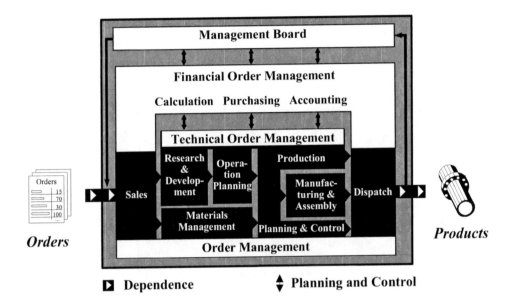

In this context, the order management process encompasses all activities and organizational units that are necessary for the transformation of orders into products. Thereby, the preliminary tasks for inquiry and offer handling are excluded. On that basis, software used for the support of the order management process is examined in further detail.

Order Management Systems

In general, an information system consists of hardware, an operating system, and the software application, as well as the appropriate data (Broy & Denert, 2001). The prevailing work focuses on business software, which encompasses administration applications (e.g., for financial accounting, etc.) and management information systems, as well as office automation and communication software (Meyers & Oberndorf, 2002). Due to the diversity of business software, the generic term order management system (OMS) is introduced and defined as follows: OMS are complex commercial off-the-shelf business software (CCOTS) which support the order management. Hence, business software for the following fields of application can be assigned to OMS (see *Figure 6*): Factory Data Collecting (FDS), Production Activity Control (PAC), Production Planning and Control (PAC), Enterprise Resource Planning (ERP), Workflow Management (WFM) or Supply Chain Management (SCM).

Figure 6: Order management systems (Berlak, 2003)

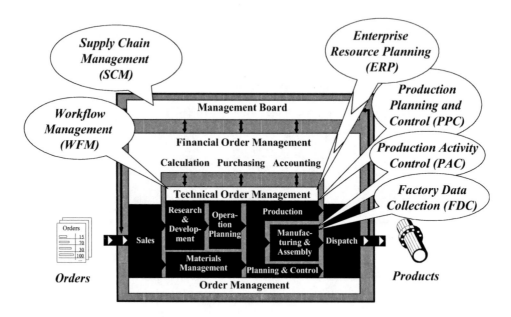

The different types of software subsumed by the term OMS are described in the following:

- A Factory Data Collection software (FDC) is a tool to receive, capture, process and analyze shop floor data by sensors or manual data input terminals (Jansen, 1993). FDC usually exists in combination with PAC, PPC or ERP software.

- Production Activity Control software (PAC) coordinates the operational implementation of production plans (Meinberg & Topolweski, 1995). However, there is no unique definition of the term PAC (Scheer, 2000). General tasks of a PAC software are machine and resource scheduling, capacity planning, and manufacturing order release, as well as order progress control (Maucher, 1998). An empirical investigation of 320 PAC applications indicates that these systems are linked in 95% of cases with a super-ordinate PPC or ERP software (Köhler, 1999). Furthermore, approximately 50 % of the examined PAC systems are connected with a FDC software in order to enable a highly realistic production activity control.

- Production Planning and Control software (PPC) is used for computer-aided planning, controlling and monitoring of the technical order management spanning the order request until the final delivery (AWF, 1985). Hence, PPC software possesses a large variety of functionality including, for example, order scheduling as well as capacity and resource planning

(Scheer, 2000). The first PPC software programs emerged in the 1950s (Maucher, 1998). In the last ten years nearly all industrial companies with more than 500 employees implemented such software (Kernler, 1995). ERP software evolved by the extension of PPC software with other business functionalities (O' Leary, 2000).

- Enterprise Resource Planning software (ERP) is an integrated and packaged software for the entire order management (Davenport, 1998). ERP packages consist of certain modules, for example, financial and accounting, selling, stock management, production, personnel management, customer care or service (Hiquet, 1998).

- A Workflow of Management software (WFM) is responsible for the processing, control and management of organizational workflows (Jablonski et. al., 1997). WFM software is evolved by technological developments in the areas of the document management systems (Gulbins et. al. 1998), active databases (Dittrich & Gatziu, 1996) and groupware software (Khoshafian & Buckiewicz, 1995). WFM systems can be used to support the activities carried out in the order management process.

- Supply Chain Management software (SCM) enables the optimization of in-plant and inter-company order management by new simulation functionality (Evans et. al., 1996). Today, SCM software is usually set up on existing ERP systems offering a memory resident simulation, analyze and configuration of a supply chain model. After planning different scenarios, the simulation results can be transferred back to the ERP software. At present, SCM vendors try to enhance their software with ERP functionality. On the other hand, ERP vendors try to include SCM simulation functionality (Harnwell, 1998).

In summary, the generic term OMS is used for the above mentioned FDC, PAC, PPC, ERP, WFM and SCM software tools. Mainly, OMS are CCOTS and therefore developed for a specific application field where they offer predefined functionality (Broy & Denert, 2002). The main difference between CCOTS and an individual software is that the CCOTS have to be adapted to a business organization before use, where as the individual software is developed for one specific customer (Cockburn, 2001). This so-called customizing of OMS is carried out by setting certain parameters and data tables within the software. For example, up to 8.000 tables and parameters must be adjusted in the OMS SAP R/3 (Hiquet, 1998). Thus, the customizing is associated with high financial expenditures for management consultants and software developers (Weiss, 2000). As a consequence, enterprises tend to "never touch a running system" once their OMS is customized (Wallace & Kremzar, 2001). This in turn stimulates an emerging dilemma: Necessary organizational changes due to turbulences on sales and procurement markets cannot be implemented due to the rigidity of an running OMS. Hence, the next section deals with the fundamentals of an OMS changeability.

Changeability of Order Management Systems

The term changeability is defined and discussed differently in literature, a unique definition did not yet intersperse itself so far (Duerrschmidt, 2001). The emphasis of past investigations was situated mainly in the disciplines of production management and economics where changeability describes a general ability of an enterprise to adapt to changing business conditions and environments (Kotter, 1996). In the software engineering community, this term is not often used and relatively uncommon. Hence, the prevailing work postulates the following model for changeability regarding CCOTS-OMS (see *Figure 7*).

CCOTS-OMS are developed according to certain goals (e.g., return on investment, market shares, etc.) and restrictions (e.g., development tools, costs, etc.) of the software manufacturer. Core requirements for the OMS result from the application field (e.g., user requirements, etc.). Due to their characteristics, CCOTS-OMS are configured to a specific organization before use (Configuration State n). During operation, OMS act as a service provider for tasks of the order management process. Hence, the changeability of OMS can be described as follows.

As long as the order management process does not change, the entire cooperation between the OMS and the organization is in a steady state. However, if the business environment changes significantly, the order management process must be adapted accordingly. The OMS ability for change consists of two change potentials, flexibility and responsiveness.

Figure 7: Context of changeability and OMS operation (Berlak & Deifel, 2002)

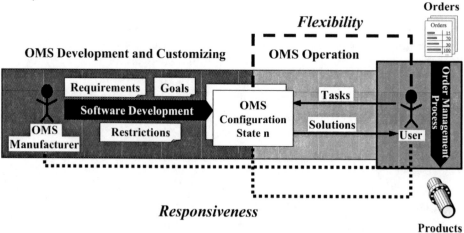

During operation of the OMS, software modifications can be achieved by the implemented software functionality. The so-called **flexibility** of the OMS describes a predefined change potential identified and implemented by the software manufacturer during the OMS development. If changes can be realized by the flexibility of the OMS, the user is able to solve the occurring problems on his own (e.g., resetting parameters, using alternate functions or data, etc.). If the existing OMS flexibility is not sufficiently supporting the changes of the order management process, another change potential must be assessed.

The so-called **responsiveness** shows the background of the predefined and implemented change potential of an OMS. Here, humans' problem-solving ability and creativity is used to modify and/or expand the OMS to deliver an optimal problem solution. For example, OMS interfaces can be used to develop additional software solutions (e.g., self-developed add-on solutions). As another opportunity, organizational changes could be initiated to solve the order management problems without using additional OMS functionalities. With a more timely and/or costly expenditure, an update of the existing OMS or, additionally, software solutions from other vendors could be installed in order to solve the problem.

In summary, the changeability of OMS can be characterized by the change potentials of flexibility and responsiveness. Hereby, flexibility is implemented in the OMS during software development. However, responsiveness means to find solutions for not assumed problems when the flexibility of an OMS is exceeded. Building upon these definitions, the cybernetic model of order management is introduced in the following.

CYBERNETIC MODEL OF ORDER MANAGEMENT

In order to communicate a mutual understanding of the interdisciplinary synergy of an organization and OMS, this cybernetic approach was developed. The term cybernetic belongs to control engineering and describes a closed feedback system that remains stable despite disturbances (Wiener, 1948). A control loop consists of a regulated system, a measurement unit and a controller. The latter affects the controlled system, whereby the success of the adjusting measure is steered. *Figure 8* presents the cybernetic model of order management.

According to this model, enterprises are treated as open systems exposed to a dynamic business environment, in which they fulfill orders by delivering products. Hence, the order management process encompasses all organizational activities for transforming customer and/or sales plan orders into products. In

Figure 8: Cybernetic model of order management (Berlak & Deifel, 2002)

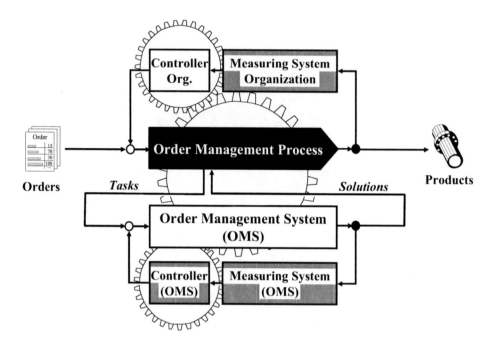

order to be competitive, a measuring system for the process' effectiveness and efficiency is used. In case of occurring deviations, changes in the order management's organization and process structure are initiated. As can be seen later, the selection of an adequate organizational change strategy is negotiated with the controller of the OMS control loop in order to select an optimal strategy for the entire company. Today, this connection is often lacking. Organizational change strategies, like moving from a MRPII based production planning towards a Kanban strategy, are often initiated without the coordination with the OMS control loop. The results range from higher efforts and less profits to a worse case stop of the implementation.

In order to ensure an optimal effectiveness and efficiency of the order management process, an adequate software support by an OMS is needed. Therefore, the OMS control loop is responsible to deliver suitable solutions for the occurring tasks and problems from the organizational control loop. Discrepancies between required and offered solutions may be identified by using a measuring system. In case of inefficiencies, the OMS has to be modified by the application of an adequate controller strategy. As mentioned before, the selection of an optimal strategy of the OMS controller works in close cooperation with the organizational control loop to achieve a global optimum. This cooperation is symbolized in *Figure 8* by the connected gear wheels. In the following, both control loops are described in further detail.

The Control Loop Organization

The main goal of the organization control loop is the efficient operation of the order management process. Therefore, a measuring system based on a key-performance-indicator (KPI) is used, based on research results from Frese (1992), Theuvesen (1996) and Werder (1999). Hence, efficiency is referred to as the decisive and decision relevant criterion for the evaluation of alternative organization structures, business processes and organizational measures. The measurement system forms the base for a comparison of actual and nominal values. The latter are determined by method tool set consisting, for example, of benchmarking techniques, time series analyses and market/customer opinion polls.

In case of exceeding KPI-specific threshold values, the organizational controller has to intervene. Hence, changes in the structural and/or sequence organization of the order management process are initiated concerning coordination, decision, information, control and motivation aspects. Therefore, the controller uses a strategy database consisting of certain strategies (e.g., outsourcing of activities). Heinen (1991) defines a strategy as the global way to reach certain goals, which represent the nominal values mentioned before. Every strategy may be determined by the attribute's expenses, benefits, restrictions, context and measures. The evaluation of expenses, benefits and restrictions of a strategy is carried out in close cooperation with the OMS controller. The same procedure takes place for the selection of an entire optimal strategy whose measures are implemented afterwards. For further details about this control loop it is referred to in Berlak (2001) or Berlakand Deifel (2002).

The Control Loop OMS

The OMS control loop acts as a service provider to deliver optimal solutions for the occurring tasks and problems of the order management process. Hence, an OMS offers several functions and services, which are recorded by an appropriate measuring system. Mainly, measuring criteria like the effectiveness, efficiency, convenience or suitability of the services are addressed. Deviations clarify that the occurring problems in the order management process cannot be solved by adequate services. For example, if a key account customer requires a daily instead of a weekly delivery, and the existing OMS has just the flexibility to plan weekly, the problem cannot be solved. In such a constellation the OMS controller must change the structure and/or the processes of the OMS. Hence, the flexibility and/or the responsiveness of the software system must be addressed for these adaptations.

In principle, four main strategies for the OMS controller can be performed. First, the entire OMS or its modules can be replaced. Secondly, the existing OMS and/or its modules can be extended by purchased or self-developed software modules. Thirdly, the OMS and/or its modules can be reengineered. And fourthly, the users can be trained. For the selection of a suitable strategy the close coordination and cooperation with the organizational control loop is substantial.

A substantial part of the OMS control loop is its coupling for the systematic evolution of a CCOTS-OMS. In Deifel (2001) a concept for process modeling is presented, which places decisions explicitly into the focal point of each software development activity. Hence, it's possible to create a holistic and systematic transition from the identified deviations of the OMS control loop, over to requirements engineering, up to the architectural software design. The developed process model describes gradual steps from system-independently structured requirements to the aspects and variations of a first architectural design.

The above mentioned flexibility of an OMS is supported by a software architecture, in which several variations are contained and whose activation is to a large extent systematically enabled. However, the responsiveness of a CCOTS is influenced by two other substantial factors. For a vendor, independent reaction and adequate disclosure and standardization of interfaces is required. On the other hand, the responsiveness of the software producer can be improved by facilitating the advancement of the OMS accordingly. This requires a systematic version-spreading and evolutionary development of the CCOTS-OMS.

In the following section, this decision-oriented approach to CCOTS-OMS software development is described in further detail.

DECISION ORIENTED SOFTWARE DEVELOPMENT

The OMS control loop has two main influences on the OMS. Firstly, it influences how the OMS should be customizable, i.e., how the shipped and installed software should be adaptable to customer's problems. The second influence refers to the evolution of the installed software. The two subjects are comparable to problems in the product line area. There a distinction between specifics and commonalties of different software systems in the same application domain is made. Customization relates to the problem of how to derive specifics of individual customers, whereas evolution is a problem of how to define a common reusable architecture for a product line. The OMS control loop results in a decision: whether a customization of the installed software suffices, whether it triggers the evolution of the OMS, or even both. Furthermore, it constrains what has to be done in the follow-up operations.

In this section, the focus is on the evolution of CCOTS-OMS. In Deifel (2001) and Deifel, Schwerin and Vogel (1999), the basics of the decision oriented software development process were presented. Here, the main ideas of this concept are sketched and related to the described OMS control loop. Firstly, the tri-section of development process models into roles, activities and work products is described. Then, an overview over elements of decision oriented development processes is given before the model of work products is introduced. Finally, techniques supporting the description of the introduced model elements are presented.

Roles, Activities and Work Products

A classical principle for modeling development processes is the distinction of the main element types' roles, activities and work products (Derniame, Kaba, & Wastell, 1999), which are shown in *Figure 9*. The distinctions aim at a clear structuring of the development processes in order to support efficient resource planning, adequate task sharing, traceability and consistency tests between different work products.

The elements of the development process are:
- **Role**: Roles define tasks and responsibilities of persons who participate on the development, so-called actors.
- **Work product**: These are central work pieces and results of the development. The most important work product is the developed CCOTS system. Further, in order to reach a systematic development, different work products are necessary to document guidelines and substantial intermediate results. Between different work products exist dependencies, which are described by means of an extra model of work products.
- **Activity**: Work products are stepwise results of development activities, which are executed by actors. Activities are triggered by predefined initial states of related input work products. They finish when their output products reach a specific final state. The execution of different activities

Figure 9: Elements of the development process

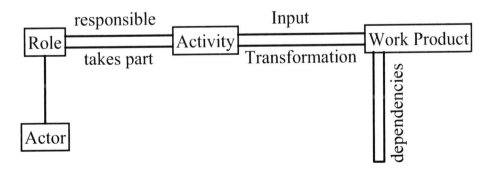

only is coupled by product states. This differentiates this from many existing process models which prescribe a certain sequence of activities.

On that basis, the next section deals with the decision oriented approach for the software development process.

Decision Oriented Software Development Process

The observation that each software development has to pass a sequence of different decision situations led to the idea to model development processes focusing on these. In principle, a decision situation consists of the following elements:

- **Problem space**: The focused problem of a decision situation.
- **Decision object**: Factors which directly influence the resulting solution. In each decision situation more than one decision object can participate.
- **Alternative**: For a given problem space, different possible solutions are defined. The derivation of alternatives is a central part of each decision situation.
- **Measurement criterion**: In order to select the best solution, alternatives have to be evaluated. Measurement criteria drive what is measured in alternatives.
- **Objective function**: With the objective function, the optimization criterion of a decision problem is described. An objective function constrains the minimization or maximization of single measurement criteria and their mutual weights.
- **Solution**: The solution represents the final selected alternative. It represents the optimum of derived alternatives with respect to the given objective function.
- **Guidelines**: Guidelines serve for the systematic derivation of alternatives.

Figure 10 gives an overview of correlations between different elements of a decision situation. The elements of a decision situation are represented by different work products, whereas one work product may even be mapped to different elements within one decision situation at the same time.

During the execution of the decision oriented software development process, the contents of assigned work products are filled stepwise. When each work product has reached a certain predefined state the decision can be made. The steps of work are made within the activities mentioned before. It is differentiated between two kinds of activities, the preparations and the decisions. Within preparations, work products are filled without any preceding decision situation. Compared to the structure of decisions is predefined of a decision situation.

Figure 10: Elements of a decision situation

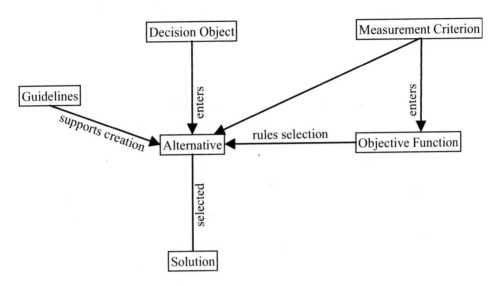

As stated in Deifel (2001), this kind of modeling of the development processes fundamentally increases traceability of development steps and their flexibility. The order of activities is only restricted by mutual dependencies of associated work products. Such dependencies will be demonstrated for work products in architectural design later on in this section.

Development activities within a decision oriented development process can be described schematically with predefined templates. Within this section only the contents of such templates can be sketched, for further details see Deifel (2001). Decisions are described with items like problem space, associated roles, decision objects, measurement criterion, objective function, solution, guidelines, restrictions and method. The template for preparations consists of the associated decision situation, roles, input- and output-work products, guidelines, motivation and method.

Work Products for Software Development

As mentioned at the beginning of this section, work products are in the eye of the decision oriented software development process. Now, the concept of modelling work products introduced in Deifel, Schwerin and Vogel (1999) as well as Deifel (2001) is presented. Important is to describe types of work products and their mutual relationships. In the following paragraphs, a concept for a model of work products is described, consisting of:

- **Product types**: Basic characteristics of a work product are described by its attributes. Product types may be aggregated of other product types.

Similarities between work product types are be expressed by hierarchical generalizations/specializations, which is used here in the sense of a classical "is a"-relationship.

- **Product relationships**: Relationships between work products can be expressed by associations. These associations have the same meaning as relationships in E/R-modeling (Chen, 1976). They can be described more precisely by attributes. Further, work products corresponding to an association can be assigned to roles with respect to the specific association.

- **Model states**: The execution of activities depends on model states. The state of a work product is represented by currently associated attributes, its' currently aggregated work products and its' associated work products. The state of an association describes currently defined associations of association types. The model state is defined by currently defined work products, their states and the state of associations.

- **Description of the model**: Within the current paper we use graphical and textual elements for describing the model of work products. A considerable description further can contain also formal techniques (Deifel, 2001). For the graphical notation it is referred to the notation of UML-class diagrams (Rumbaugh, Jacobson, & Booch, 1999).

Work Products – Decision Oriented Development

Within activities, work products are adequately mapped to the elements of the corresponding decision situation. Due to the same contents, alternatives and the solution of a decision situation are allocated to the same product types. In order to manage complex decision situations, alternatives may be structured hierarchically to divide the problem space into problem parts. To represent this, AND- and OR-aggregations are used. AND-aggregations denote the decomposition of a problem space into corresponding problem parts and OR-aggregations denote alternatives for a corresponding problem part.

DECISION ORIENTED ARCHITECTURAL DESIGN

In the last section, a model for decision oriented software development was presented. Deifel (2001) describes how to elicit requirements for CCOTS and how to develop a consistent requirements specification, which reflects a compromise between customer needs, development costs and development time. The elicitation for requirements is done within the cybernetic model of order management described in the above section. Within this section, a systematic architectural design for CCOTS-OMS, with an intensive use of a model of work products, is outlined. At the beginning, a definition of the term software architecture is given. Then, the concepts of aspects and variations are sketched. In the end, a model of work products for architectural design is presented.

Software Architecture

In literature (Shaw, Garlan, 1996; Jacobson, Griss, & Jonsson, 1997), the most common understanding of software architecture is that it represents a hierarchical decomposition of a software system into subsystems. Each of these subsystems defines some unit of the entire software and is interconnected via interfaces to other components by predefined communication mechanisms. Despite this common understanding, these terms are usually used in very different contexts. Hence, a new approach defined a formal model based on FOCUS (Broy & Stolen, 2001) to get a more precise understanding of these technical terms (Bergner, Rausch, Sihling, & Vilbig, 1999).

In general, software architectures aim at the fulfillment of content requirements, with respect to certain decision requirements, by using some general design principles for the decomposition of the software system. In this context, Boehm (Shaw & Garlan, 1996) talks about an intermediate abstraction between user needs and the final system structure that helps to bridge the gap between user requirements and the software. Others motivate the purpose of software architectures by their support for some pre-selected requirements (Jacobson, Griss, & Jonsson, 1997) like supporting development, maintenance, reuse and evolution of a software.

In the context of this work, software architectures consist of both the decomposition of the system into its subsystems, as well as a mapping from applied design principles to the resulting subsystems. Design principles are represented in this product model by so-called architectural styles. It should be accentuated here that this mapping of an intermediate abstraction to the final system structure is no sufficient motivation for the existence of software architectures. For a decision oriented design, the objective function and the corresponding measurement criteria, i.e., why a specific design principle has been chosen, have to be documented as well.

Aspects and Variations

This subsection sketches a first structuring of requirements into aspects and variations. Both base on the principle of the separation of concerns (Dijkstra, 1976; Tarr, Osher, Harrison & Sutton, 1999), which analyses a problem space with respect to different concerns and describes those separately. Together with research efforts in aspect oriented programming in the late nineties this classical approach regained popularity. New attempts aim at the integration of such basic concepts even in earlier phases (Clarke, Tarr & Osher, 1999; Kiczales, Lamping & Mendhekar, 1997; Walker, Baniassad & Murphy, 1999). In the following, instead of the term concern the term aspect is used synonymously. Also it is assumed that CCOTS can be decomposed reasonably into aspects.

Briefly, each product of a product type aspect describes a specific aspect of requirements from a CCOTS. It consists of the attribute description, which informally describes the aspect. Each aspect aggregates all associated requirements. Generally, requirements can be aggregated to different aspects. For example, in financial software the aspects could be billing, balancing, graphical representations or statistics, etc. In this case, the separation focuses on required functionality of the software system.

Usually, some requirements and, consequently, aspects are not mutually independent. In order to indicate this, the association type "correlates" is introduced. For example, usability and input/output are two separate aspects of a CCOTS. High usability can only be reached if especially the input/output of a software can be accessed comfortable with respect to the users' needs. To indicate that usability has an effect, the association "correlates" is used.

Different customers ask for different requirements, even within the same application area of a CCOTS. Therefore, differences and commonalties have to be described adequately. This description has to be independent from a realization structure in order to fully contain customers' requirements and to avoid an unintentional multiple realization of the same requirements within different parts of a CCOTS. Further, requirements have to be abstracted from individual customers due to the large number of CCOTS-OMS customers.

Such varying requirements are modeled within the model of work products with variation-types and variations. Variation-types are a specialization of aspects and allow respectively describe variations from different perspectives. In addition to requirements, each variation-type aggregates, mutually excluding variations. A variation aggregates requirements of the variation-type to which it belongs. A variation-type may be, for example, the country language for textual output of a software system. Variations of this variation-type are, e.g., English, German and French. Some requirements are aggregated to each variation of a variation-type. They describe the commonalties of a variation-type, which is called a common kernel. Every other requirement of the variation-type is aggregated to exactly one variation. Hence, all requirements which are aggregated to a variation and which do not belong to the kernel describe the specifics the variation. The identification of common kernels helps to identify reuse potentials in the software to be developed.

Due to time and cost limitations, a CCOTS manufacturer cannot realize all customer requirements. Furthermore, between different variation-types, varia-

Table 1: Overview of relationship-types

Associations			Description
Correlates	Variation-type	Requirement	The realization of a requirement is not independent of a variation-type
expects	variation	variation	If the first variation is activated, then the second variation also has to be activated
excludes	variation	variation	Associated variations may not be activated at the same time
wish	variation	variation	Associated variations should be preferred in realization
correlates	variation-type	aspect	At least one of the requirements which are aggregated to the aspect correlates with the associated variation-type

tions, aspects and requirements are different kinds of relationships, which have to be taken into account during development and during runtime. For example, some variations of a variation-type may require variations of another variation-type in order to fulfill its purpose. *Table 1* gives a short overview of the introduced relationship-types.

Description of Variations

In order to describe aspects and variations, extensions of existing specification techniques are needed. It can be distinguished between so-called external specifications and internal. External specifications serve for giving an overview over an existing model of development products. For this purpose UML-class diagrams specialized by stereotypes are used. Product types are represented by stereotypes of UML-classifiers and association types are represented by stereotypes of UML-relationships. Thus, earlier approaches for describing variations of product lines are extended by so-called feature trees (Lam, 1998; Hamer, van der Linden, Saunders & te Sligte, 1998; Davis, 1995; Traz, 1995; Griss, Favaro & d'Alessandro, 1997) and integrated with more general approaches, like class diagrams.

Further specifications describe technical contents of development products in detail. For a comprehensive description of a CCOTS, relationships of internal descriptions to versioning, variations and realization states of requirements also have to be specified. Specifications which describe detailed technical contents and their relationships to the mentioned issues are called internal specifications. In order to reuse well-established description techniques like UML-notations or other tabular descriptions, coloring techniques in order to represent such additional aspects are used. For graphical techniques, background coloring is used by partitioning the drawn graph with Voronoi diagrams and coloring the areas. In tabular specifications cells are colored. This approach generalizes earlier approaches for describing specific aspects in singular description techniques like ER-diagrams, state-diagrams and system structure-diagrams (Kang, Cohen & Hess, 1990; Cheong, Anande & Jarzabek, 1998) or state-charts and activity-charts (Harel, Lachover & Naamad, 1990). To distinguish different variations, different presentation styles for graphical elements (e.g., dotted instead of solid lines) or labels (e.g., italic instead of normal font) are used.

Architectural Elements

Now, the product types for architectural design are described. *Table 2* gives an overview of the mapping of decision elements work products describing architectural work products.

In this context, the work products architectural style, architectural alternative and software architecture represent software architectures in a general sense and therefore can be described with an architecture description. However, they are different in their role in the decision oriented design. For each role, different additional aggregations or associations are necessary for documenting the complete content of a product. To demonstrate this difference, separate products are defined. Architectural elements are described separately, the terms content requirement and decision requirement should be clarified. The terms differentiate requirements for software with respect to their use in the software architecture. Content requirements denote those requirements that directly have

Table 2: Overview decision elements

Decision element	Architectural work product
Decision object	Content requirement
Measurement criterion	Decision requirement
Guidelines	Architectural styles
Alternative	Architectural alternative
Objective function	Objective function
Solution	Software architecture

Figure 11: Elements of architectural design

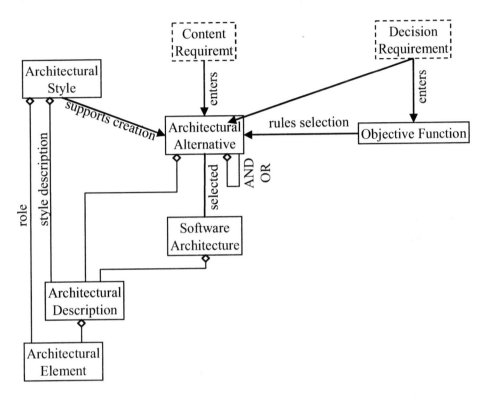

any representation in a software system. Examples for this are all functions software has to fulfill. Compared to this, decision requirements cannot be found directly in software architecture. They are fulfilled more or less in different alternatives. For example, maintainability is a decision requirement. The following paragraph briefly sketches content and purpose of the different architectural elements. For a detailed description it is referred to Deifel, Schwerin and Vogel (1999).

The construction of architectural alternatives in the decision-oriented design depends mainly on content requirements and architectural styles (see *Figure 11*). Further, existing software parts must be taken into account and reduce the possible space of architectural alternatives. The architectural alternatives with their AND- and OR-aggregations span a space of possible software architectures. The final software architecture is a composition of selected architectural alternatives. Each architectural alternative describes a part of a software architecture, which shall fulfill a subset of requirements.

Architectural styles represent experienced knowledge for good architectural design in history and support the derivation of new architectures. They are descriptions of generic architectures, which are independent of specific software systems and of specific content requirements. Architectural styles support the construction of architectural alternatives.

Finally, the software architecture represents a unique decision of alternative architectures. The software architecture is the basis for all further development steps. It documents the complete architecture and the rationale which lead to this decision.

Architectural alternatives, architectural styles and the final software architecture have to be described in an appropriate way. For this purpose, the products architecture description and element are defined. Architectural elements may be refined in an adequate way, like component, interface, connector, protocol, architectural style, etc. In Deifel, Schwerin and Vogel (1999) one refinement solution is described. Other refinements are possible as well.

The architectural description describes the constituents of architecture and their relationships. Hence, it represents a typical description of software architecture. Compared to this, an architectural element is a generic element of an architecture description, which usually is related to a large variety of sub-types. It describes a part of an architecture description.

ACTIVATION STYLES

In the last section, the general view at architectural design as a process of different development decisions was sketched. Now, the impact of variations on architectural design is described. Hence, for a software design, requirements and variations have to be selected and especially their activation styles and their technical realization mechanisms have to be chosen.

Selecting Activation Style: With the activation style of a variation, the way users of a CCOTS can activate their specific variations is meant. Briefly, activation styles of predefined variations can be classified into parameterization and modularization (Conrade & Westfechtel, 1997; Karhinen, Ran & Tallgren, 1997). By parameterization, the software realizes all possible combinations of different variations within one product. In this case, setting configuration parameters of this product activates the variations. Compared to this, modularization denotes software that is separated into different modules. Here, a user can set his configuration state by selecting and combining appropriate modules. A special case for modularization of a CCOTS is the separation of a software into different products which are shipped independently. As is later shown, criteria which influence the selection for activation kinds come from customer requirements, marketing, development and logistics.

Selecting Realization Mechanism: Depending on the selected activation style, a matching realization mechanism has to be chosen. This step may be supported by configuration management, by special techniques within programming languages (e.g., inheritance and polymorphism) or directly by manually programming branches within the program flow.

The decision for the activation style and appropriate realization mechanisms for variations is one of the first steps of architectural design. The rest of this section concentrates on activation styles. Hence, important decision requirements for different activation styles are presented.

Decision Requirements for Selecting Activation Styles

For each variation type an adequate activation style has to be selected. Generally, a larger modularization comes together with higher logistical efforts and a stronger cross-linking of modules. Further, the selected activation style constrains applicable realization mechanisms and consequently influences development costs and time. In the following, main absolute criteria and relative criteria, which are both adapted from the taxonomy for requirement changes introduced in Deifel and Salzmann (1999), are presented.

Absolute Criterion: Time of Change: This duration indicates when a change has to be done:

- *Runtime:* The change has to be done during runtime of the software. For example, production systems may change their configuration without stopping the production.
- *No Runtime:* The change can be done when the software is not running.

Absolute Criterion: Product Separation: In order to increase the return on investment, a marketing strategy may be to reach a clever separation of the CCOTS into different products which are sold independently.

- *Product Separation:* The CCOTS can be separated into different products.
- *No Product Separation:* Every variation has to be sold within one integrated product.

Absolute Criterion: Delivery Time: Closely related to the product separation criterion is the development and logistics criterion on delivery time. Suppose different variations of a CCOTS can be developed concurrently. Then the most flexible way is that the variations can be delivered asynchronously as well.

- *Synchronous Delivery:* all variations are delivered synchronously after a CCOTS has been developed. This leads to easier test procedures and an easier logistics.
- *Asynchronous Delivery:* the completion time of different variations is different. This leads to a more flexible development.

Both criteria, "product separation" and "delivery time," require the possibility to modularize the CCOTS. Note that this is incorporated with an increasing number of modules; the system complexity and logistics efforts increase as well (Karhinen, Ran & Tallgren, 1997).

Relative Criterion: Change Frequency: Another customer criterion is to support requirement changes adequately within the software in order to reach a high usability. Depending on the change frequency, the need for a comfortable configuration of the software system is different. Two different periods can be distinguished:

- *Long-term periods:* the intermediate time between two requirement changes is relatively long.
- *Short-term periods:* the intermediate time between two requirement changes is relatively short.

Activation Styles

Now, four activation styles, which can be found in practice, are presented. It is not taken into account the possibility to define variations with script programming and open interfaces. It is presumed that a variation already is developed and can be activated. The main difference between the activation styles concerns "how" and "when" a user has to choose the activation of a variation. It can be distinguished between purchase time, installation time and runtime. First, activation styles are introduced and then later related to decision requirements.

Activation Style: Setting of Runtime Options: Here, all variations of a variation type are purchased and installed at once on a computer. A user can activate variations during runtime by changing settings of the program, e.g., switching radio-buttons or control-buttons within predefined windows.

Activation Style: Automatic Configuration/Runtime Installation: This activation style does not presume that all variations have to be purchased and consequently installed on a computer. The software can be extended with new variations during runtime (e.g., the addition of plug-ins in commercial web-browsers). This presumes two steps: An automatic installation of new variations and, afterwards, an automatic reconfiguration of already installed software. The new functionality is included within modules that are connected to the already installed software. Hence, the user is passive and responsible for making the new module available.

Activation Style: Installation Selection: Here a user activates a variation during the installation time of the software. In this case he buys all functionality of a variation type together with the purchased package. During installation he selects which variations should be activated. Usually installation selection is supported by installation programs or by editable configuration files. The main reason for using installation selection is the possibility to support static changes like static modularization (i.e., dividing the software into parts which can be exchanged when the software is not running), or the static setting of program options. Changes of activations of variations are done by reinstallations of the software.

Activation Style: Purchase of Different Products: A software producer may develop software as a package of different separately offered products. In this case a customer has to select variations by purchasing adequate products. The activation/deactivation of a variation is done by separate installations/de-installations corresponding products.

Decision Situation for Activation Styles

At first sight, the presented activation styles seem to be very simple. But the main reason for the presentation of the different styles becomes clearer if the selection criteria are mapped to activation styles within a decision situation.

Table 3 shows such mapping.

Table 3: Mapping of activation styles with a decision situation

		Runtime options	**Runtime installation**	**Installation selection**	**Purchase of different products**
Absolute	Time of change	Runtime	Runtime	No Runtime	No Runtime
	Modularization	No	Yes	No	Yes
Relative	Change frequency	Short	Short	Long	Long

Note again that all required absolute criteria must be fulfilled in a selected activation style. Compared to this, relative criteria should be fulfilled as far as possible. As can be seen in the table, each activation style allows a different combination of the two absolute criteria. Therefore in order to cover all "must"-cases, each activation style is necessary.

Finally, a summary and an outlook for future research activities is given.

CONCLUSION

The objective of this chapter is to give advice on how to enhance the changeability of order management systems (OMS). OMS are here referred to complex commercial off-the-shelf (CCOTS) software used to support the order management, like, e.g., enterprise resource planning software (ERP). In this context, the order management process encompasses all activities and organizational units of an enterprise, which are necessary to transformation, customer and/or sales plan orders, into deliverable products. Due to the turbulences on sales and procurement markets, the permanent need for change will be a defining feature in the future business landscape. However, far too often these organizational changes can not be implemented as intended due to the lacking ability of today's CCOTS-OMS.

In order to enhance the changeability of OMS and organizations, the cybernetic model of order management was introduced. This model covers organizational and information-technical views on order management applying systems and control theory to couple business processes and supporting software adequately. The organizational control loop is responsible to ensure the effectiveness and efficiency of the order management process by initiating structural and/or process changes of the business organization in case of identified inefficiencies.

Closely cooperated is the OMS control loop, where OMS are regarded as service providers for tasks and problems from the order management. Inefficiencies of provided services lead to adaptations of OMS structure and/or processes. The OMS control loop is connected to the software development by means of the presented decision-oriented approach. Hereby, software development is seen as a collection of activities, mainly structured by decisions. The decision orientation uses work products for describing aspects, variations and architectural elements. Aspects and variations serve for structuring requirements of the whole market of an OMS. Basing on those architectural elements helps to systematically derive an architectural design, which is easily changeable due to a high traceability of the underlying model of work products.

Future research should focus on the profound specification of the presented cybernetic approach. Further, the architecture derivation should be focused in more detail, e.g., finding mechanisms, which support a systematic realization of presented activation styles.

REFERENCES

Anderson, D. M., & Pine, B. J. (1997). *Agile product development for mass customization*. Chicago: Irwin.

Ausschuss fuer Wirtschaftliche Fertigung, E.V. (Ed.), (1985). AWF-Empfehlung – Integrierter Einsatz in der Produktion. Eschborn: AWF.

Bergner, K., Rausch, A., Sihling, M., Vilbig, A., & Broy, M. (1999). A formal model for componentware. In M. Sitaraman & G. Leavens (Eds.), *Foundations of component-based systems*. Cambridge: Cambridge University Press.

Berlak, J. (2001). Changeable order management. In A. D' Atri, A. Solvberg& L. Willcocks (Eds.), *Proceedings of the OESSEO 2001-Open Enterprise Solutions: Systems, Experiences and Organizations*. Rome: Luiss Edizioni.

Berlak, J. (2003). *Methodik zur struktuierten Auswahl von Auftragsabwicklungssystemen*. Unpublished doctoral dissertation, Utz, Munich.

Berlak, J., & Deifel, B. (2002). Activation styles for changeable Order Management Systems. In M. Khosrow-Pour (Ed.), *Issues and trends of Information Technology management in contemporary organizations* (pp. 70-74). Hershey, PA: Idea Group Publishing.

Bower, J. L. (1994). Jack Welch: General Electric's revolutionary. *Harvard Business Review*, 4, 1-22.

Broy, M., & Denert, E. (2000). *Software pioneers: Contributions to software engineering*. Berlin: Springer.

Broy, M., & Stolen, K. (1999). *Specification and development of interactive systems: FOCUS on streams, interfaces, and refinement*. Berlin: Springer.

Chakravarthy, B. (1997, Winter). A new strategy framework for coping with turbulence. *Sloan Management Review*, pp. 69-82.

Chen, P.P. (1976). The entity-relationship model – Towards a unified view of data. *ACM Transactions on Database Systems*, *1*(1), 9-36.

Cheong, Y. C., Anande, A. L., & Jarzabek, S. (1998). *Handling variant requirements in software architectures for product families*. Las Palmas: ARES II.

Chopra, S., & Meindl, P. (2000). *Supply chain management: Strategy, planning and operations*. New York: Prentice Hall.

Clarke, S., Tarr, P., & Ossher, M. (1999). *Designing for evolution with subjects*. Los Angeles: ICSE'99.

Cockburn, A. (2001). *Agile software development*. New York: Addison-Wesley.

Conradi, R., & Westfechtel, B. (1997). *Towards a uniform version model for software configuration management*. Boston: Harvard University Press.

Darr, W. (1992). *Integrierte Marketing-Logistik: Auftragsabwicklung als Element der marketing-logistischen Strukturplanung*. Wiesbaden: DUV.

Das, T. K., & Elango, B. (1995). Managing strategic flexibility: Key to effective performance. *Journal of General Management, 20* (3), 60-74.

Davenport, T. H. (1998). Putting the Enterprise in the Enterprise System. *Harvard Business Review*, 7-8, 122-131.

Davis, M. J. (1995). *Adaptable reusable code*. Seattle: SSR'95.

Deifel, B. (2001). *Requirements Engineering komplexer Standardsoftware*. Munich: Technische Universitaet Muenchen.

Deifel, B., & Salzmann, C. (1999). *Requirements and conditions for dynamics in evolutionary software systems*. Proceedings of the International Workshop on the Principles of Software Evolution, IWPSE99, Fukuoka.

Deifel, B., Schwerin, W., & Vogel, S. (1999). *Work products for integrated software development*. Munich: Technische Universitaet Muenchen.

Derniame, J. C., Kaba, B. A., & Wastell, D. (1999). *Software process: Principles, methodology, and technology*. Berlin: Springer.

Dijkstra, E. (1976). *A discipline of programming*. New York: Prentice Hall.

Dittrich, K. R., & Gatziu, S. (1996). *Aktive Datenbanksysteme: Konzepte und mechanismen*. Bonn: MITP.

Emery, F. E., & Trist, E. L. (1965). The causal texture of organizational environments. *Human Relations, 18,* 21-32.

European Commission (Ed.). (1996). *Definition of small and medium-sized enterprises*. Brussels: European Commission.

Evans, G. N., Naim, M. M., & Towill, D. R. (1996). Educating the supply chain: An holistic approach. *International Journal of Materials and Product Technology, 11* (5/6), 464-476.

Forrester, J. W. (1961). *Industrial dynamics*. Boston: Pegasus Communications.

Fredenall, L. D., & Hill, J. E. (2000). *Basics of supply chain management*. New York: Lewis Publishers.

Frese, E. (1992). *Handwoerterbuch der Organisation*. Stuttgart: Schaefer-Poeschel.

Griss, M., Favaro, J., & d'Alessandro, M. (1997). Featuring the reuse driven software engineering business. *Object Magazine, 11*, 37-45.

Gulbins, J., Seyfried, M., & Strack-Zimmermann, H. (1998). *Dokumentenmanagement*. Berlin: Springer.

Hafen, U., Kuenzler, C., & Fischer, D. (2000). *Erfolgreich restrukturieren in KMU*. Zurich: VDF.

Hamer, P., van der Linden, F., Saunders, A., & te Sligte, H. (1998). *An integral hierarchy and diversity model for describing product family architectures*. Las Palmas: ARES II.

Harel, D., Lachover, H., & Naamad, A. (1990). Statemate: A working environment for the development of complex reactive systems. *IEEE Transactions on Software Engineering, 16* (4), 240-255.

Harnwell, C. (1998). Supply Chain Management - mehr als "nur" ERP-Systeme. *IT Management, 11*, 27-29.

Heinen, E. (Ed.). (1991). *Industriebetriebslehre: Entscheidungen im Industriebetrieb*. Wiesbaden: Gabler.

Hiquet, B. D. (1998). *SAP R/3 implementation guide*. London: Macmillan Technical Publishing.

Jablonski, S., Böhm, M., & Schulze, W. (Eds.). (1997). *Workflowmanagement: Entwicklung von Anwendungen und Systemen*. Heidelberg: dpunkt.

Jacobson, I., Griss, M., & Jonsson, P. (2001). *Software reuse*. New York: Addison Wesley.

Kang, K., Cohen, S., & Hess J. (1990). *Feature-oriented domain analysis feasibility study*. Pittsburg: Carnegie Mellon University.

Karhinen, A., Ran A., & Tallgren T. (1997). *Configuring designs for feuse*. Boston: Harvard University Press.

Kernler, H. (1995). *PPS der 3. Generation: Grundlagen, Methoden, Anregungen*. Heidelberg: Huethig.

Khoshafian, S., & Buckiewicz, M. (1995). *Introduction to groupware, workflow and work group computing*. New York: Wiley.

Kiczales, G., Lamping, J., & Mendhekar, A. (1997). *Aspect-oriented programming*. Berlin: Springer.

Köhler, C. (1999). Der elektronische Leitstand – Befehlsempfaenger oder Partner der Werkstatt ? *VDI-Z, 132* (3) , 14-20.

Kotter, J. P. (1996). *Leading change*. Boston: Harvard Business School.

Lam, W. (1998). A case study of requirements reuse through product families. *Annals of Software Engineering, 5*, 253-277.

Maucher, I. (Ed.). (1998). *Wandel der Leitbilder zur Entwicklung und Nutzung von PPS-Systemen*. Munich: Hampp.

Meinberg, U., & Topolewski, F. (1995). *Lexikon der Fertigungsleittechnik*. Berlin: Beuth.

Meyers, B. C., & Oberndorf, P. (2001). *Managing software acquisition: Open systems and COTS products*. New York: Addison-Wesley.

Milberg, J., & Reinhart, G. (Eds.). (1997). *Mit Schwung zum Aufschwung: Muenchner Kolloquium 1997*. Munich: Utz.

O' Leary, D. E. (2000). *Enterprise resource planning systems*. Cambridge: Cambridge University Press.

Reinhart, G., Duerrschmidt, S., Hirschberg, A., & Selke, C. (1999). Reaktionsfaehigkeit fuer Unternehmen: Eine Antwort auf turbulente Maerkte. *ZWF, 94* (1/2), 21-24.

Rumbaugh, J., Jacobson, I, & Booch, G. (1999). *The unified modeling language reference manual.* New York: Addison-Wesley.

Scheer, A. W. (Ed.). (2000). *Aris: Business process modeling.* Berlin: Springer.

Schreyoegg, G. (1999). *Organisation: Grundlagen moderner Organisationsgestaltung.* Wiesbaden: Gabler.

Shaw, M., & Garlan, D. (1996). *Software Architecture – Perspectives on an emerging discipline.* New York: Prentice Hall.

Tarr, P., Ossher, H., Harrison, W., & Sutton, S. M. (1999). *N degrees of separation: Multi-dimensional separation of concerns.* Los Angeles: ICSE'99.

Tetenbaum, T. J. (1998). Shifting paradigms: From Newton to chaos. *Organizational Dynamics, 26* (4), 21-32.

Theuvesen, L. (1996). Business reengineering. *Zeitschrift fuer betriebswirtschaftliche Forschung, 48* (1), 65-82.

Traz, W. (1995). DSSA: Pedagogical example. *ACM Software Engineering Notes, 6,* 49-62.

Vollmann, T. E., Berry, T. E., & Whybark, D. C. (1997). Manufacturing planning and control systems. New York: McGraw-Hill.

Walker, R. J., Baniassad, E. L. A., & Murphy, G. C. (1999). *An initial assessment of aspect-oriented programming.* Los Angeles: ICSE'99.

Wallace, T. F., & Kremzar, M. H. (2001). *ERP: Making it happen: The implementers' guide to success with enterprise resource planning.* New York: John Wiley & Sons.

Weiss, A. (2000). *Getting started in consulting.* New York: John Wiley & Sons.

Werder, A. V. (1999). Effizienzbewertung organisatorischer Strukturen. *Wirtschaftswissenschaftliches Studium, 28* (8), 412-417.

Wiener, N. (1948). *Cybernetics.* New York: MIT Press.

Chapter III

ERP System Acquisition: A Process Model and Results from an Austrian Survey

Edward W. N. Bernroider
Vienna University of Economics and Business Administration, Austria

Stefan Koch
Vienna University of Economics and Business Administration, Austria

ABSTRACT

This chapter introduces the ERP software acquisition process based on a rational or normative decision-making approach embedded within the wider ERP system lifecycle. It presents five hypotheses closely related to practical problems during ERP system acquisition, which were derived from a review of recent academic literature and suggestions from students, practitioners and researchers. Based on perceptions of an empirical survey of Austrian organizations, the hypotheses and every stage of the proposed acquisition process model were investigated. Special consideration was given to the differences between small to medium and large organizations. It was assumed that these differ in several phases of the acquisition process. As most ERP system suppliers are today striving to penetrate the market segment of small to medium enterprises, with the market for large organizations mostly saturated, this point warrants particular interest.

INTRODUCTION

An enterprise resource planning (ERP) system is a software infrastructure embedded with "best practices," respectively best ways to do business based on common business practices or academic theory. The aim is to improve the cooperation and interaction between all the organizations' departments, such as the products planning, manufacturing, purchasing, marketing and customers service department. ERP is a fine expression of the inseparability of IT and business. As an enabling key technology as well as an effective managerial tool, ERP systems allow companies to integrate at all levels and utilize important ERP applications, such as supply-chain management, financials and accounting applications, human resource management and customer relationship management (Boubekri, 2001). ERP systems promise the development and sustainment of competitive advantage in the global marketplace through enhanced decision support; reduced asset bases and costs; more accurate and timely information; higher flexibility or increased customer satisfaction (Davenport, 1998; Davenport, 2000; Poston & Grabski, 2000; Rizzi & Zamboni, 1999). But the far-reaching structural changes following an ERP software implementation can also be disastrous, as examples (Bingi, Sharma & Godla, 1999; Buckhout, Frey & Nemec, Jr., 1999; Scott, 1999; Scott & Vessey, 2002) show. A market research company reported that 70% of ERP implementations fail to achieve their corporate goals (Buckhout et al., 1999). Because of the high risks involved, exploring early stages of the ERP lifecycle becomes very important.

In this chapter we focus on the early stage of evaluating and selecting an ERP system prior to implementation. We also focus on the decision-making situation faced by small and medium-sized enterprises (SMEs). This is of particular importance because SMEs are more and more experiencing the need for integration, especially for inter-organizational integration, and expecting ERP software to fulfill these needs. The availability of relatively inexpensive hardware is fostering this situation (Gable & Stewart, 1999). In general, decision-making in SMEs features much greater constraints on the ability to gather information in order to reduce uncertainty about their investment (Cobham, 2000).

On the other side, ERP vendors are in search for new challenges to generate higher revenues and have turned to the small and medium-sized market segments. In the last years, ERP software packages sales flattened. A saturation of the market, as most large organizations have already implemented an ERP solution, decreased the annual ERP market growth (PDC, 1999). By 1998 approximately 40% of companies with annual revenues over one billion USD had implemented ERP systems (Caldwell & Stein, 1998). The small and medium-sized market segment is far from being saturated (PDC, 1999). The total European midsize market for IT products and services surpasses 50 billion dollars per year (Everdingen, Hillegersberg & Waarts, 2000).

In this chapter we will analyse the ERP software acquisition by firstly introducing an acquisition process model embedded within the wider lifecycle of an ERP solution. Secondly, we show characteristics and, especially, specificities attributed to small to medium-sized enterprises (SMEs) for each stage of the ERP system acquisition process. The chapter concludes with the discussion of the research findings and implications for further research and practice.

METHODOLOGY

This chapter draws on results from recent studies published in academic literature and from results of an empirical investigation of ERP decision-making in Austrian organizations conducted by our research institute between December 1998 and March 1999. For the empirical work a design of a questionnaire was employed. On completion of the pilot testing, the mailing, together with separate, prepaid envelopes, followed. In all cases, the senior management of the IT-department was contacted. 813 Austrian small/medium and large-size organizations were addressed and a return rate of 17% was achieved, which corresponds to 138 valid returns. The data was analyzed using a statistical package. Non parametric statistics, such as chi-square, were calculated to test the independence of responses between small or medium-sized and large organizations. When analyzing the strength of a relationship between two variables the Spearman rank correlation coefficient has been used instead of the Pearson correlation coefficient because this analysis has been conducted only with ordinal scaled variables. For comparison of two independent samples that were not normal distributed (tested using Kolmogorov-Smirnov), a Mann-Whitney U-test was employed.

Of the 138 answers received, 22 (or 15.9%) belonged to small or medium-sized organizations. The remaining majority (116 questionnaires or 84.1%) was classified as large enterprises. Classification was performed using data on number of employees and turnover following the definition proposed by the Commission of the European Community (EC, 1996). A consequence arising from the different group sizes is that the precision of the estimates concerning the population characteristics of large organizations is likely to be more reliable compared to the case of smaller organizations, but the statistical tests employed account for the different sample sizes.

THE ERP LIFECYCLE

Firstly, we want to position the acquisition process within a wider ERP system lifecycle, which was originally proposed by (Esteves & Pastor, 1999). It

Figure 1: An ERP lifecycle model (Esteves & Pastor, 1999)

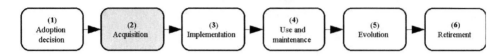

covers six different stages that an ERP system passes during its life within an organization (see *Figure 1*).

In the **adoption decision phase** managers decide to invest in a new enterprise resource planning system to replace the current information system infrastructure in place. The new ERP system is expected to address the organizations' critical business challenges and to improve the organizational strategy and performance. The rational decision-making process begins with the statement of problems and situational goals. Thus, the phase includes the definition of system requirements, its goals, allowed costs and expected benefits.

The **acquisition phase** comprises the selection of the ERP package that best fits the requirements of the organization to minimize the need for customization. This decision is based upon an different sub-stages covering the gathering of all necessary information, the evaluation and comparison of the considered system alternatives (Stefanou, 2001) and making the choice. If a consulting company has not been engaged already in the first stage of the ERP lifecycle, it is likely that it will enter at this stage to support the organization and especially to follow in the implementation phase.

The **implementation phase** deals with the customization, respectively parameterization and adaptation of the ERP package chosen. The implementation phase is usually undertaken with the help of consultants who provide "best ways" to implement and offer trainings. This area also comprises the implementation of all hardware and software related resources needed to introduce the ERP system to the organization. Besides these technical changes, the implementation of an ERP system induces organizational changes, which causes direct consequences on information flow, knowledge, culture, people, and tasks. There is a mutual, bi-directional relationship between the technical and organizational aspects (T. H. Davenport, 1998).

In the **use and maintenance phase** the product should be used in a way that returns expected benefits and minimizes disruption. Therefore the system in use and the effected business processes should be regularly controlled and verified with the goals and benefits formulated in earlier stages of the lifecycle. The functionality, usability, and adequacy to the organizational processes must be monitored and maintained, because malfunctions need to be prevented or corrected and special optimization requests must be met. Also, general systems improvements have to be implemented.

In the **evolution phase** additional capabilities are integrated into or extended to the ERP package to obtain additional benefits. Such an extension, for example, can be customer relationship management (CRM) or supply chain management (SCM) modules.

The substitution of the chosen ERP system will become necessary in the **retirement phase**, when new technologies appear or the ERP system becomes inadequate to the business' requirements. The lifespan of an ERP solution varies greatly depending on the success of the earlier stages in the lifecycle model (Al-Mudimigh et al., 2001). Examples have shown that the far-reaching structural changes following an ERP software implementation can also be disastrous. It may be even be necessary to roll back the entire implementation process if important organizational needs can not be met by the newly introduced enterprise information system. Considering ERP software decisions with its complex and far-reaching implications, poor decision-making can result in disastrous situations. Therefore, especially in the early stages of decision-making, the right actions must be taken to avoid expensive and business threatening consequences. This chapter focuses on phase two of this lifecycle, which involves the selection of the "best" ERP solution as perceived by the decision makers. The framework outlined in this chapter and the investigated research questions represent a further step towards understanding the decision-making process for ERP investments and differences made by SMEs and large organizations. The stage of system acquisition will be analysed based on a general process model for decision making derived from literature, which was slightly adopted for the special needs of selecting an ERP system. For all relevant stages within this model the findings contributing to the introduced research hypotheses will be analyzed.

FEEDBACK LOOPS WITHIN THE ERP-LIFECYCLE MODEL

It has to be noted that various feedback relationships exist in the described ERP lifecycle model. For example, the adoption decision phase should also include an analysis of the impact of adoption at a business and organizational level. Because of the many specificities of different ERP solutions, a thorough understanding of the impact after implementation can only be achieved with a concrete solution as basis for the analysis. The definition and evaluation of system alternatives are steps which take place in the next stage covering the acquisition of the required solution. Therefore an information feedback loop would be necessary between stages one and two (see *Figure 2*).

Figure 2: Feedback from stage 2 to 1

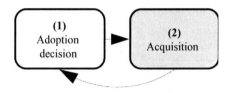

All relevant feedback connections concerning the acquisition stage were incorporated in the following ERP software acquisition process model.

AN ERP SOFTWARE ACQUISITION PROCESS MODEL

The acquisition stage of the ERP lifecycle model involves the evaluation and thereafter selection of the ERP system. Factors such as functionality, price, training and maintenance services are analyzed and the contractual agreements are also defined. In this phase, it is also important to analyze of the return on investment of the product selected. Thus, the acquisition stage is not a single activity that takes place all at once. The process consists of several different activities that take place at different times and that may be repeated. Based on general purpose stage models (Griffin & Pustay, 1996; Moorhead & Griffin, 1998; Simon, 1960) an ERP package decision model was designed (Bernroider & Koch, 2000) (see *Figure 3*). This model was formalized by the Event-driven Process Chains (EPCs) (Aalst, 1999; Scheer & Habermann, 2000) process modeling technique used by some of the leading tools in the field of business process engineering such as SAP R/3 (SAP AG), ARIS (IDS Prof. Scheer GmbH), LiveModel/Analyst (Intellicorp, Inc.) and Visio (Visio Corp.). This rational or normative model of decision-making follows a systematic, step-by-step approach and suggests that managers apply logic and rationality in making the best decisions. Rationality implies that individual behavior has some purpose and that individual actions are systematic and logical in the pursuit of goals. Rationality has been a fundamental assumption in many disciplines like economics, organizational theory and corporate strategy (Ranganathan & Sethi, 2000). At the level of individual decisions, rationality implies gathering information pertinent to the decision, analyzing the information gathered, and generating and evaluating alternatives to make a final choice. Boynton & Zmud (1987) reported that many of the assumptions and premises that underlie the current planning literature reflect a rational model of organizational decision processes. Recent findings report a positive impact of rationality on decision effectiveness in IT decisions (Ranganathan & Sethi, 2000) and in the strategic management area (Dean & Sharfman, 1996; Priem, Rasheed & Kotulic, 1995).

The rational decision-making model supplies a structural design for the second stage of the described ERP lifecycle model, namely the ERP acquisition phase, and comprises the following five steps:

A)   *Composition of the Project Team:* Due to the special importance of group decisions in the selection process of ERP solutions (as described in the next section) the general purpose decision model, which does not incorporate this stage, was extended by this first stage of the acquisition model.

Figure 3: An ERP software acquisition process model

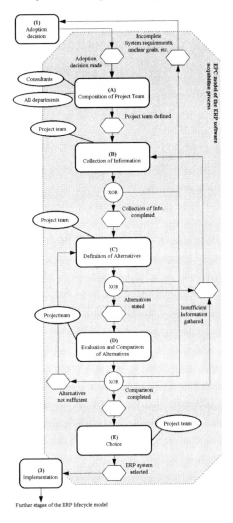

B)   *Collecting Information*: The second stage, where all information relevant for the problem identified is collected. It may be necessary to restate the problem formulation. For this case there is a feedback to stage 1.

C)   *Definition of Alternatives*: In this stage all relevant alternative solutions to the identified problem are conceived using the collected information. It may not be possible to conceive all relevant alternative solutions with the information collected. Also, the problem formulation may be incomplete. For both cases a feedback link exists either to stage 2 or stage 3.

D)   *Evaluation and Comparison of Alternatives*: Every alternative solution needs to be analyzed in order to allow a comparison. During analysis, it might occur that the problem is not well defined (back to stage 1) or that information may be missing (back to stage 2) or that other alternatives must be found (back to stage 3).

E)   *Choice*: The selection within the various solution alternatives and contractual agreements.

In the next section we will describe characteristics of the acquisition model with an emphasis on differences between small to medium and large organizations.

RESEARCH HYPOTHESES

The research hypotheses presented below were derived from recent findings published in academic literature and suggestions from students, practitioners and researchers of our institute in the field of information system evaluation (see also Bernroider & Koch, 2002). The investigated hypotheses were closely related to practical problems, especially management pitfalls, often showing up when implementing and thereafter operating the chosen system, e.g., a low employee motivation.

Hypothesis 1: Most companies are choosing a participative evaluation strategy in the ERP system decision-making process.

An ERP decision produces not only large technical changes, but also large organizational changes (managerial and institutional changes) that affect almost all employees in an organization. Many organizations have undertaken an ERP system decision and implementation (often together with major business process change initiatives) over the past 10 years. It has been indicated (Guha, Grover, Kettinger & Teng, 1997) that not only the technical aspects play a significant role in a successful decision and implementation process. The effective balancing of forces in favor of a change over forces of resistance is also an important task, which is also a major element in change management theory (Kettinger & Grover, 1999; Stoddard & Jarvenpaa, 1995). Organizations, groups, or individuals will resist changes that are perceived as a threat (Davenport, 1993; Guha et al., 1997). The principles of change management especially apply to ERP system implementation (Aladwani, 2001). It is important that the employees relate to the new software environment. On that condition, and with better change management practices, staff motivation will be higher. As has been argued (Appleton, 1997; Davenport, 1993; Hammer & Champy, 1993; Montazemi, Cameron & Gupta, 1996; Willcocks & Sykes, 2000), the participation of the people affected by the system, and knowing the business processes, leads to better decisions and a higher rate of acceptance later on (Guha et al., 1997). In Tayler (1998) possible benefits arising from a participative type of team structure include the motivational improvement of local participation and attention to individual quality of working life, as well as the necessary attention to strategic purpose and to reciprocal and coordinative social roles. On the other hand, it has to be noted that a participative form of decision-making might lead to game playing behavior if one or more parties try to influence the decision process to arrive at their preferred solution (O'Leary, 2000). Given this situation, we suggest that the majority of organizations implementing an ERP solution relied on a participative evaluation strategy. Based on this assumption we have already introduced the first stage "Composition of Project Team" in the ERP acquisition model.

Hypothesis 2: Organizations apply formal evaluation techniques other than conventional financial methods in the ERP system selection process.

The evaluation of information systems, especially ERP solutions, is one of the rather difficult problems to tackle in IT management. Nevertheless, at least one methodology from the vast set of evaluation techniques must be chosen in order to have a tool for an effective and transparent comparison of the different choices of action investigated. Only conventional financial and economic evaluation techniques alone will not suffice. Research in IT has extended the range of tools to include productivity measures, return on management and information economics, to name only a few, and various taxonomies of methods have been put forward (Bannister & Remenyi, 1999; Jones & Hughes, 1999; Kontio, 1996; Lawlis, Mark, Thomas & Courtheyn, 2001; Remenyi, 1991; Sedigh-Ali, Ghafoor & Paul, 2001).

Decision makers tend to describe their decisions as being based to a greater or smaller extent on instinct or individual experiences. The more complex the decision, the more likely this seems to be. We suggest that such a defection from the solid ground of rational decision-making should be avoided. For every ERP software decision, formal evaluation methodologies should be applied. It has been confirmed that IT executives who systematically collected information and analyzed it made more effective decisions than those who did not (Ranganathan & Sethi, 2000).

Hypothesis 3: SMEs apply less formal and less complex evaluation tech-niques than large organizations in the ERP system selection process.

SMEs are usually much more informal and unstructured in their manage-ment style or definition of strategy. This allows them to compete in a very dynamic and competitive environment through high flexibility and responsive-ness. This is a major premise for SMEs to be always close to their markets and customers. Regarding IT investments, many SMEs often seem to lack an explicit IT plan or strategy, or even a defined IT budget (Dans, 2001). Dans even states that decisions to adopt a particular technology are in many cases driven by personal attitudes or perceptions of the firm's owner, rather than by any formal cost-benefit or strategic analysis. Gable & Stewart (1999) proposed that a decisional specificity attributed to SMEs is less usage of formal models when evaluating SAP R/3 systems. Thus, we propose that SMEs apply less formal and less complex evaluation techniques than large organizations in the ERP system selection process.

Hypothesis 4: Higher flexibility is valued higher by smaller organizations.

As already noted, smaller organizations tend to be more flexible than larger ones. Their organizational structure is less rigid and can be changed more easily. The same applies to their business processes. Therefore, and also because they face greater environmental uncertainty due to lesser influence (Gable & Stewart, 1999), smaller organizations have the need and also the means to be more flexible. As the information systems in use have to be aligned with the business strategy and the current business processes, they have also to offer more flexibility to fulfill this requirement. The information systems in smaller organizations should therefore offer the possibilities to implement the current business processes, which might not necessarily follow the standards which are derived from larger organizations, and to be changed easily in order to accom-modate changes to these processes. It can be assumed that this necessary requirement for increased flexibility will also affect the evaluation and selection of ERP packages.

Hypothesis 5: Smaller organizations spend less effort during all stages of the decision-making process.

Smaller organizations face more severe restrictions on their resources, including, among others, financial and human resources. This "resource poverty" also constitutes part of the organizational specificity of smaller organizations (Gable & Stewart, 1999). Slack resources are often scarce or nil (Dans, 2001). It can therefore be assumed that this factor plays a role in the context of ERP selection. This might include, for example, the ways in which information regarding alternatives and their respective quality is gathered, and also the composition and size of the project team responsible for the decision-making.

EMPIRICAL FINDINGS

In this section and for every stage of the ERP decision-making process model, we will report findings contributing to the proposed research hypotheses. We show the results of our empirical investigation, which we also compare within the proposed acquisition model with recent findings from other empirical studies in order to receive an up-to-date description of important aspects concerning ERP software selection.

Stage A – Project Team Composition

As shown in Bernroider & Koch (2000), four different types for the structure of the selection group were identified from more specific data gathered:

i)   Top-management decisions with the inclusion of external consultants (adopted by 17.6% of the organizations).
ii) Centralized decision-making characterized by a strong focus on the IT and organizational department, with only small participation of other internal departments and no employment of consultants (10.9%).
iii) Participative decision-making (35.3%).
iv) Others, respectively diverse structures without a perceivable classification (36.1%).

Hypothesis 1 ("Most companies are choosing a participative evaluation strategy in the ERP system decision-making process") is strengthened by the fact that participative decision-making has been employed by the majority of the organizations. No differences were found indicating that SMEs utilize the participative form more or less extensively than large organizations. In each of the four cases analyzed in Verville & Halingten (2002), the acquisition teams' composition was also interdisciplinary, with team members coming from various departments.

Considering *Hypothesis 5* ("Smaller Organizations spend less effort during all stages of the decision-making process"), the study has shown that smaller organizations use project teams for evaluation and decision-making which are considerably smaller (Bernroider & Koch, 2000). In SMEs, the team size is in the mean 4.82 compared to 9.82 persons for larger organizations. As fewer persons mean less costs, this already contributes to the hypothesis in this early stage of the decision-making process. It can also be noted that SMEs tend to adopt a centralized decision within the IT and organizational department more often in relation to large organizations, maybe because of either a resulting reduction in costs or a lack of know-how in other departments.

Stage B – Collecting Information:

The results of the empirical study strengthen *Hypothesis 5* ("Smaller organizations spend less effort during all stages of the decision-making process") in the context of information gathering. The data showed that smaller organizations employ less diverse approaches, and also show a tendency for less expensive methods (Bernroider & Koch, 2000). For example, the analysis of a prototype or an evaluation by external consultants are used extensively by larger organizations only. Methods such as presentations by ERP system vendors and sending of a requirements catalogue are, in contrast, used by nearly all organizations. In the mean, smaller organizations used 3.05 different approaches, larger ones 3.88 (out of eight different possibilities provided). To obtain data from different information sources is pointed out as being very important for companies engaged in ERP software selection in order to be able to cross-check and verify information, which might be crucial for implementation and usage success later on (Verville & Halingten, 2002).

Stage C – Definition of Alternatives:

Considered alternatives in the decision-making process of Austrian enterprises were ERP solution from SAP (87.5% of the organizations), BaaN (44.5%), Oracle (32.5%), Navision (16.0%), J.D. Edwards (9.2%), Peoplesoft (5.0%) and other, smaller suppliers (47.1%) (Bernroider & Koch, 2000). A similar situation was presented by the Department of Information Engineering at the Institute of Information Systems at the University of Bern (Knolmayer, von Arb & Zimmerli, 1997) for Swiss organizations. In both studies a strong presence of other, smaller suppliers was detected. This hints at a need for more specialized and less complex systems.

Stage D – Evaluation and Comparison of Alternatives:

Seventy-seven point three percent of the organizations used some sort of formal evaluation model in the ERP decision-making process. When excluding conventional financial methods, the rate drops to 30%, which contradicts

Hypothesis 2 ("Organizations apply formal evaluation techniques other than conventional financial methods in the ERP system selection process").

In order to investigate *Hypothesis 3* ("SMEs apply less formal and less complex evaluation techniques than large organizations in the ERP system selection process") the different types of formal evaluation approaches in SMEs and large organization need to be analyzed. The data showed that smaller enterprises use, for the most part, only static investment methods, while large organizations also employ dynamic methods or other methods, such as utilization ranking analysis or even Real Options (Taudes et al., 2000; Trigeorgis, 1996). The use of these methods correlates significantly with the size of the organization. *Hypothesis 3* is therefore strongly supported by the results of our study. It can be assumed that smaller organizations often rely on hermeneutic approaches (Bannister & Remenyi, 1999), defined as methods of interpretation of data which use non-structured and non-formal approaches to decision-making at the expense of the usage rate concerning more complex methods.

The last statement indirectly supports *Hypothesis 5* ("Smaller Organizations spend less effort during all stages of the decision-making process"), as the application of more complex models would necessitate more effort.

Using the results of the study undertaken, differences in the weights attributed to selection criteria were observed (Bernroider & Koch, 2000). Contributing to *Hypothesis 4* ("Higher flexibility is valued higher by smaller organizations") several aspects dealing with flexibility were rated differently. Goals to be achieved by the ERP implementation dealing with this point, e.g., increased organizational flexibility or improved innovation capabilities, were rated as less important by smaller organizations. While this might seem counter-intuitive at first glance, it supports the notion that smaller organizations are more flexible from the start and therefore do not perceive an ERP package as a means to increasing their flexibility, in contrast to larger organizations. On the other hand, characteristics of the ERP systems concerned with the flexibility of the software itself, e.g., adaptability to business processes and flexibility to future changes, are rated higher. It can be seen that achieving a fit between the processes implemented by the ERP solution and the organization's idiosyncratic ways of working is more important for smaller organizations, which more often have some specific, not industry-standard processes. These results are also in accordance with the findings of another survey on ERP adoption in European midsize companies (Everdingen et al., 2000). The authors also found that fit with current business processes and flexibility were the highest rated criteria for information system selection.

Stage E – Choice:

The situation regarding the solutions chosen is similar with the solutions considered. SAP's dominance of the market place was clear (chosen by 69.8%

of the organizations). Again, smaller companies have captured quite a large market share (23.3%), with Oracle (13.8%) and BaaN (11.2%) being the only other contenders of larger size (Bernroider & Koch, 2000). Both the leading position of SAP and the relatively large market share for smaller suppliers are in accordance with the findings of a comparable European survey of midsize companies (Everdingen et al., 2000).

Pertaining to *Hypothesis 4* ("Higher flexibility is valued higher by smaller organizations") and in accordance with the results detailed for Stage D ("Evaluation and Comparison of Alternatives"), the higher rating of SMEs for flexibility-related criteria concerning ERP system alternatives also affects smaller organizations' selection of vendors. For example, the software supplied by BaaN, which is believed to be more flexible than the rival SAP product (Markus & Corenelis, 2000), is chosen more often. SAP R/3, on the other hand, is selected more often by large organizations.

Hypothesis 5 ("Smaller organizations spend less effort during all stages of the decision-making process") concerning Austrian companies is proved when investigating overall duration and costs for decision making including all phases, which is significantly lower for SMEs. The mean duration is 17.57 weeks compared to 30.04 weeks, the costs are about 30.000 Euro compared to 77.000 Euro for larger organizations. While the results given for several phases above have also hinted at the correctness of this hypothesis, these findings prove the difference between organizations of different size.

CONCLUSION

In this chapter the acquisition process for the evaluation and selection of ERP packages was explored. We have presented an ERP software acquisition process model. Special consideration was given to the differences between small/medium and large organizations. It was assumed that these differ in several phases of the decision-making process. As most ERP system suppliers are today striving to penetrate the market segment of small to medium enterprises, with the market for large organizations mostly saturated, this point also warrants particular interest.

We have formulated five hypotheses closely related to practical problems, which were derived from a review of recent academic literature and suggestions from students, practitioners and researchers. Using the acquisition process model and results of empirical studies, the hypotheses relevant for each stage were investigated. In *Table 1* the investigated research hypotheses and the verdict from our analyses is summarized.

The organizational specificities of smaller organizations, e.g., their lack in resources of both financial and human nature, had a great effect on the

Table 1: Investigated hypotheses and verdict from the empirical analysis

No.	Hypothesis	Verdict
H1	Most companies are choosing a participative evaluation strategy in the ERP system decision-making process	Indicated
H2	Organizations apply formal evaluation techniques other than conventional financial methods in the ERP system selection process	Partly disproven
H3	SMEs apply less formal and less complex evaluation techniques than large organizations in the ERP system selection process	Partly proven
H4	Higher flexibility is valued higher by smaller organizations	Partly proven
H5	Smaller Organizations spend less effort during all stages of the decision-making process	Proven

characteristics of the acquisition process. For example, it has been found that while a high percentage of organizations adopt some sort of participative form of decision making, as is also proposed by many researchers and practitioners, smaller organizations show a higher tendency to a centralized form centered in the IT department, and also use teams of much smaller size in the whole process. In addition, the decision in this group of smaller organizations is based on less complex models and less diverse and less expensive methods of information gathering. The criteria for the selection of a particular ERP system were also different, as smaller organizations, which mostly are more flexible today and have a pressing need to conserve this, do not see an ERP package as offering them a chance to become more flexible, but demand a high flexibility from the software itself, so as to be able to adapt it to their current, not necessarily industry standard business processes, and to be able to quickly adapt to new process changes the environment might make necessary. The decision-making process overall can be shown to take both less time and cost for smaller organizations.

Further research would be needed to deal with the differences between small/medium and large organizations for every stage of the ERP system lifecycle. Especially the stage usage and maintenance of the chosen package might also differ between these types of organizations. The findings should then be condensed into one coherent process framework for the whole ERP lifecycle in organizations.

REFERENCES

Aalst, W. M. P. v. d. (1999). Formalization and verification of event-driven process chains. *Information and Software Technology, 41*, 639-650.

Aladwani, A. M. (2001). Change management strategies for successful ERP implementation. *Business Process Management Journal, 7* (3), 266-275.

Al-Mudimigh, A., Zairi, M., & Al-Mashari, M. (2001). ERP software implementation: An integrative framework. *European Journal of Information Systems, 10*, 216-226.

Appleton, E. L. (1997). How to survive ERP. *Datamation, 43*, 50-53.

Bannister, F., & Remenyi, D. (1999). Value perception in IT investment decisions. *The Electronic Journal of Information Systems Evaluation, 2* (2).

Bernroider, E., & Koch, S. (2000). *Differences in characteristics of the ERP system selection process between small or medium and large organizations*. Paper presented at the Sixth Americas Conference on Information Systems, Long Beach, California.

Bernroider, E., & Koch, S. (2002). A framework for the selection of ERP packages for small to medium and large organizations. In L. Hossain, J. D. Patrick & M. A. Rashid (Eds.), *Enterprise Resource Planning: Global Opportunities and Challenges* (pp. 206-222). Hershey, PA: Idea Group Publishing.

Bingi, P., Sharma, M., & Godla, J. (1999). Critical Issues Affecting an ERP Implementation. *Information Systems Management Decision, 16* (3), 7-14.

Boubekri, N. (2001). Technology enablers for supply chain management. *Integrated Manufacturing Systems, 12* (6), 394-399.

Boynton, A. C., & Zmud, R. W. (1987). Information technology planning in the 1990s: Directions for practice and research. *MIS Quarterly, 11* (1), 59-71.

Buckhout, S., Frey, E., & Nemec, Jr., J. (1999). Making ERP succeed: Turning fear into promise. *IEEE Transactions of Engineering Management, 27* (3), 116-123.

Caldwell, B., & Stein, T. (1998, 30 November). New IT Agenda. *Information Week,* pp. 30-38.

Cobham, A. (2000). *Making Bad Decisions: Firm size and investment under uncertainty* (Working Papers from Queen Elizabeth House). Oxford: University of Oxford.

Dans, E. (2001). IT investment in small and medium enterprises: Paradoxically productive? *The Electronic Journal of Information Systems Evaluation, 4* (1).

Davenport, T. H. (1993). *Process innovation: Reengineering work through information technology*. Boston, MA: Harvard Business School Press.

Davenport, T. H. (1998). Putting the enterprise into the enterprise system. *Harvard Business Review*, 121-131.

Davenport, T. H. (2000). *Mission critical - Realizing the promise of enterprise systems*. Boston, MA: Harvard Business School Press.

Dean, J. W., & Sharfman, M. P. (1996). Does decision process matter? A study of strategic decision making effectiveness. *Academy of Management Journal, 39* (2), 368-396.

EC. (1996). *Empfehlung der Kommision betreffend die Definition der kleinen und mittleren Unternehmen* (Amtsblatt der Europäischen Gemeinschaften No. L 107/4). Brussels: Commission of the European Community.

Esteves, J., & Pastor, J. (1999). *An ERP lifecycle-based research agenda.* Paper presented at the International Workshop on Enterprise Management Resource and Planning Systems (EMRPS), Venice, Italy.

Everdingen, Y. V., Hillegersberg, J. V., & Waarts, E. (2000). ERP adoption by European midsize companies. *Communications of ACM, 43* (4), 27-31.

Gable, G., & Stewart, G. (1999). *SAP R/3 implementation issues for small to medium enterprises.* Paper presented at the Fifth Americas Conference on Information Systems, Milwaukee, Wisconsin.

Griffin, R. W., & Pustay, M. W. (1996). *International business: A managerial perspective.* Reading, MA: Addison-Wesley Publishing Company.

Guha, S., Grover, V., Kettinger, W. J., & Teng, J. T. C. (1997). Business process change and organizational performance: Exploring an antecedent model. *Journal of Management Information Systems, 14* (1), 119-154.

Hammer, M., & Champy, J. (1993). *Reengineering the Corporation.* New York: Harper Collins Publisher.

Jones, S., & Hughes, J. (1999). IS Value and investment appraisal. *The Electronic Journal of Information Systems Evaluation, 2* (1).

Kettinger, W. J., & Grover, V. (1999). Special Section: Toward a theory of business process change management. *Journal of Management Information Systems, 12* (1), 9-30.

Knolmayer, G., von Arb, R., & Zimmerli, C. (1997). *Erfahrungen mit der Einführung von SAP R/3 in Schweizer Unternehmungen (Experiences gained from SAP R/3 Implementations in Swiss Organizations)* (Study of the Department Information Engineering at the Institute of Information Systems). Bern: University of Bern.

Kontio, J. (1996). *A case study in applying a systematic method for COTS selection.* Paper presented at the 18th International Conference on Information Systems, Cleveland, Ohio.

Lawlis, P. K., Mark, K. E., Thomas, D. A., & Courtheyn, T. (2001). A formal process for evaluating COTS software products. *IEEE Computer, 34* (5), 58-63.

Markus, L. M., & Corenelis, T. (2000). The enterprise systems experience: From adoption to success. In R. Zmud (Ed.), *Framing the domains of IT management research: Glimpsing the future through the past.* Cincinnati, Ohio: Pinnaflex Educational Resources.

Montazemi, A. R., Cameron, D. A., & Gupta, K. M. (1996). An empirical study of factors affecting software package selection. *Journal of Management Information Systems, 13* (1), 89-106.

Moorhead, G., & Griffin, R. W. (1998). *Organizational behavior: Managing people and organizations* (5th ed.). Boston, MA: Houghton Mifflin Company.

O'Leary, D. E. (2000). *Game playing behaviour in requirements analysis, evaluation and system choice for enterprise resource planning systems.* Paper presented at the 21st International Conference on Information Systems, Brisbane, Australia.

PDC. (1999). *ERP Software 99 Germany: The ERP software industry in Germany, Markets and strategies, 1997-2003.* Paris: Pierre Audoin Conseil.

Poston, R., & Grabski, S. (2000). *The impact of enterprise resource planning systems on firm performance.* Paper presented at the 21st International Conference on Information Systems, Brisbane, Australia.

Priem, R. L., Rasheed, A. M. A., & Kotulic, A. G. (1995). Rationality in strategic decision processes, environmental dynamism and firm performance. *Journal of Management, 21* (5), 913-929.

Ranganathan, C., & Sethi, V. (2000). *Assessing the impact of decision process on effectiveness of strategic IT decisions: A triangulation approach.* Paper presented at the 21st International Conference on Information Systems, Brisbane, Australia.

Remenyi, D. S. J. (1991). *A guide to measuring and managing IT benefits.* Oxford: NCC Blackwell.

Rizzi, A., & Zamboni, R. (1999). Efficiency improvement in manual warehouses through ERP systems implementation and redesign of the logistics processes. *Logistics Information Management, 12* (5), 367-377.

Scheer, A.W., & Habermann, F. (2000). Making ERP a success: Using business process models to achieve positive results. *Communications of ACM, 43* (4), 57-61.

Scott, J. E. (1999). *The FoxMeyer Drugs' Bankruptcy: Was it a failure of ERP?* Paper presented at the Fifth Americas Conference on Information Systems, Milwaukee, Wisconsin.

Scott, J.E., & Vessey, I. (2002). Managing risks in enterprise systems implementations. *Communications of the ACM, 45* (4), 74-81.

Sedigh-Ali, S., Ghafoor, A., & Paul, R. A. (2001). Software engineering metrics for COTS-based systems. *IEEE Computer, 34* (5), 44-50.

Simon, H. A. (1960). *The new science of management decision.* New York: Harper & Roy.

Stefanou, C.J. (2001). A framework for the ex-ante evaluation of ERP software. *European Journal of Information Systems, 10*, 204-215.

Stoddard, D. B., & Jarvenpaa, S. L. (1995). Business Process Redesign: Tactics for Managing Radical Change. *Journal of Management Information Systems, 12* (1), 81-107.

Taudes, A., Feurstein, M., & Mild, A. (2000). Options analysis of software platform decisions: A case study. *MIS Quarterly, 24* (2), 227-243.

Tayler, J. C. (1998). Participative design: Linking BPR and SAP with an STS approach. *Journal of Organizational Change, 11* (3), 233-245.

Trigeorgis, L. (1996). *Real options: Managerial flexibility and strategy in resource allocation*. Cambridge, MA: The MIT Press.

Verville, J., & Halingten, A. (2002). An investigation of the decision process for selecting an ERP software: The case of ESC. *Management Decision, 40* (3), 206-216.

Verville, J. C., & Halingten, A. (2002). A qualitative study of the influencing factors on the decision process for acquiring ERP software. *Qualitative Market Research: An International Journal, 5* (3), 188-198.

Willcocks, L. P., & Sykes, R. (2000). The role of the CIO and IT function in ERP. *Communications of the ACM, 43* (4), 32-38.

Chapter IV

The Second Wave ERP Market: An Australian Viewpoint

Andrew Stein
Victoria University, Australia

Paul Hawking
Victoria University, Australia

ABSTRACT

This chapter presents the market penetration of SAP systems in the Australian market together with an analysis of three mini-case study implementations. The implementations showcase a global rollout, a global consolidation and a "greenfields" small to medium implementation, and present the diverse range of implementations that are occurring in the Australian ERP marketplace. The global ERP industry blossomed in the 1990s, automating back office operations and, in the new century, moves have been made to introduce a "second and third wave" of functionality in ERP systems. Research up-to-date has been limited, especially in the relation to market penetration, of these new "second wave" products in the Australian region. The trend in 2000/01 was for upgrades and restructure in preparation for the move to e-commerce. In 2002, there has been an expanded focus on mysap.com, small to medium enterprises and the expansion into "third wave" products. This chapter looks at the market movement and demographics of companies that have implemented SAP software, the dominant ERP vendor within the Australian marketplace, and will focus on the trends that are impacting the Australian ERP market.

INTRODUCTION

ERP sales now represent a significant proportion of total outlays by business on information technology infrastructure. A recent survey of 800 U.S. companies showed that almost half of these companies had installed an ERP system and that these systems were commanding 43% of the company's application budgets (Carlino, 1999a). The global market for ERP software, which was $16.6 billion in 1998, is expected to have a compound annual growth rate of 32%, reaching more than $66 billion in sales by 2003 (Carlino, 1999b), and is estimated to have had 300 billion spent over the last decade (Carlino, 2000). More recent estimates show a slowing in demand for core ERP systems with an increasing emphasis on upgrades and extended functionality "bolted on" existing systems. There are several reasons for this diversification of ERP systems: integration of business processes, need for a common platform, better data visibility, lower operating costs, increased customer responsiveness and improved strategic decision making (Iggulden, 1999). The primary objective of this chapter is to ascertain the level of ERP implementation in Australia and to profile the demographics of the companies that had implemented this software. SAP Australia was chosen as the study vector, as it is reported as dominating the ERP market in Australasia (IDC, 1999). The first phase of the study, as presented in this chapter, provides an analysis of SAP clients in Australasia broken down by industry sector, organisation size, and types of software implemented. The second phase of the study evaluates the ERP modules implemented as per industry sector and organisation size. This helps to identify implementation trends for companies considering implementing an ERP system. The second phase will also present three SAP implementation mini-case studies to highlight the range and type of organisations moving or upgrading in the ERP marketplace.

ERP MARKET PENETRATION

Market penetration of ERP systems varies considerably from industry to industry. A recent report by Computer Economics, Inc. stated that 76% of manufacturers, 35% of insurance and health care companies, and 24% of Federal Government agencies already have an ERP system or are in the process of installing one (Stedman, 1999). Over 60% of the U.S. Fortune 1000 companies are using ERP systems and this has resulted in the major ERP vendors targeting small to medium enterprises (SMEs, also known as SMBs) to generate new sales (Stein, 1999; Piturro, 1999). This has seen the development of new implementation methodologies and modifications of ERP systems to reduce implementation complexity and the associated costs. Vendors are also extending beyond their core ERP systems to support web-based applications, e-commerce, and customer-relationship management.

The five leading ERP vendors (SAP, Oracle, Peoplesoft, JD Edwards, and Baan), account for 62% percent of the total ERP market revenue (Carlino, 1999b). SAP is the largest client/server and mainframe ERP software vendor with approximately 39% market share. The company has approximately 27,800 employees and 17,500 customers in 110 countries (SAP, 2002) representing 44,500 installations. Curran and Kellar (1998) sought to establish the extent that SAP software had been adopted by major US companies (see *Table 1*). Despite the enormous growth in the use of ERP systems, there is very little research associated with these products (Gable & Rosemann, 1999). This lack of research is further exacerbated when applied to the Australasian region.

A search of current research literature did not reveal any studies that have attempted to quantify the level of ERP usage in the region. Two proprietary reports have been produced related to ERP usage in Australia, however both of these studies had relatively small samples. The Gartner Group's ERP and FMIS Study (1998) surveyed 3,783 Chief Financial Officers and achieved a valid response rate of approximately 11%. This included only 72 responses from companies that had implemented an ERP system from one of the five leading ERP vendors. Nolan and Norton's SAP Benchmarking Survey (2000) surveyed 270 companies that had implemented SAP's ERP software and achieved a 16% response rate.

Table 1: US market SAP penetration (Curran & Kellar, 1998)

6 out of the top 10 Fortune 500 companies	7 of the top 10 petroleum companies
7 out of the top 10 most profitable companies	6 of the top 10 electronics companies
9 of the 10 companies with the highest market value	8 of the top 10 chemical companies
7 of the top 10 pharmaceutical companies	8 of the top 10 food companies

SAP Asia-Pacific

The managing director (Bennet, 2002) of SAP Australia was quoted recently:

> "What we're seeing here now is that Australian ... businesses are gradually and steadily rolling out IT systems that will enable them to take advantage of and grab opportunities when the global economy bounces back."

He was reporting on the expansion of mySAP.com licenses in the Asia-Pacific region and the move to "*second wave*" products. MySAP.com is a new term used to describe SAP's range of products. The term "*second wave*" refers to the expansion of the existing core R/3 system with either third party "bolt-on" products or SAP new products. Along with the move to added functionality, SAP Australia moved to restructure their internal business units (Bennett, 2001). The Sales area was reorganised into three units: Public Sector & Financial, Telco/Utilities and Manufacturing/Mining. The Marketing and Alliance areas were merged and all staff received training in customer engagement. These moves were all configured to move the focus from the product to the customer, which seems to take account of the need to build the business through customer retention and value adding, rather than plumbing new markets. One additional market that is being (Bennett, 2001) explored is the small to medium market. In Australia, there are 10,000 small-medium businesses (SMBs) with the subsidiaries of multi-nationals constituting 40% of the SMBs. The further changes impacting upon SAP Australia have a more global impact, with operations being globalised in 2001 and services in 2002.

RESEARCH METHODOLOGY

The first phase of the study presents the results of an analysis of customer information from SAP Australia. Victoria University is a member of the SAP University Alliance Program. This program was established to develop and deliver ERP education and to promote ERP research in Australasia. In accordance with these guidelines, SAP regularly provided confidential customer data files to the University. The first data file was the customer file that contained information such as client name, contact, implementation date and version details. The second file contained information like name, go-live date and module, which was supplied bimonthly. The two files were combined into a database and cross-referenced with external sources to include financial and other pertinent demographic data pertinent to the enterprises. This data was then loaded in SPSS v10 and analysed with standard statistical measures.

The second phase of the study presents three mini-case studies. Case study research methodology was used as the chapter presents an exploratory look at implications of second wave ERP implementations. Yin (1994, p. 35) emphasises the importance of asking "what" when analysing information systems. Yin goes further and emphasises the need to study contemporary phenomena within real life contexts. Walsham (2000, p.204) supports case study methodology and sees the need for a move away from traditional information systems research methods, such as surveys, toward more interpretative case studies, ethnographies and action research projects. Several works have used case studies (Chan, 2001; Lee, 1989; Benbasat et al., 1987) in presenting information systems research. Cavaye (1995) used case study research to analyse inter-organisational systems and the complexity of information systems. The data collection process included examination of existing documentation, content analysis of email, interview of actors and direct observations.

RESULTS

Customers

A customer according to SAP is an organisation who is using SAP software. In Australia and New Zealand this includes SAP itself, the 17 universities (which are part of SAP University Alliance), SAP implementation partners and the traditional business users of the software. As mentioned previously, SAP has approximately 17,500 customers in 110 countries with 387 SAP customers in the Australasian region. Of these, 329 were based in Australia and 58 in New Zealand. The customers are spread across all industry sectors. SAP uses its own industry sectors to categorise its customers, as illustrated in *Table 2*. SAP Australia includes additional categories to classify its customers compared to the SAP worldwide figures. Although the worldwide figures have less categories, there is an additional "Other" category (11.9%) which does not appear in the Australasian data. It must be remembered that the worldwide data would include the data for the Australasian region. The major sector where SAP software has been implemented in Australasia is the Public Sector (16.5%). Further analysis of the Public Sector category indicated that SAP customers were predominantly at both the Federal and State government levels with only two customers at the Local government level. At State level, the New South Wales and Queensland Governments are the main customers. The Public Sector category reveals a significant difference between Australasian and SAP worldwide, which could be a reflection of the multiple levels of the Australian political system. Also, each department within the governments is classified as a separate customer by SAP. Anecdotally however, SAP admits that they have a very high market penetration in this sector in the Australasian region compared to the rest of the world. The next highest category in the Australasian figures is the SAP Service Providers (11.4%). SAP, up until recently, considered themselves as a software developer and vendor. They did not consider themselves as software implementers and accordingly formed partnerships with a number of companies to perform this role. These were usually the major accounting and IT consulting companies. The "SAP Service Providers" category includes these implementation partners. It is necessary for these companies to internally install the different versions of the SAP software to provide a development and training environment for their consultants. The figures for this category in the Australasian region are comparable with the worldwide figures (11.4% compared with 10.0%).

Table 2: Customers by SAP industry type; Australasia and worldwide

Industry Sector	Australasia Customers (N=387)	World Customers(N=17,583)
Sap Public Sector	16.5%	3.0%
Sap Service Provider	11.4%	10.0%
Sap Consumer Products	8.3%	9.7%
Sap High Tech & Electronics	5.9%	11.1%
Sap Retail	5.9%	6.4%
Sap Chemicals	5.4%	8.5%
Sap Higher Education & Research	5.2%	0.7%
Sap Utilities	4.4%	4.1%
Sap Mining	4.1%	*
Sap Telecommunications	2.8%	3.4%
Sap Media	2.6%	2.2%
Sap Engineering & Construction	2.6%	9.7%
Primary Metal & Steel	2.6%	*
Sap Automotive	2.3%	5.4%
Sap Banking	2.3%	2.0%
Transportation & Storage	2.3%	*
Sap Oil & Gas	2.3%	3.2%
Forest Products & Paper	2.3%	2.8%
Sap Pharmaceuticals	2.1%	3.1%
Metal Products	2.1%	*
Building Materials, Clay & Glass	1.8%	*
Sap Insurance	1.6%	1.9%
Textiles Production	1.3%	*
Sap Aerospace & Defence	0.8%	1.5%
Sap Healthcare	0.5%	2.4%

* SAP worldwide has an "Other" category at 11.9%

The major discrepancy between the Australasian and worldwide figures occurs in the Higher Education and Research category (5.2% and 0.7% respectively). This can be explained by how SAP Australasia classifies its customers. The 17 universities that are part of the SAP University Alliance program in Australasia have been included in this category. These universities receive the software free of any cost, which is in contrast to the three universities within Australia that are using SAP software as a business system. It would appear that the worldwide figures only include universities that have purchased the software. There are approximately 170 universities in the Americas which are part of the SAP University Alliance Program. If they were included in the worldwide figures, then the category percentage would be far higher than its present value (0.7%). This reinforces the assumption that the worldwide figure only includes universities that have purchased the software. SAP produces a pre-configured version of their software designed specifically for the Higher Education and Research sector. However, none of the universities within Australasia have purchased this version, rather opting for the standard version of the SAP software. There are many other discrepancies between the Australasian and worldwide figures, especially in the Engineering & Construction and Healthcare sectors, which cannot be explained at present. This is a potential direction for further research. In the Nolan and Norton (1999) study it was concluded that the majority (55%) of SAP customers were from the Consumer and Industrial Markets classification (*Table 3*). Even though the study had a smaller sample and was limited to Australian customers, their findings are indicative of the Australasian market when compared with *Table 2*. The major discrepancy between our analysis and Nolan and Norton's is in the

Table 3: Australian customers, Nolan & Norton industry type (Nolan & Norton, 1999)

Industry Sector	Australia Customers (N=43)
Consumer & Industrial Markets	55%
Public Sector	16%
Energy and Natural Resources	14%
Health Care and Life Services	5%
Information/Communication/Entertainment	5%
Financial	5%

Higher Education sector. This, however, would be for the same reason outlined earlier. The size of the enterprise is an important factor when considering market penetration. Traditionally, SAP was restricted to larger organisations due to its complexity and associated costs. As mentioned, SAP, as well as the other ERP vendors, have developed a number of strategies to reduce implementation costs in an attempt to make their software more affordable to mid-range organisations (Piturro, 1999). The customer data was classified by revenue to provide an indication of the size of companies implementing SAP software. Business Review Weekly (2000) annually produces the BRW1000, which is a ranking by revenue of the largest listed, private, government and foreign enterprises operating in Australia. Using the BRW figures, financial data was obtained for 146 of these companies (*Table 4*).

There was difficulty sourcing data for the remaining companies as they were either public sector organisations (16.5%), universities (5.2%), or subsidiaries of larger companies. Companies using SAP software represent over $205.6 billion in annual revenue. According to *Table 3*, the majority of companies (60%) had annual revenues over $500 million, which supports the notion that large companies are the dominant market for ERP vendors. However, 40% of the companies had revenues under the $500 million, with the lowest

Table 4: Customers (N=146) by size (revenue) (Nolan & Norton, 1999)

Size $millions	Customers %
>1000	38%
750-1000	8%
500-749	14%
250-499	20%
<250	20%

Table 5: BRW analysis of SAP breakdown (BRW, 2000)

The largest 5 employers use SAP	2 out of top 3 diversified resources companies
3 out of top 5 private companies	2 out of top 3 diversified industrials companies
4 out of top 5 public companies	2 out of top 3 energy companies
2 out of top 3 building materials companies	4 out of top 5 communication companies
3 out of top 5 mining companies	

being $58 million. The large percentage of smaller companies reflects the shift in ERP vendors' strategy in recent years to target small to medium enterprises. Future research comparing the date of implementation to the size of the company could further test the effectiveness of this strategy. This will help determine whether market penetration of smaller companies has been a recent occurrence. Previously, figures were presented on market penetration in the Fortune 500 US companies (Curran & Kellar, 1998). Using the BRW1000 list, similar statistics can be produced for Australian companies who have implemented SAP software.

A recent report identified the top 100 IT users in Australia. Using the SAP customer list it was determined that nine out of the top 12 IT users were SAP customers and 45% of the total list were also SAP users.

Implementations

From 1989 to July 2000, 387 customers implemented or were in the process of implementing SAP software. This does not include update or upgrade implementations. A break down of the initial year of implementation for each customer is included in *Table 6*.

The data indicates that approximately 65% of companies have had their ERP systems for at least two years. Nolan and Norton (2000) grouped implementations into levels of maturity. They argued that when evaluating costs of an ERP implementation, the company's previous experience with ERP systems should be considered. Their maturity classifications were:

- Beginning – implemented SAP in the past 12 months,
- Consolidating – implemented SAP between one and three years,
- Mature – implemented SAP for more than three years.

Table 6: Customer implementations by year (Nolan & Norton, 2000)

Year	Number of Implementations	%
1989/94	13	3.4%
1995	28	7.2%
1996	41	10.6%
1997	62	16.0%
1998	109	28.2%
1999	72	18.6%
2000	45	11.6%
Not specified	17	4.4%

Applying the maturity classification to the above data indicates that the majority of Australasian companies are in the Consolidating stage (58.4%), followed by the Mature phase (37.2%), and the Beginning phase (11.6%).

The increasing numbers of implementations leading up to 2000 reflect companies implementing solutions to the Y2K problem. A recent study by the Institute of Management Accountants (2000) found that 64% of companies surveyed had initiated an ERP project to redress their Y2K issues (Krumwiede et al., 2000). This could also partially explain the decrease in implementations after 2000. Additionally the post-2000 decrease would also be due to the introduction of a consumption tax (Goods and Services Tax) in Australia in June 2000. Many organisations would have focused their information technology expenditure on modifying their existing systems to calculate and record this new tax. The data indicated that although there were 387 customers, this represented 711 instances. An instance is a separate implementation of SAP software, usually for the purpose of handling data for a separate company within the overall enterprise or used to support an installation of one of SAP's software solutions. *Table 7* provides details of the different SAP products and the number of implementations. SAP has developed two major releases of their ERP software. The first was R/2, which was mainframe based, while R/3, their newer client server based version was released in 1992. In addition to their ERP software, they released a range of products that were referred to as the *"second wave"* products. These products were basically enhancements to the ERP software. They included Business Information Warehouse (BW), Knowledge Warehouse (KW), Strategic Enterprise Management (SEM), Customer Relationship Management (CRM) and Advanced Planner and Optimisation (APO). SAP recently has grouped its *"second wave"* products and R/3 with added e-Commerce functionality (Workplace/Portal and Marketplace) and referred to it as mySAP.com.

Table 7: Second wave implementations by year (Bennett, 2001)

Software	Pre-2001 Implementations	Live 2001 Implementations	User Segment	Key Market
R/3	506	N/a	N/a	All
CRM	69	29	>50	AU/NZ
eProc	56	12	>50	AU/JP/SG
BW	263	110	1-20	AU/JP
APO	73	15	1-20	AU/NZ
Workplace	122	31	>20	AU/Korea

SAP's major sales in the Australasian region have been its R/3 product. The 506 R/3 implementations represent 374 customers, which indicates that many of these customers are now adding value to their ERP implementation by purchasing the "*second wave*" products. Even though SAP is attempting to develop new markets for their R/3 product, it would be expected that the sales of the "*second wave*" products will increase, while sales of R/3 will decrease due to market saturation. It could be argued that the implementation of "*second wave*" products is a measure of maturity of the ERP implementation. It would be expected that companies would not be implementing any of the "*second wave*" products until their ERP implementation was fully functional. Therefore, there would be a relationship between a company's experience with SAP R/3 as defined by Nolan and Norton's (2000) maturity classification and the implementation of the "*second wave*" products. MySAP.com is touted as SAP's eBusiness solution that facilitates back-end and front-end integration.

The "marketplace" component provides a foundation for collaborative eBusiness. The data supplied by SAP will provide a basis for determining the extent of eBusiness solutions implementation by many of the leading companies in Australasia. A direction for future research would be the relationship between levels of maturity as defined by Nolan and Norton and the adoption of eBusiness solutions. Chris Bennett (Bennett, 2001) signalled this move into added functionality when he commented,

> "All these wins and conversion programs signal the next stage in the e-commerce environment."

To look at the spread of business activity of SAP Asia-Pacific three case studies are presented: a global roll-out representing a full R/3 with extensive second wave functionality, the national upgrade showing the conglomeration of disparate systems into one R/3 roll-out, and, finally, the SMB roll-out. Each case will show a diversity of implementations, features and impacts.

MINI-CASE STUDY 1:
THE GLOBAL ROLL-OUT

In 2001, Cadbury Schweppes instigated project PROBE (Programme Realisation Of Benefits Enabled ERP). This is not just an ERP rollout, but a global project to re-engineer the existing processes and systems to capture expected benefits. The enterprise developed eight guiding principles in a Future Business Process Model (FBPM, see *Figure 1*). The PROBE global project involves 13,000 users in 27 business units spanning 15 countries. The first rollout

Figure 1: Future Business Process Model (FBPM) (BCO5651, 2002)

Master Data	Organisation Capability
Knowledge Management	Global Standards
Shared Activities	E-Business
Sales & Operations Planning	End to End E-Enabled ERP Systems

was conducted in 19 sites across Australia involving 1,500 users. Countries that were involved included Australia, New Zealand, USA, UK, Sweden, South Africa, Germany, Canada and Belgium, with Price Waterhouse Coopers as the Global implementation partner.

The FBPM divides the business into seven areas that are used for the process design (see *Figure 2*). Each of these areas is decomposed into groups, processes and tasks and then into transactions. The process and data design have produced upwards of 450 flowcharts.

Once the processes are disassembled they are then analysed and built into a new business process.

The decomposition of existing processes to yield new processes promises to yield major benefits (see *Figure 3*).

Figure 2: FBPM, process mapping

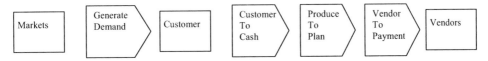

Figure 3: Cadbury Schweppes blueprint benefits

Cross functional	Performance measures included
Integrated	Job roles included
Finite number of end-to-end scenarios	Benchmarked on SAP best practice
Consistent, common & routine approach to data	Benchmarking fully enabled

Figure 4: Five track implementation (BCO5651, 2002)

Program Management	Go-Live Change Integration Technical Infrastructure Systems Integration Process & Data Design	Local Implementation

This re-engineering process is extensive and Australia was selected as the first go-live before it is to be rolled out world-wide. The choice of Australia as test site is interesting, as the head office is sited in the United Kingdom. The systems to be implemented go from the supply chain to CRM. The implementation follows five tracks (see *Figure 4*).

A variation of ASAP was utilised for implementation with the main phases being Blueprint Input, Blueprint Internalisation, Local Realisation, Final Preparation and Go-live Support. The global roll-out is all-encompassing in scope. The next mini-case looks at a national upgrade for the "Big Australian."

MINI-CASE STUDY 2:
THE GLOBAL CONSOLIDATION

Broken Hill Proprietary (BHP) is the "Big Australian." For decades, BHP was the largest Australian company and mirrored the resource nature of Australia's economy in the 20th century. In 2001, BHP merged with the UK-based Billiton Corporation to form BHPbilliton, one of the largest resources enterprises in the world. In Australia, BHP had commenced a global consolidation of its ERP systems. Throughout the company (BHP, 2001) there were 27 different ERP systems, including several different ERP platforms operating on a number of hardware platforms. Whilst many of the systems were SAP, they had been implemented differently and master data had been defined differently depending on what industry and country it was to support. This made it very difficult to compare data from the different areas of the company. The new implementation, known as GSAP, would focus exclusively on SAP and be based on common definitions of master data across the company. Added functionality was incorporated in the "upgrade," including knowledge management (KM), advanced planner and optimiser (APO) and business warehouse (BW). All systems are to be hosted on two servers, one based in Australia and the other in

America. The scope of the rollout was expected to exceed $AUD200 million. The Billiton Corporation was also a SAP customer before the merger. The common definition of master data developed by BHP and the global consolidation has extended to include the Billiton Corporation. The total project is now expected to exceed $AUD600 million.

MINI-CASE STUDY 3:
THE "GREENFIELDS" SMALL TO MEDIUM ENTERPRISE

Tyco Flow Control is an Australian-based (SAP, 2002a) subsidiary of Tyco International. The company found that, due to a number of acquisitions over recent years, their manufacturing and corporate systems faced a number of difficulties when providing connectivity between the various business units. The company decided to implement SAP R/3 in its Unistrut division. Unistrut manufactures and markets a wide range of metal framing systems and electrical and mechanical support systems. The scope of the project was to support the full planning cycle from forecasting and budgeting to detailed production scheduling. The company implemented SAP's sales and distribution, production planning and controlling modules, as well as the advanced planning and optimisation (APO) solution. The total cost of the project was $AUD2.5 million. The company found post-implementation a number of benefits, including the reduction of physical inventory, counting to a daily job with no additional person-power from a task, which occurred twice a year involving 15 people over three days.

DISCUSSION

The use of ERP systems in Australasia is well established with many leading companies implementing these types of systems. The companies represent all industry sectors with the Public Sector being most dominant. The companies vary in size and the products implemented. Sales have slowed since 2000 and it will be interesting to follow future sales' trends and directions. Research related to the extent of ERP implementation has been limited. This study into the ERP (SAP) market in Australasia provides a foundation for future research into the adopters of ERP systems. The data that SAP has provided to the university is invaluable and will enable researchers to conduct ongoing research into the various implementation trends associated with these products. Throughout the chapter there are indications of the type of research in progress as an extension of this initial study as well as future directions. These studies, other than contributing to the gamut of knowledge associated with ERP products and information systems, will be a valuable resource to companies considering the implementation of this type of software. It is envisaged that these series of studies will provide benchmarks for various aspects of ERP implementations. Originally, ERP systems were developed to support very large companies in a narrow range of industries. As this market became saturated, the ERP vendors have added functionality to enable them to explore new markets. The data presented in this chapter reflects the diversity of ERP implementations in terms of company size, industry sector and functionality. In the Australasian region many companies are now looking at how to get added benefits from their initial investment in their ERP system. They are increasing the level of functionality offered by their ERP system or implementing some of the "bolt on" solutions such as data warehousing and customer relationship management.

It appears that many companies were pushed down the ERP path by year 2000 compliancy and/or poor disparate systems. These implementations have matured to a certain extent, enabling companies to investigate how they can further leverage their investment in the ERP system. The second wave of implementations are proactive, compared to the reactive nature of initial implementations, and are strategic in nature, forming the basis for future initiatives.

CONCLUSION

This chapter has presented the emerging market positions of SAP Australia and the necessity to be agile and pursue new markets in order to remake the business. The three emerging markets are the upgrade value adding markets, the "*second wave*" added functionality market and the small-to-medium market. Further research needs to maintain a focus on the emerging themes of ERP business and to do this it will be necessary to further track new implementations, new products, the success of these new products in the marketplace and the emerging role of implementation partners. Several emerging trends that should be the basis for further study include virtual supply chains, employee self-service modules, employee/enterprise portals, and the ability of these portals to interface SAP and non-SAP systems.

REFERENCES

BCO5651, (2002). Presentation of Global Rollout, Enterprise Implementation Seminar, Victoria University, April 20th, 2002.

Benbasat, I., Goldstein, D., & Mead, M. (1987). The case research strategy in studies of information systems. *MIS Quarterly, 11* (3), 369-386.

Bennett, C. (2001). SAP Update, delivered to ASUG Plenary, December.

Bennett, C. (2002a). SAP expands mySAP.com user base with new contracts and additional licenses. Retrieved May 16, 2002 fromhttp://www.sap.com/australia/company/press/2002/0508.asp.

BHP (2001). BHP SAP Update, delivered to ASUG Plenary, December.

BRW (2000). The BRW1000. *Business Review Weekly* Retrieved on October 20, 2000 from http://www.brw.com.au/stories/19991113/intro.htm.

Carlino, J. (1999a). AMR research predicts ERP market will reach $66.6 billion by 2003 Retrieved January 7, 2000 from http://www.amrresearch.com/press/files/99518.asp.

Carlino, J. (1999b). AMR research unveils report on enterprise application spending and penetration. Retrieved January 7, 2000 from http://www.amrresearch.com/press/files/99823.asp.

Carlino, J. (2000). AMR research predicts enterprise application market will reach $78 billion by 2004. Retrieved January 8, 2002 from http://www.amrresearch.com/press/files/.

Cavaye, A. (1996). Case study research: A multi-faceted approach for IS. *Information Systems Journal, 6* (3), 227-242.

Chan, R., & Roseman, M. (2001). Integrating knowledge into process models: A case study. In *Proceedings of the Twelfth Australasian Conference on Information Systems*. Southern Cross University, Australia.

Curran, T., & Kellar, G. (1998). *SAP R/3 Business Blueprint*. Prentice Hall, NJ.

Farley, D. (1998, March). Defining enterprise resource planning. *APICS*.

Gable, G., & Rosemann, M. (1999, November 1-2). ERP in university teaching & research: An international survey. In *Proceedings of the 3rd Annual SAP Asia Pacific Institutes of Higher Learning Forum Maximizing the synergy between teaching, research and business, Singapore.*

Gartner Group, (1998, November). ERP and FMIS Study. Sydney: Gartner Group.

IDC (1999). ERP Market Statistics. Sydney: IDC.

Iggulden, T. (Ed.) (1999, June). Looking for Payback. *MIS*, 75-80

Krumwiede, K. R., & Jordan, W. G. (2000, October 31). Reaping the promise of enterprise resource systems. *Institute of Management Accountants*. Retrieved August 9, 2000 from http://www.erpsupersite.com/scream/nov/1/sm-20001101a.htm.

Lee, A. (1989). Case studies as natural experiments. *Human Relations, 42* (2), 117-137.

Nolan & Norton Institute (2000). *SAP Benchmarking Report 2000*. KPMG Melbourne.

Piturro, M. (1999, September). How midsize companies are buying ERP. *Journal of Accountancy, 188* (3), 41-47.

SAP (2002a). SAP Best Practice Awards. Retrieved October 5, 2002 from http://www.sap.com/.

SAP (2002b). SAP Corporate Profile. Retrieved October 5, 2002 from http://www.sap.com/company/profile_long.htm.

Stedman, C. (1999, August 16). What's next for ERP? *Computerworld, 33* (33), 48-49.

Stein, T. (1999, January 4). Big strides for ERP. *InformationWeek, 715,* 67-69.

Walsham, G. (2000). Globalisation and IT: agenda for research In *Organisational and Social Perspectives on Information Technology* (pp. 195-210). Boston, MA: Kluwer Academic Publishers.

Yin, R. (1994). *Case study research, design and methods,* (2nd edition). Newbury Park: Sage Publications.

Chapter V

Enterprise Application Integration: New Solutions for a Solved Problem or a Challenging Research Field?

Joachim Schelp
University of St. Gallen, Switzerland

Frederic Rowohl
University of St. Gallen, Switzerland

ABSTRACT

When closing the loop back to legacy systems, data warehousing is becoming a general IT integration topic, which is — partly — discussed under the label enterprise application integration. This article enables the interested reader to identify current problems in enterprise application integration. It shows solutions reached in previous research efforts, as well as solutions provided by today's software vendors. Finally, it sums up the pending gaps and open research fields.

INTRODUCTION

For many years, the integration aspect has been a main topic in both theory and practice of computer science. The overall aim is to integrate heterogeneous applications across processes in the whole enterprise. During the last decade, several approaches have been made in both research and practice to establish such integrated information systems (Mertens, 1966; Scheer 1995; Merttens, 1995). The theoretic approach often is to propose new application systems or architectures. For example, Scheer (1995) and Mertens (1995) worked on reference models for the integration of applications (and data). Other approaches focus on data flows, processes or functions.

Still today, there is an increasing demand for integrating applications in the business area. Pending integration efforts, like data warehousing projects, are to be extended to bring their results back to legacy systems, e.g., to feed customer relationship management systems. New business models require the adoption of new technologies without leaving enough time to build up completely new systems: existing applications have to be extended by connecting them to new application types bearing these new technologies. The development of horizontal applications is an example of this trend (Winter, 2000).

Although several approaches were developed to integrate existing applications, software vendors still present new toolkits based on new technologies to address the specific needs of enterprise application integration problems. As these technologies are not mentioned explicitly in the existing approaches for application integration, we have to ask whether these approaches fulfill today's needs and represent the state of the art in application integration. Main problems occur in both increasing complexity and dynamics of today's businesses and information technologies, as well as in varying decentralized architectures. Furthermore, for most of the approaches presented in research, existing applications or architectures are discarded in favor of new ones without referring to or even *integrating* the existing set of systems.

This article derives specific problems occurring from integration and requirements for the integration of existing heterogeneous applications regarding current business needs. After an initial discussion, we will show the result reached in several research projects in the past and compare them with the problems and requirements described before. In a third step we ask for current solutions provided by both software vendors and the scientific community. Again, we will compare these solutions with the problems and requirements described initially. Finally, we show the gaps still pending and deduce the open research problems. A short conclusion will round up this paper.

CURRENT REQUIREMENTS FOR INTEGRATION OF APPLICATIONS

As stated above, still today integration is an urgent need for companies. This has several reasons, which result from the rapidly evolving technological environment and the fast adoption in business processes:

- New technologies enable new application types, opening new distribution channels for companies. For example, in the banking area there are not only ATM-networks as an additional front-end to the customers but also WWW- or WAP-interfaces. And again, new technologies like UMTS are at the horizon (EITO, 2001).

- Because of the internet, there is an urgent need for enabling online transactions instead of the old-fashioned batch processes. Batch processing methods require time frames which customers do not accept when initiating online transactions.

- New applications for customer relationship management extend the need for transferring analytical data from data warehouses back into transactional systems. This remarkably impacts performance, access, and data organization for these systems. Data has to be organized by subjects and not only by relations, online transactions are required as well as short request times. These are challenges for both analytical and transactional systems, which today fulfill only one or two of these requirements.

- Integrated solutions, like enterprise resource planning systems, reach their limits when new technologies must be incorporated. Therefore, additional tiers must be introduced in the information system environments to add an additional transformation layer between old and new applications.

To sum up these problems, we can derive the following requirements. The above problems can be united to *complexity* (in different ways), *compatibility* (e.g., to exchange data), and limited *capacity* of existing systems.

- The higher a legacy systems' data, function, and process models' complexity is, the more complex is an integrated logical view on them. But this is required to couple the systems together. Therefore, there is a strong requirement to build integrated logical models of different levels of complexity.

- Especially old legacy systems have limited means of importing or exporting data in foreign formats. To exchange and convert data between different systems, metadata has to be collected, structured, and exchanged. Therefore methods and tools for metadata management are required which can enable data quality issues as well.

- From a more technical point of view, additional application layers are required as the older legacy systems are often working at their capacity limit. Because of little system performance, sometimes they cannot export and import data to additional systems even if they have the functionality to do this. The resulting enhanced IT landscape of a company must be planned and maintained.

These requirements are a challenge. As technological improvements are still at the beginning, companies are urged to work with continuously changing environments. Heterogeneity in the IT-landscape within an enterprise will be an ongoing challenge, which has to be met by IT-concepts and strategies as well as by middleware applications in use.

The addressed requirements can be met on a more conceptual and on a more technical level. Conceptual approaches developed in the previous decades are discussed in the following section, technical solutions as well as current conceptual work are presented later.

PREVIOUS INTEGRATION APPROACHES

Since the early 1970s, the need for integration and concepts of integration of enterprise applications has been a broadly discussed topic in the computer science community. Several existing suggestions have been made and further developed in literature. However, not all were implemented in practice, so a proof of concept has not been made for each proposed solution. With today's increasing demand for integration models, the view of existing approaches could give an indication of recent research efforts. This chapter gives an overview of existing integration models and procedures.

Different views on integrated information management can be distinguished (Mertens, 1995):

1. *Integration object*
    The integration object can be data, functions, processes, methods, and programs.
2. *Direction of integration*
    The direction of the integration can be horizontal or vertical.
3. *Range of integration*
    The integration can take place in one area of an enterprise, in the whole enterprise, or between different enterprises.
4. *Degree of automation*
    The intended degree of automation can be full automation or automation in parts.

Concerning the integration object, recent models focus on both data and functions, and partially on processes. The other views are secondary and often

Figure 1: Integration of data and functions (Mertens, 1995)

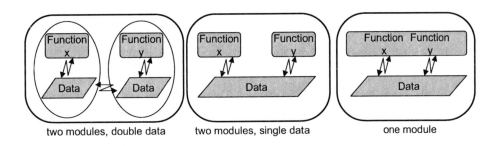

follow the integration object. Different levels of integration of data and functions are shown in *Figure 1*. In the left figure, two systems exchange and process data automatically. This is a very simple way of integration, but the data has to be stored redundantly. In the middle figure, different applications use the same database. The data has to be modeled in an appropriate way to integrate it in one database. In the right figure, the functions are linked together on a technical level. The result is an integration of functions (see also Mertens, 1995, p. 24).

Basically, existing integration models can be divided in data oriented, function oriented, and others (Mertens & Holzner, 1992).

Data Oriented Integration Models

The models developed by Vetter, Scheer and Rauh are good examples for data oriented integration concepts. At least Scheer's model is known beyond German speaking countries, because of his model's (ARIS) role in the customization process for enterprise resource planning systems like SAP R/3.

"Conceptual Data Model" by Vetter (1990)

Vetter separates in his Conceptual Data Model different phases of development, namely the design of the object system, the information system, the database concept, and the processes. He defines a bottom-up approach when he develops the enterprise wide data model by joining the separated data models of applications from the business departments. The aim is to develop an extensive data model of the informational environment.

"ARIS" by Scheer (1991)

Scheer developed "Architecture of Integrated Information Systems (ARIS);" a framework for development, optimization and realization of integrated applications. The "ARIS-House" (*Figure 2*) is an architecture combining multiple views and levels of integration.

Figure 2: The "ARIS-House" (Scheer, 1991)

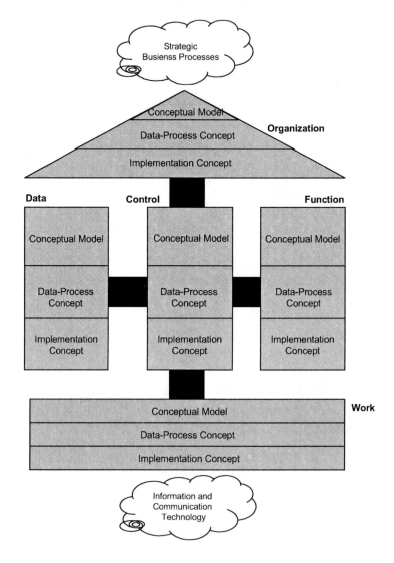

He defines process chains as the starting point of the development of the system architecture. The process chains are assigned to separated levels: on the application level there are single proceedings, on a higher level the process types and the standard processes. On this level, the enterprise information systems are allocated. On a meta level the general process model is defined.

The development of ARIS consists of four phases. First is the analysis of the process chains. Second is the modeling of the conceptual model, followed by the design of the data-process concepts. The fourth and last step is the design of the implementation concept. Phases 2 to 4 are subdivided by different views (function, organization, data, control). The conceptual data model is an important element of ARIS, whereon the focus on data integration is based.

ARIS consists of entity relationship models for different functional areas, in detail for production, technology, procurement, sales, human resources, accountancy and administration. The ARIS-approach is top-down because of the definition of process chains from an external point of view.

UFM-UDM by Rauh (1990)

Rauh developed a function model of the enterprise (UFM) and a data model of the enterprise (UDM) and combined them. The UDM should be a complete description of the enterprise from a data point-of-view. The data are assigned to functions, such as procurement, production, sales, human resources and accountancy, management, controlling, and information management. These functions again are divided into strategic, tactical, and operative functions. The aim is to base the function model on an enterprise wide data model.

Function Oriented Integration Models

The two function-oriented integration models presented here were developed from a more theoretical point of view.

"Kölner Integrationsmodell (KIM)" by Grochla (1974)

In the mid 1970s Grochla developed, at the University of Cologne/Germany, the "Kölner Integrationsmodell (KIM)" (Cologne Integration Model). The KIM is an integrated total model for planning, realization and control tasks of information systems. Data-proceeding jobs are seized within and between the enterprise areas of procurement, logistics, production, sales etc. The model consists of a literal and a graphical part.

In the literal part, a task description list, a channel list and a connector list are separated. The channel list describes how the tasks are combined and work together, the connector list brings tasks together with others. The graphical part exists of models for the named tasks — planning, realization, and control. The KIM is very detailed and extensive. The focus is not on databases but on functions in the enterprise information system environment.

Integrated Information Processing by Mertens (1995)

Mertens divides, in his model of integrated information processing (the 11th edition), horizontal and vertical integration (*Figure 3*). The main focus for the horizontal integration aspect (which is more interesting in this context) is the value chain of an enterprise. Therefore, he mainly deals with the coherence of processes (e.g., procurement) and does not start with an integrated enterprise-

Figure 3: Total concept of the integrated information processing (Mertens, 1995)

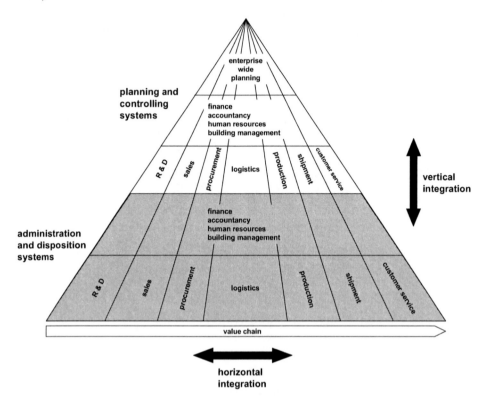

wide data model. His model is defined as text, in a function tree, a data flow plan, and in different tables.

Although he points out that there is a risk for interrupting business processes when taking a view from departments or sections of an enterprise, and not from the process point of view (1995, p. 4), Mertens deals with the functions within areas like R&D, sales, procurement, logistics, production, etc. His model is likewise a total integration model and comprises the whole organization.

Other Approaches for System Integration

Integration is an implicit issue within the various approaches in business process (re-)engineering — especially when this topic is discussed from information technology's point of view. One of these approaches, Scheer's Architecture of Information Systems (ARIS) was discussed in a previous section. During the last decade a wide range of other business process engineering approaches were discussed. As most of them have a subset of the power in expressiveness or range of models, the following discussion will focus on SOM (Semantic Object Model), which is object-oriented and is different from the other approaches.

Introduced by Ferstl and Sinz in 1990 (Ferstl & Sinz, 1990), the SOM is another approach to model business processes. It is targeted on enterprise planning, business process modeling, and the specification of business application systems. Enterprise planning is done to identify all relevant objects within the company's universe, as well as outside. Then these objects are used as a base for the more detailed specification of the business process model from the behavioral perspective. The processes are split up in transactions between two objects. Transactions control and execute exchanged services and messages.

The business process model can be modeled from different perspectives: the interaction model specifies the flow between objects and the process event scheme shows the events related to transactions in a way similar to petri nets.

Similar to ARIS, there is a special modeling tool available for the SOM approach. In contrast to ARIS, it keeps only one meta model in its repository and all graphs are generated from that model. Also, every modification made from one perspective will modify the central model and, accordingly, the other perspectives (Ferstl et al., 1994). Also based on this central model, the third modeling goal in the approach will be supported: the specification of business application systems to ease its implementation.

As most business process (re-)engineering approaches, SOM is aimed to build a new application system from scratch. The tools accompanying these approaches are helpful to reduce the complexity of the according data, function, and process models, respectively, to handle them. But the resulting application is still complex and a closed one. When further applications have to be integrated, the right solution from this point of view is to develop a new application.

CURRENT APPROACHES TO APPLICATION INTEGRATION

The heterogeneous environment of information systems leads to both many integration problems and big challenges for system architects. Historically, built information infrastructures collided with claims made by current e-business needs. Related business processes are divided on different islands of hardware and software. EAI is demanded when business processes on different information platforms must be contracted. Currently, breaks in media and inappropriate human-to-machine interfaces are a standard in today's information environments. First steps of solving the problems lead to point-to-point connections between single applications. But the massive need for integrated systems in e-business can not be met with m*n single connection points. Experts say that after the database segment and the enterprise resource planning (ERP) segment,

EAI-applications will be next to become a big market of standard software tools (Nußdorfer, 2001). Therefore, the next section describes the solutions provided by the market before some of the theoretical work in this field is discussed.

EAI Solutions Provided by the Market

EAI-tools link different data sources and applications at the application or process level. They portray business logic through process modeling and workflow control, less than connecting systems, technically or semantically on the functional or data level. They present a dedicated transaction platform, either as a central hub-and-spoke model or as a distributed bus-oriented approach (Knapp, 2001).

Integration can be done at three different layers of applications: on the presentation layer, on the function layer, or on the data layer. Integration at the *presentation* layer is quite simple because the respective information is put together at the user interface. The user is able to work with different programs at one interface. It is possible to add features like workflow or validation rules. The disadvantage of this solution is the system performance because of the additional software layer upon existing programs. Implemented functions can be used further when the integration is made at the *function* layer. The applications communicate on interfaces and either exchange data or call a function. Integration at the *data* layer uses the data sources directly. This method is useful when data must be exchanged between different applications. Problems arise in understanding the data models and the business logic. Furthermore, the interfaces must be adapted when changes at the data models are made; the administration tasks are quite intensive.

EAI and middleware are often used synonymously. But as experts point out, EAI actually is the logical development of known middleware concepts. The middleware works on a lower level of abstraction, either synchronous or asynchronous, and is message oriented or transaction oriented. However, the method of EAI is more likely comparable to tools from the extraction-transformation-loading (ETL) area in data warehousing. Both provide the unit of data (Knapp, 2001).

"[...]middleware is a general term for any programming that serves to 'glue together' or mediate between two separate and usually already existing programs" (TechTarget.com, 2001). Many software producers offer their tools under the term middleware, whereas their marketing departments talk about EAI-solutions. However, the market can be subdivided in five different categories (Oberdorfer, 2001):

1. *Remote Procedure Call (RPC) Technique*
   With RPC functions on, a remote computer can synchronously be started by using a network. This oldest middleware technology comes from the 1970s and is used for most distributed object technologies.

2. *Database Access Middleware*

    This middleware enables the access on remote databases. Today, standards like Open Database Connectivity (ODBC) or Java Database Connectivity (JDBC) are accepted and supported by most databases. Database access middleware is suitable for access at the data layer only.

3. *Message Oriented Middleware (MOM)*

    MOM is used for the exchange of messages between applications. This service is an asynchronous method for integration. Each participant can be a sender or receiver, and the middleware plays the role of the post. Messages can be sent and received either with the messaging method or through defined interface. Products are, e.g., MQSeries by IBM, MSMQ by Microsoft, Java Message Service (JMS).

4. *Distributed Object Technology (DOT)*

    With the DOT, objects are distributed in a network and can be called by defined interfaces. Today's applications often work with object-oriented languages, so DOT plays an important role for EAI. Problems occur in the complexity of the interfaces. Products are, e.g., DCOM by Microsoft, CORBA by the OMG, Java2 Enterprise Edition (J2EE) by Sun.

5. *Transaction Oriented Middleware*

    In this technique, transaction processing monitors (TPM) handle the communication of different applications. TPMs are the central node of the application logic and are named as the first generation of today's application servers. The procedures are based on single transactions. TPMs ensure the integrity of the transactions and manage the resources. Products are, e.g., Tuxedo by BEA, MTS by Microsoft, CICS by IBM.

Different methods are often used in combination. In addition to this, some of the current buzzwords introduced by vendors (e.g., web services) can be seen as extensions or a further development of these five above-mentioned middleware technologies.

In contrast to the approaches mentioned above, applications are loosely coupled when integrated within an EAI project. In addition to the concepts mentioned before, also mixed architectures are possible. An example may be the integration of a portal system with existing transactional systems. A messaging-based approach may cause problems under certain circumstances, especially when transactional systems are running with a high load, close to their capacity limits, and with a slow response time. The solution may be to store data redundantly in a separate data store and to query only selected, most current data from the transactional systems (e.g., stock information) and to keep data like user profiles in this separate data store. An example of such an architecture is depicted in *Figure 4*.

The aim of using middleware components is to generate consistent data structures in information systems. Moreover, EAI integrates business processes

Figure 4: Example of a mixed EAI-architecture

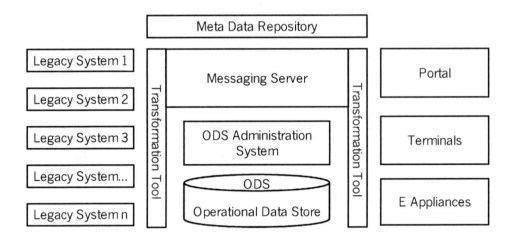

and data, but not only data like middleware does. On the other hand, middleware is basic for EAI-tools. While middleware does not provide a central control instance and leaves the business logic in the applications, EAI is process oriented and manages business logic and processes in a central authority. Uncoupling technology and applications enables the reuse of the single parts.

EAI ranks on a higher level than the single application or information system (and therefore middleware) does. The challenge of EAI is the aim to integrate existing systems on the one hand and, on the other hand, to define the business logic on a meta level (from technology point of view). The starting point in EAI-projects must be the existing business logic and process connections realized in the applications. Hence, EAI primarily is technology driven, and business driven secondarily.

EAI in Literature

There is not much research work done explicitly on enterprise application integration yet. Most sources stating EAI in their title simply document concepts and systems implemented in practice. But when the focus is widened, there is a lot of work concentrating on middleware, data base systems, data warehousing, systems architecture, portals, etc., addressing integration issues as well. Concerning the components shown in *Figure 4*. There are a wide range of ongoing research projects that focus on different aspects like, e.g., extraction, *transformation* and load tools or meta data (see Marco, 2000; Poole et al., 2002) and, accordingly, repositories used in data warehousing in a similar way.

The current EAI discussion, led by vendors of EAI tools, is often dominated by messaging concepts and web services. The underlying middleware concepts are well discussed in the scientific community. Also, EAI topics initiated by vendors from related fields have a well-known base in research. An example is the transfer of analytical data from the data warehouse back to transactional systems. This may be the case when customer relationship management tools are introduced and an architecture as described in *Figure 4* is chosen. Storing data redundantly for transactional purposes is a concept discussed — again — in the data warehouse field and is known as the usage of operational data stores (Inmon, 1999).

Like the vendors, the researchers enter the EAI arena from different starting points as well. For example, research work in (enterprise) portals faces the problem of integrating different application systems to feed the portal with data (Linthicum, 2001). Like research on portal technology, the research on collaboration technologies may be another starting point: the core of an application integration solution may also consist of a workflow management system (Kloppmann, 2001). Solutions like this may reflect the importance of the underlying business processes more than some of the EAI vendors' approaches concentrating on integration technology only.

Finally, standardization becomes more and more important for EAI projects. Standards for data exchange show their potential, not only in the inter-company communication, but also in the intra-company communication between different applications. Therefore, current standardization efforts to establish an EDI successor based on XML (Kotok & Webber, 2002) are also relevant for EAI.

Although a wide range of research efforts in fields related with enterprise application integration are ongoing, the number of publications dedicated to EAI is fairly small (e.g., Ruh et al., 2001; Linthicum, 2000), and most of them are still in the early stages of research work.

COMPARING EXISTING AND NEW INTEGRATION CONCEPTS WITH CURRENT REQUIREMENTS

The previous chapter showed that vendors meet the technological challenges and that most of the scientific approaches concentrate on the conceptual view. The "traditional" scientific approaches are too simple to be helpful; building a new integrated application is a clear solution, but when facing limited time and budgets, this integrated application is too complex to be a useful solution. Additionally, when integrating further applications, the answer cannot be to build a new integrated one when considering limited time and budgets.

Therefore, the early scientific solutions mentioned above are helpful to address some of the complexity problems. They help to handle the complexity of data, function, and process models by structuring them and — partly — offering the tools to do that in a structured and well-documented way. But they are useful to document existing structures only. They are not connected to metadata repositories controlling ETL — or messaging tools. At the least, all documentation work has to be done twice.

The more theoretic approaches are helpful, but not satisfying, as they do not provide methods to model different applications and the relationships concerning data, functions, and processes between them. They do not provide methods for an integrated interface management, integrated metadata collection and structuring, nor means to assure data quality — at least not in an integrated way. The process models for these approaches fit to ordinary application development and often rely on prototyping, which is not adequate when the functionality for data exchange is not implemented at the required full extent.

The solutions offered by software vendors are focused on technical issues only. They offer tools to convert data between various formats, to exchange data between different kinds of data storage systems, and to establish communication between older legacy and newer internet applications. Also, they offer tools to manage metadata and to interchange it with the operational systems as well as with other tools.

On the other hand, they do not offer tools to model the integration. Data quality is recognized as an important problem, but the organizational side of this challenge is not addressed. The same is true for metadata management or the planning and maintenance of an IT landscape of a company. Most tools cover one of the topics mentioned only, few more than one. And no tool or integrated set of tools covers everything mentioned.

Theoretical as well as practical solutions address only parts of these complex problems. An integrated approach is still missing. The basic elements of such an approach to be developed are presented in the following section.

Table 1: Integration issues and their coverage in some research approaches

		Vetter	ARIS	Rau	KIM	Mertens	SOM
Integrated models for	Data	•	•	•			o
	Functions		•	•	•	•	•
	Processes		•			•	•
Metadata	Management		o			o	o
	Tools		o				o
	Methods		o			o	o
IT	Planning		o			o	o
	Maintenance		o			o	o
(•: fully covered, o: partly covered)							

OPEN RESEARCH ISSUES AND OUTLOOK

An integrated approach to address the problems mentioned above must cover—among others—the following topics:

- Metadata management as described before.
- Data quality management as described before.
- Data standards (XML, etc.) are to be chosen to exchange the data between various operational applications.
- Transformation models are required to transform exchanged data between these systems.
- Project management has to address chains of integration projects, as integration is an ongoing task and cannot be done doing single and separated projects alone.
- The complex information technology infrastructure must be structured and planned to increase the flexibility of the overall IT-system of a company. Infrastructure development has to follow the evolution of the company's business and process models and not vice versa.

To address these issues existing methods and tools, especially in the data warehousing field, have to be reviewed. Some methods and tools can be enhanced, additional tools and methods have to be defined and proofed in projects.

REFERENCES

Barker, R. (1990). *CASE*Method^{TM}: Entity Relationship Modeling*. New York: Addison-Wesley.

Emmerich, W., & Gruhn, V. (1990). *Software Process Modelling with FUNSOFT Nets* (Software-Technology Memo No. 47). Dortmund.

European Information Technology Observatory (EITO), & European Economic Interest Grouping (EEIG) (Ed.) (2001). *European Information Technology Observatory, 2001*. Frankfurt.

Ferstl, O. K., & Sinz, E. J. (1990). Objektmodellierung betrieblicher Informationssysteme im Semantischen Objektmodell (SOM*). Wirtschaftsinformatik, 32* (6), 566-581.

Ferstl, O. K., & Sinz, E. J. (1994). From business process modeling to the specification of distributed business application systems: An object-oriented approach. *Bamberger Beiträge zur Wirtschaftsinformatik No. 20*.

Ferstl O. K., Sinz, E. J., Amberg, M., Hagemann, U., & Malischewski, C. (1994). Tool-based business process modeling using the SOM approach. *Bamberger Beiträge zur Wirtschaftsinformatik No. 19*.

Grochla, E., et al. (1974). *Integrierte Gesamtmodelle der Datenverarbeitung.* München.

Grünauer, K. M. (2001). *Supply chain management: Architektur, werkzeuge und methode.* (Ph.D. thesis, St. Gallen, 2001).

Inmon, W. H. (1999). *Building the Operational Data Store*, 2nd ed., New York et al.

Kloppmann, M., Leymann, F., & Roller, D. (2001). Enterprise Application Integration mit Workflow Management. *HMD, 2137*, 23–30.

Knapp, C. (2001, March 23) Intelligente Verbindungen - Mit EAI Prozesse und Workflow übergreifend steuern. *Computerwoche Extra*, 2, p. 11

Kotok, A., & Webber, D. R. R. (2002). *ebXML – The new global standard for doing business over the internet.* Boston: New Riders Publishing.

Linthicum, D. S. (2000). *Enterprise application integration.* Reading, MA: Addison-Wesley.

Linthicum, D. S. (2001). *B2B application integration: e-Business–enable your enterprise.*Reading, MA: Addison-Wesley Professional.

Marco, D. (2000). *Building and managing the meta data repository: A full lifecycle guide.* New York: Wiley Publishing.

Mertens, P. (1966). Die zwischenbetriebliche Integration der Datenverarbeitung im Einkaufs- und Lieferwesen. *Zeitschrift für Datenverarbeitung*, 4, 207.

Mertens, P. (1995). *Integrierte Informationsverarbeitung, 1* (10).

Mertens, P., & Holzner, J. (1992). Eine Gegenüberstellung von Integrationsansätzen der Wirtschaftsinformatik. *Wirtschaftsinformatik, 34* (2), 5.

Nußdorfer, R. (2001, March 23). Der Markt hebt langsam ab—Enterprise Application Integration in Deutschland. *Computerwoche Extra*, 2, 4-7

Oberdorfer, R. (2001). Allround-Adapter—EAI: Ordnung in Unternehmens-anwendungen. *iX: Magazin für professionelle Informationstechnik*, 5, 136-139.

Poole, J., Chang, D., Tolbert, D., & Mellor, D. (2002). *Common warehouse metamodel: An introduction to the standard for data warehouse integration.* New York: John Wiley & Sons.

Rauh, O. (1990). *Informationsmanagement im Industriebetrieb – Lehrbuch der Wirtschaftsinformatik auf Grundlage der integrierten Datenverarbeitung.* Herne, Berlin.

Ruh, W. A., Maginnis, F. X., & Brown, W. J. (2001). *Enterprise Application Integration: A Wiley Tech Brief.* New York: John Wiley & Sons.

Scheer, A.-W. (1991). *Architektur integrierter Informationssysteme.* Berlin: Springer-Verlag.

Scheer, A.-W. (1995). *Wirtschaftsinformatik*. Studienausgabe, Berlin: Springer-Verlag.

UBIS GmbH (Ed.) (1993). *BONAPART™: Model your business – Objektorientierte Unternehmensmodellierung mit BONAPART™*. Berlin.

Vetter, M. (1990). *Strategie der Anwendungssoftware-Entwicklung: Planung, Prinzipien, Konzepte* (2nd ed.). Stuttgart: B. G. Teubner.

WhatIs.com. (2001) Content. Retrieved from http://whatis.techtarget.com/definitionsSearchResults/1,289878,sid9,00.html?query=middleware

Winter, R. (2000). Zur Positionierung und Weiterentwicklung des Data Warehousing in der betrieblichen Applikationsarchitektur. In R. Jung, & R. Winter, (eds.), *Data Warehousing Strategie — Erfahrungen — Methoden — Visionen* (pp.127-139). Berlin: Springer-Verlag.

Chapter VI

The Effects of an Enterprise Resource Planning System (ERP) Implementation on Job Characteristics – A Study Using the Hackman and Oldham Job Characteristics Model

Gerald Grant
Carleton University, Canada

Aareni Uruthirapathy
Carleton University, Canada

ABSTRACT

As organizations undertake the deployment of integrated ERP systems, concerns are growing about its impact on people occupying jobs and roles in those organizations. The authors set out to assess the impact of ERP implementation on job characteristics. Using the Hackman and Oldham Job Characteristics Model as a basis, the study assesses how ERP affected work redesign and job satisfaction of people working in several Canadian federal government organizations.

INTRODUCTION

Work redesign occurs whenever a job changes, whether because of new technology, internal reorganization, or a whim of management (Hackman & Oldham, 1975). In order to adopt new technologies, companies have to introduce significant organizational changes which require an overall work redesign. Many organizations use work redesign as a tool to introduce planned change: whether it is an organizational change or a technological change, work must be redesigned to introduce new work routines.

During the mid 1990s, many medium and large companies started implementing enterprise resource planning (ERP) systems from companies such as Baan, PeopleSoft, SAP, and Oracle. Survey results based on data collected from 186 companies from a broad cross section of industries that implemented SAP highlighted eight important reasons why organizations initially chose to implement SAP. These reasons were the following: to standardize company processes, to integrate operations or data, to reengineer business processes, to optimize supply chain, to increase business flexibility, to increase productivity, to support globalization, and to help solve year 2000 problems (Cooke & Peterson, 1998).

An ERP implementation is not only an IT change but also a major business change. It is critical for organizations and their employees to understand this, because only then will the issue of communicating change and its effects to employees attain equal standing with the implementation of technical changes. ERPs have embedded processes, which impose their own logic on a company's strategy, organization and culture. Companies have to reconcile the technological imperatives of an enterprise system with the business needs of the organization (Davenport, 1999).

During an enterprise system implementation, organizations have to reallocate human resources to the project. Employees must be trained in new skills and work alongside outside consultants to transfer knowledge about the systems and the process (Welti, 1999). With a process system, departments located separately are encouraged to move closer together so that managers can work with the process system more effectively. Structural reorganization allows easy interaction between different functional groups. For example, all those involved in order fulfillment are located together to share the same facility and get a better view of the entire process. Top management's strong commitment is critical for a successful implementation of an ERP system. The new organizational structure allows top management to have a stronger influence on the organization's integrated functions. An enterprise system also has a paradoxical impact on a company's organizational culture (Davenport, 1999); an integrated system increases the pressure for the eradication of strictly functional organizational culture. A new, more collaborative, organizational culture is expected to emerge as the functional units work through an integrated system.

In this chapter, we explore the impact of ERP implementation on work redesign. Two questions motivate this research: (1) To what extent does ERP implementation lead to work redesign? (2) What is the impact of ERP-initiated work redesign on employee job satisfaction? We address these questions by investigating the experience of organizations in the Canadian Federal Government that implemented SAP R/3 using the Hackman-Oldham (1975) as a theoretical lens. The rest of the chapter will proceed as follows: We begin with a general discussion of theories of work redesign followed by a brief overview of the Hackman and Oldham Job Characteristics Model. We then discuss the Job Characteristics Model and ERP-initiated work redesign. Following an overview of the research method, we present the results of the survey and interviews. After a brief discussion, we highlight some implications for organizations adopting ERP systems.

THEORIES OF WORK REDESIGN

The implementation of an ERP system such as SAP R/3 can have a dramatic effect on the style, structure, and culture of the organization. When this occurs, work redesign is inevitable. Employees, who have undergone training with the process system and acquired greater knowledge interacting with it, need tasks assigned that use these skills. Employees who find it difficult to work with the enterprise system need non-system jobs assigned to them. Performance evaluation and career advancement should reflect the organizational changes. Work redesign around the process system should not only increase the efficiency of the company but also provide the organizational participants with enriched work. Task design should result in work itself providing the employees with the motivation to perform well, and increasing on-the-job productivity. Most of all, jobs need to be designed in such a way that they provide employees enjoyable work by putting their skills and talents to use.

How can individuals be motivated at work? Researchers in human behavior science have been trying to answer this question for a long time. It has been a difficult question to answer because individuals are different from one another. In the mid 1970s, researchers considered work redesign as the solution to motivating employees at work. Case studies of successful work redesign projects indicate that work redesign can be an effective tool for improving both the quality of the work experience of employees and their on-the-job productivity

(Hackman, 1975). A number of researchers have studied work redesign over the years. The table below provides an outline of the theories espoused and their basic assumptions.

Researchers	Theory	Basic Assumptions
Frederick Herzberg (1959)	Two Factor Theory	Hygiene factors are necessary to maintain a reasonable level of satisfaction in employees, which are extrinsic and are related to the job context. They are pay, benefits, job security, physical working conditions, supervision policies, company policies and relationships with co-workers. Motivating factors are intrinsic to the content of the job itself. These are factors such as achievement, advancement, recognition and responsibility. It is these factors that bring job satisfaction and improvement in performance.
Douglas McGregor (1960)	Theory X and Theory Y	McGregor's Theory X assumes that employees are lazy and unwilling to produce above the minimum requirements. By contrast, Theory Y assumes that people are not by nature passive or resistant to organizational objectives. The essential task of management is to arrange organizational operations in such a way that employees achieve their own goals by directing their efforts towards organizational objectives.
Turner and Lawrence (1965)	Requisite Task Attributes Model	They used six requisite task attributes, such as variety, required interaction, knowledge and skill, autonomy, optional interaction and responsibility to calculate a requisite task attribute index (RTA). They found strong links between attendance, worker's involvement and attributes of the work.
William Scott (1966)	Activation Theory	When jobs are dull or repetitive it leads to low levels of performance because dull jobs fail to activate the brain. However, when jobs are enriched, it leads to a state of activation and enhances productivity.

HACKMAN AND OLDHAM JOB CHARACTERISTICS MODEL

In 1975, Hackman and Oldham proposed a comprehensive Job Characteristics Model for work redesign in modern organizations.

Hackman and Oldham (1975) argued that task dimensions could represent the motivating potential of jobs and proposed that individuals would be motivated towards their job, and feel job satisfaction, only when they experienced certain psychological states. They identified these critical psychological states: experienced meaningfulness of work, experienced responsibility for outcomes of the work, and knowledge of actual results of the work activities. The belief is that the positive effect created by the presence of these psychological states reinforces motivation and serves as an incentive for continuing to do the task. In order to produce these psychological states, a job should have certain core characteristics. Hackman and Oldham found that skills variety, task identity and task significance facilitated experienced meaningfulness at work; the level of autonomy in a job increases the feeling of personal responsibilities for work outcomes. They also found that when a job has good feedback, it provides the employee with increased knowledge of the actual results of the work activities. The Job Characteristics Model suggested that growth need strength (GNS) is a moderator, which affects the employees' reactions to their work. Hackman and Oldham used a job diagnostic survey (JDS) to test their Job Characteristics Model, obtaining data from 658 employees working on 62 different jobs in seven organizations.

Figure 1: Hackman and Oldham Job Characteristics Model (1975)

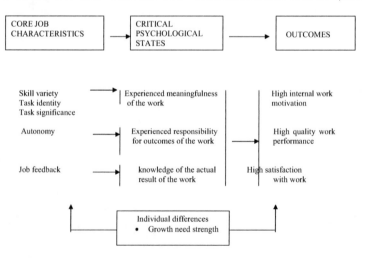

Source: J. R. Hackman & G.R. Oldham, work redesign (Reading, MA: Addison-Wesley Publishing Co., 1980)

RESEARCH BACKGROUND

Selected Canadian Government organizations have implemented SAP R/3 software as the enterprise system to replace their legacy systems. Before the SAP implementation, the Federal Government organizations had information systems that their in-house IT departments built and managed. With the decision to use the SAP system, there was limited time to prepare the necessary foundation for a successful implementation. The SAP implementation brought significant changes into these organizations. SAP project teams were formed in every functional unit and a speedy implementation began. These project teams worked alongside outside SAP consultants and spent a great deal of time configuring the system to suit the particular needs of the industry. Functions decentralized across Canada had to be centralized, resulting in the splitting, merging and re-alignment of departments and the establishment of new groups. Employees received new jobs with new roles and responsibilities. Employees moved from one location to another so they could work closely with peers from other functional units. The normal routines of work were disturbed, which frustrated many employees who struggled to familiarize with the new process system. When the process was centralized, jobs moved from different parts of Canada to one location. During a normal hiring process, employers match the employees' skills, abilities and responsibilities with the job profile; however, such matching did not take place when reassigning jobs during SAP implementation, as there was insufficient time to do so.

RESEARCH METHOD

An exploratory research carried out in nine government organizations with forty-seven SAP users attempted to establish how work redesign involving SAP systems took place. A questionnaire containing questions based on the components of the Job Characteristics Model was sent to all federal government organizations where SAP system was implemented. The overriding objective of this research was to develop a clear understanding of how the implementation of an Enterprise Resource System generated work redesign in organizations, and whether such work redesigns provided the organizational participants with job satisfaction. Thus, the survey tried to get answers for two questions: "To what extent does enterprise resource planning implementation lead to work redesign?" and "What is the impact of ERP initiated work redesign on employee job satisfaction?"

RESULTS

We use the job characteristics contained in the Hackman and Oldham model to present and discuss the results of the surveys and interviews.

Skill Variety

The research found that 75 percent of the respondents agreed that they used more skills with SAP than they did before. With the legacy systems, they had only to understand a limited number of processes and perform them repetitively; with SAP, they had to be very analytical and clearly understand their part in the whole process. SAP users employed a variety of skills and talents when they tried new processes and deal with the software. However, some managers were of the view that using more skills and talents largely depended on the set of skills the employees possessed. Employees who had stronger computer skills would use them much more than would those who were less computer literate.

Task Identity

When asked about task identity, 55 percent of the sample agreed that they knew their work outcomes in the process system. An employee working with the accounting module and in charge of the general ledger will be responsible for creating, changing and maintaining the ledger. The nametag attached to each SAP transaction allows employees to identity how their work interacts with the whole organization, thus individual employees know who is doing what and whether data is correctly processed. The system will also detect errors made by individual employees. However, there are security features, such as role-based authorizations, protocols and digital signatures, which prevent them from accessing all information. Some managers argue that these features considerably reduce task identity for employees.

Autonomy and Task Significance

More than 80 percent of those who answered the questionnaires agreed that the process system provided employees with autonomy and independence at work. An integrated system provides the users with the necessary information to perform their work. When a new transaction takes place, the information is instantly available company-wide. Managers prepare reports and allow their employees to do their own queries and to retrieve appropriate data. Some managers, however, raised doubts about whether the process system provided employees with autonomy, since they considered SAP to be a highly standardized system that forced individual employees to work within a given framework with little flexibility. For example, a receiver must immediately enter relevant data into the system upon receipt of products. The employee cannot wait until the next day, because that causes many mismatches in the system. In an integrated system, every interaction becomes important, with even small transactions having a large impact on the organization. This may be the reason why over 55 percent of the respondents felt that their work with the SAP system was more significant to the organization than it was before. With the SAP system, individuals need to know what is driving the system and to where it is being driven, because it depends on individuals to provide accurate and timely data. For example, before the integrated system, a payroll clerk counted the time for each employee and passed the information to the compensation section clerk; however, in the process system, this data drives the whole system, making the payroll clerk's task more significant.

Feedback from Job and Supervisor

When asked about feedback from the job itself, more than 60 percent of the sample said that they often received feedback from their job. However, the feedback appeared to be more from other individuals rather than directly from the system. Some believe that when you deal with the system on a day-to-day basis with different people doing different activities, one individual may identify and communicate mistakes made by another. An integrated system such as SAP facilitates this quick error detection. In this study, only 40 percent of the sample indicated that they received feedback from their supervisors; managers set the task parameters, and it was up to individual employees to complete the job without having to report back to their supervisors because the transaction records are all in the process system. Because everyone who was involved in getting the job done knew who was doing what and the progress of the task, there was no immediate need for a formal feedback. Organizations participating in the study were working on setting up formal feedback channels as employees adapt to the process system.

On average, 60 percent of the sample agreed that the process system provided them with an enriched job with characteristics such as autonomy, task identity, task significance, skill variety, and feedback from both the job and the supervisor. Some job characteristics, specifically autonomy, task identity and task significance were stronger than others were.

Meaningfulness in Work

In this research, more than 80 percent of the sample showed that they experienced meaningfulness in their work with the SAP system. This sense of accomplishment came when individuals overcame the challenges presented by the process system and learned to work around the constraints of the system. The process system also allowed users to work with peers from other departments; they were able to compare what they were doing and learn from each other, discovering correct functionality and developing the necessary solutions for problems. These experiences were meaningful and employees felt satisfied with their work performance.

Of all the variables suggested by the Job Characteristics Model, only task significance had significant correlation with experienced meaningfulness, demonstrating that this group of SAP users experienced meaningfulness when they felt that their job was significant to the whole organization. On the other hand, feedback from the job and supervisor had a moderate rating individually but correlated significantly with experienced meaningfulness (although not predicted by the model). From this, we reason that, for this particular sample of SAP users, task significance led to experienced meaningfulness and that, even when they received moderate levels of feedback from job and supervisor, they still experienced meaningfulness.

Experienced Responsibility

According to the model, autonomy leads to the psychological state of experienced responsibility. The correlation between these two variables was very poor in this study and not as predicted by the Job Characteristics Model; however, other job dimensions - task identity and task significance - correlated more strongly with experienced responsibility. We conclude that, for this group of SAP users, experienced responsibility did not come from the level of independence they had, but from other job dimensions such as task significance and task identity.

Knowledge of Task Outcomes

Job and supervisor feedback provide employees with knowledge of task outcomes. In this research, there was a significant correlation between knowledge of results and feedback from the job, this being the only job dimension that predicted knowledge of task outcomes suggested by the job characteristic model. The system provides users with periodic feedback on transactions, allowing SAP users to do things faster and better since employees immediately know the results of their work. However, there was no significant correlation between knowledge of results and feedback from the supervisor, further supporting the low rating indicated for feedback from supervisor. Although not predicted by the model, other job dimension variables such as skill variety and task identity had strong relationships with knowledge of outcomes. These findings suggest that, for this particular sample of SAP users, skill variety and task identity provided them with knowledge of their work outcome as much as feedback from the job. Nevertheless, the nature of the SAP system does not provide direct results from work - it only contains and provides updated information about the many transactions that take place within an organization.

Growth Need Strength

In theory, growth need strength plays a mediating role between job dimensions and the affective outcomes. This moderating effect was not found in our research. The participants who had high growth need and those who had lower growth need both reacted the same way to job dimensions. Nor was there any difference in their psychological states. When the SAP system was implemented, it collapsed all the working levels to support the software. Employees from all levels were taken from their jobs and put to work on the process system. These organizations did not have clear career advancement paths in place to identify talent with the process system.   In many federal organizations, personnel turnover during and after SAP implementation was significant. These may be the reasons why growth need did not influence how individuals reacted to their jobs with the process system.

DISCUSSION AND IMPLICATIONS

The analysis of the five core job characteristics and the three critical psychological states in the Job Characteristic Model provided a snapshot as to how users felt about their new jobs when working with a process system such as SAP R/3. Initially, working with the SAP system was not motivating for employees in these organizations, as they did not understand how their jobs were going to change and could not perform their tasks effectively. They struggled to carry out their responsibilities. When work units went "live" with the system, the error rates were generally high. However, as time passed and SAP users became more comfortable with the integrated system and got to know their exact roles and responsibilities, they became more motivated in their jobs. The whole work environment forced employees to change their behavior towards work; the legacy systems disappeared as the new system took over. Work redesign initiated by the process system provided employees with opportunities for personal growth by giving them an opportunity to work with world-class integrated system technology and acquire skills that increase their value in the labor market. In most organizations, after a year of SAP adoption, employees are happier with the system and complaints have reduced tremendously. As employees successfully overcame the constraints of the process system, they experienced more satisfaction at work.

Implications for Organizations Adopting ERP System

There are some steps companies can take to improve the transition from the legacy system to the ERP system. First, organizations need to have in place strategies for managing IS enabled change during each phase of the implementation. These strategies will favorably affect employees and give them information on how their jobs are going to change, reducing the level of resistance. When management decides to implement ERP, they should communicate this decision to all organizational levels. Change strategies should emphasize that the process system implementation is not an IT change, but a business change. Employees need to understand the business objectives the organization is trying to achieve through implementing a process system. Change agents should be working with all functional units to address the concerns of the employees who will undergo major work changes. They should have good communication and negotiation skills to be able to influence the mindset of the employees and create a favorable response to the process system.

Second, organizations should ensure that there is a strong project management process in place. When organizations implement many SAP modules at the same time, each module should have a subproject manager. There should be a clear structure in assigning work to people within the process system. When assigning responsibilities, it is important to match job profiles with skills, talents and previous experience. Management should evaluate employees and discuss with each individual how his or her job is going to change and whether the individual is willing to take up new responsibilities. They should also explain the guidance and help that will be available for individuals to cope with the changes. In many government organizations, supervisors spend considerable time testing the modules; actual users should also participate in the testing process to allow them to understand the process system and give them opportunities to try transactions in different ways.

Third, a SAP implementation budget should allocate sufficient funds for SAP training. The prospective user requires training in the particular module in which he or she is going to work. Some government organizations used the concept of training the trainers; a group of employees received training and then they trained other users. This type of training is not suitable for a complex system like SAP. In some Canadian federal government organizations some departments received more training than others did; this is also not suitable for an integrated system because all departments should have the expertise for a successful adoption of the process system - all departments need equal training. Organizations often cut short the training phase when they have only a short time frame in which to implement the system; this should not be the case. Users should know how to operate the system in order to work comfortably with it; they need clear manuals that teach them about the system. These manuals should document the many processes in the system, thereby reducing some of the difficulties the users encounter and facilitating self-learning. SAP users also need post-implementation training to allow them to find solutions to their own unique problems.

Finally, when organizations hire SAP consultants, they must take the time to investigate whether the consultants have the expertise and knowledge in particular industry practices. Hiring consultants with SAP knowledge alone is not enough to solve the day-to-day problems of SAP users, as the consultants must understand the internal business environment of the organization. In addition, the services of consultants should be engaged in different phases of the SAP implementation. In some of the organizations where this research was conducted, consultants were available only at the initial stages of SAP implementation; when the SAP users got to know the system and had questions and doubts, there were no consultants to help them - the employees had to spend more time in figuring things out for themselves. Organizations need control over what the consultants are doing, periodically auditing the services of the consultants and making sure they transfer knowledge to the users.

CONCLUSIONS

Redesigning work in organizations is a very challenging undertaking because every individual needs a job profile that matches his or her skills and knowledge. Even if one job is changed in an organization, many of the interfaces between that job and the related ones need to be changed also, creating a chain of changes. When an organization implements an enterprise planning system such as SAP R/3, work has to be redesigned extensively. It is a challenging task for managers to allocate work and for employees to get used to new ways of doing the job. Paying attention to people issues is critical element in achieving success from an enterprise system.

REFERENCES

Cooke, P. D., & Peterson, J. W. (1998). *SAP implementation: Strategies and results*. New York: The Conference Board Publication, Inc.

Davenport, T. (1998), Putting the enterprise into the enterprise systems. *Harvard Business Review*, 76 (4), pp. 121-131.

Hackman. J.R. (1975). On the coming demise of job enrichment. In E.L. Cass & F.G. Zimmer, (eds.), *Man And Work In Society*. New York: Van Nostrand-Reinhold.

Hackman, J.R., & Oldham, G.R. (1975). Development of the job diagnostic survey. *Journal of Applied Psychology*, 60 (2), pp. 159-170.

Hackman, J.R., & Oldham, G.R. (1976). Motivation through the design of work: Test of a theory. *Organizational Behavior and Human Performance, 16* (2), pp. 250-279.

Hackman, J.R., & Oldham, G.R. (1980). Motivation through the design of work. In *Work Redesign* (pp. 71-99). MA: Addison-Wesley.

Hammer, M. & Stanton, S. (1999). How process enterprises really work. *Harvard Business Review, 77*(6), pp. 108-118.

Herzberg, F., Mausner, B., & Bloch-Snyderman, B. (1959). *The motivation to work (2nd Ed.)* New York: John Wiley & Sons.

Mayo, E. (1945). *The social problems of an industrial civilization.* Boston: Harvard University Press.

McGregor, D. (1966). *Leadership and motivation.* MA: The M.I.T Press.

Scott, W. E. (1966). Activation theory and task design. In *Organizational behavior and human performance* (pp. 3-30).

Turner, A.N., & Lawrence, P. R. (1965). *Industrial jobs and the worker.* Boston, MA: Harvard University, Graduate School of Business Administration.

Welti, N. (1999). *Successful SAP R/3 implementation: A practical management of ERP project.* Addison-Wesley.

Chapter VII

Context Management of ERP Processes in Virtual Communities

Farhad Daneshgar
University of New South Wales, Australia

ABSTRACT

A methodology is proposed for sharing the contextual knowledge/resources that flow within ERP processes in virtual communities. Context is represented by a set of relevant collaborative semantic concepts or "objects." These are the objects that are localised/contextualised to specific sub-process within the ERP process. Two sets of objects are identified: (i) objects that make up a community member's actual contextual knowledge/resources with regards to the ERP process, and (ii) objects that make up the required contextual knowledge that various sub-processes/tasks expect from the member to possess for successful execution of those tasks. The excess of the objects in (ii) compared to those in (i) are identified and are put within the focus of the community member in order to enable the member to effectively participate in various collaborative interactions within the community's ERP process(es).

INTRODUCTION

The main motivation for this chapter is to introduce a specialised version of an existing awareness-based ERP methodology (Daneshgar, 2001) for *Virtual Communities,* or VCs for short. To this end, the primitives, *focus* and *nimbus,* that seem to have relevance to the VCs are explicitly incorporated into this existing ERP methodology.

According to the *interactionist* school in social psychology, awareness is maintained if each person *actively* provides a kind of *nimbus* by which s/he selectively exposes some of his/her properties (that is, their activities, etc.) to the others. According to this school, pairwise interactions between people occur either by *nimbus* (an object's presence), or by *focus* (its attention); the more an object is within one's focus, the more aware the person is of it. Also, the more an object provides a nimbus, the more aware others will be of it (Benford et al, 1995).

In this chapter the writer, being primarily member of both the CSCW (Computer Supported Cooperative Work) and the Knowledge Management research communities, introduces a conceptual framework for ERP processes in virtual communities which possesses the following attributes:

- As before, this extended framework emphasises the collaborative nature of the ERP process, in the sense that *awareness* and *knowledge-sharing* issues within the ERP process are explicitly addressed

- In addition, it identifies collaboration requirements of the actors within VCs, with VCs being regarded as a sub-class of the business community in which members work flexibly anywhere and at anytime. The collaboration requirements of the actors within the community are defined in terms of resources and knowledge that the actors require in order to perform their tasks within the community.

- And finally, the proposed framework is affected by the latest trend that is currently occurring within the field of Knowledge Management. According to this trend, we are reaching the end of the second generation of Knowledge Management/sharing, with its focus on tacit-explicit knowledge conversion as triggered by the SECI model of Nonaka (Nonaka, 1991). The third generation requires the clear separation of context, narrative and content management and challenges the orthodoxy of scientific management (Snowden, 2002). It is argued in this chapter that people in VCs require certain level of contextual knowledge about various resources/knowledge related to the collaborative nature of the ERP process, such as Who?, Doing what?, Using what resources? What skills?, etc. This type of *contextual* knowledge is now being distinguished from the actual *content* of the knowledge/resource itself. Such contextual knowledge is a pre-requisite to the VC members' effective involvement in various interactions within the ERP processes. In other words, and as far as the writer is aware, the methodology presented in this chapter is the first in its kind that ultimately fits into the *context management/sharing* category of the context- narrative-content taxonomy in the field of Knowledge Management as briefly mentioned before.

More specifically, the contextual knowledge is represented here by a set of relevant objects that have been localised/contextualised to actors within the ERP process in VCs. These objects make up channels within which the actual collaborative resources or *contents* (of knowledge and/or physical resources) within the ERP process flow; hence the term *contextual knowledge*.

Two sets of objects are identified: (i) objects that make up a community member's *actual contextual resources/knowledge* and are actually possessed by the community members, and (ii) objects that make up various *required contextual resources/knowledge* that are imposed by the (nature of the) tasks that these members perform within the community and, therefore, are expected from them as they perform the task. Within the (relative) context of an actor performing an ERP-related task in the VC, the excess of the objects in (ii) over those in (i) are identified by the framework. As the next step for enhancing collaboration and resource/knowledge sharing within the ERP process, these excessive objects are either explicitly put within the *focus/access* of the actor, or these objects themselves evaporate a kind of *odour/nimbus* in order to attract attention of the actor, or a combination of both.

Like many existing ERP frameworks/models, the proposed framework is also based on a widely accepted assumption that a corporate-wide information system consists of a set of potentially related subsystems. As a result, channels within which the contextual collaborative resources/knowledge flow among these subsystems must be identified, and required resources be planned. The proposed methodology treats an ERP process as a *collaborative process,* and, as a result, a set of collaborative semantic concepts are used for representation of the ERP process. This process representation consists of multiple interrelated subprocesses, with each subprocess in turn being composed of one or more simple tasks (as opposed to the collaborative tasks explained later), or *tasks* for short. Each task requires certain resources (including knowledge) for achieving its local goal or purpose, as well as certain other resources/knowledge for achieving its collaborative goals with others within the ERP process. The term *task resource* is used to describe resources (including knowledge) required for performing a task with no regard to the task's collaborative resource requirements. On the other hand *collaborative resource* is used to describe additional resources required by a task in order to collaborate with others through their tasks.

Each task is performed by a *role* and each role is played by a human agent, called *actor,* although there is no representation for the *actor* in the proposed framework, and the actor is indirectly identified by the *role* that they play at any time within the ERP process. When an actor performs a task collaboratively with another actor, then we call the task a *collaborative task* that consists of a pair of (simple) tasks, each played by a different role; hence a need for additional set of (collaborative) resources in order for the collaboration to be realised.

Another unique characteristic of the proposed framework is that it regards effective communication or information/resource exchange among the actors as being closely related to the level of awareness an actor has. An actor's awareness level is closely related to his/her extent of contextual knowledge with regards to various aspects of the ERP process and, as mentioned before, is distinct from the actual content. Examples include who (the role) is doing what (the task), how, using what resources, what skills, etc. Have a look at this familiar scenario:

> " ... If our systems had been communicating, the instant the record closed out in our system the sales guys would have known it ... There are three forecasts for monthly sales and I couldn't reconcile them. Accounting uses some kind of dollarized forecast for cash planning purposes. The sales guys are using their Ouija boards and other sorcery to figure out what deals they will close ... entering the data, especially since it is done only once, requires extensive formal procedures" (Jacobs & Whybark, 2000, pp. 12-13).

A PROCESS AWARENESS METHODOLOGY FOR ERP IN VCS

This section introduces a methodology for identifying awareness requirements of actors in an ERP process within VCs. Such requirements can then be used to plan various resources within the enterprise. The steps for this methodology follow:

Step 1

Develop a conceptual representation model for the ERP process using a set of collaborative semantic concepts. This model shows all the activities within the ERP process in the form of various tasks that are performed by actors, by assuming certain roles using two categories of resources: *task resources* and *collaborative resources*. This conceptual model is called *ERP Process Map*. Detailed description of the ERP Process Map is given in the following section.

Step 2

Measure the *actual levels of awareness* of each role that exists on the ERP Process Map using the Awareness Model. Actual level of awareness is a property of the actor; and the role simply inherits such awareness from the actor who plays it. Depending on its numeric value, this actual level of awareness may consist of a subset of collaborative semantic concepts or objects that make up the ERP Process Map. These collaborative semantic concepts are:

(i)   roles,
(ii)   tasks,
(iii) task resources, and
(iv)   collaborative resources.

As an example, we may identify the following subprocesses/subsystems in an ERP process:

* Financial Accounting (FA)
* Order Processing (OP)
* Customer Service (CS)
* Financial Reporting (FR)

We can say that FA subprocess consists of a set of *tasks* identified by FA_T1, FA_T2, FA_Tn; OP subprocess may consists of tasks OP_T1, OP_T2, etc. Role R1 may play FA_T1, FA_T2 and OP_T1, whereas role R2 may play FA_T4, FR_T1 and FR_T6. R1 needs *task resource* PR_R1_FA_T1 for performing FA_T1 task (shown by an arc connecting R1 to FA_T1), and R2 needs task resource PR_R2_FR_T1 for performing FR_T1 task (shown by the arc connecting R2 to FR_T1), etc. Let us assume that the two tasks, FA_T2 and FR_T1, are executed collaboratively and for this collaboration to occur a *task resource* TR_FA_T2_FR_T1 is required (shown by an arc connecting FA_T2 to FR_T1). A graphical representation of this ERP process is shown in *Figure 1*.

Figure 1: An example of an ERP Process Map with two roles, six simple tasks, and one collaborative task

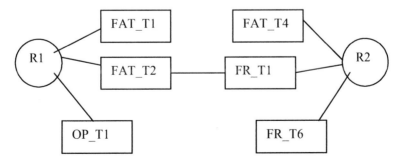

To measure the actual level of awareness of an actor, s/he must be exposed to all the objects that exist on the ERP Process map and be asked to identify those objects that s/he is aware of. The selected pool of objects is then fed to the *awareness model* that is the second component of the proposed framework. A cardinal number will be arrived at that reflects the role's actual level of awareness. These levels are explained in the following section in more detail.

Step 3

The actor's actual level of awareness is then compared against the *required level of awareness* as specified by (or, being a property of) the task that a role may perform within the process. This *required level of awareness* is the minimum level of awareness that is expected from any role who intends to perform this task. The factors that may affect the value are organisational culture as well as nature of task itself. This value reflects the fact that without such minimum level of awareness the actor will not be able to perform the task properly. A comparison between the actual level of awareness of the actor and the required level of awareness of the task will result in one of the following two outcomes:

1. **Either:** the required level of awareness of the task is equal to, or less than, the actual level of awareness of the role. This indicates that the role is qualified, or has sufficient level of awareness for taking up the task as the awareness requirements of the task are satisfied.

2. **Or:** the required level of awareness of the task exceeds the actual level of awareness of the actor. This indicates that the role does not possess required awareness. In other words, the actor is not aware of a set of objects within the ERP Map and therefore the next step must be followed.

Step 4

In order to remove the above awareness gap in VCs, special attention needs to be given to the specific nature of VCs. In traditional business processes, the concept of 'nimbus' has not been given much attention in actual implementations of systems that support collaboration and sharing of artefacts and resources. In VCs, where people and work are distributed over the times/space taxonomy, issues related to nimbus, such as selectively desire to hide, and yet to participate effectively within the community, odour (selectively giving others access to personal knowledge/skills/resources), and any other factor that VC members selectively use to represent themselves to others, become quite relevant when dealing with the sharing of knowledge and resources. On the other hand, clear separation of content and context, as mentioned before, will have a particular implication in VCs. Contents of knowledge/resources are more absolute and fixed than the context/channels within which knowledge/resource flow and/or are shared. Both as a result of this, as well as due to the nature of the VCs, the same context can be seen by different people differently, depending on a combination of the degree of willingness of the object to expose itself (nimbus), as well as the eyesight of the viewer (focus). In other words, the awareness of actors in VCs depends on both his/her *focus* as well as the others' *nimbus*.

Following section further clarify details of Step 4 of the proposed methodology.

COMPONENTS OF THE FRAMEWORK

The proposed framework consists of the following two components:

(i)   a connected graph as a conceptual model for the ERP process (called ERP Process Map), and

(ii) a new model for *process awareness* in the form of a set of algorithmic procedures that can be used to parse the above graph in order to identify various objects that constitute various levels of awareness associated with various roles and tasks within the ERP process.

Process Map

ERP Process Map is a planning and analysis tool that models the ERP collaborative process using a limited number of *collaborative semantic concepts* (or *objects*) that are linked together through various resources (including the knowledge). These concepts are briefly discussed below. Readers are advised to refer to Daneshgar (2000) for full details.

Task (Also Called 'Simple Task')

Definition: Objects with a set of attributes and *actions* to achieve a specific process goal using certain resources.

Representation: It is uniquely identifiable by a combination of one or more of its attributes (e.g., required level of awareness, goal, ID number, description, etc.), as well as its actions. In *Figure 1* simple tasks are graphically represented by vertices FAT_T1, FAT_T2, FAT_T4, FR_T1, FR_T6 and OP_T1.

Action

Definition: A sequence of goal-directed steps.

Representation: Actions are secondary concepts in the proposed framework and therefore there is no direct graphical representation for the "actions." They are embedded within the task objects.

Collaborative Task

Definition: is composed of two (or more) *simple tasks* that share the same *collaborative resource* and have a common goal.

Representation: Collaborative tasks are graphically represented by the associated simple tasks and the shared collaborative resource arc that links the tasks together. The only collaborative task in *Figure 1* is the pair of FAT_T2 and FR_T1.

Actors

Definition: These are human agents that enact a set of simple tasks by playing a set of *roles*.

Representation: There is no direct graphical representation for these objects. Actors are embedded within the *roles* that they play within the ERP process.

Role

Definition: A set of norms expressed in terms of obligations, privileges, and rights.

Representation: Roles are graphically represented by vertices of the connected graph. In *Figure 2*, roles are shown by filled circles.

Task Resource

Definition: This object represents resources that a role utilises in order to perform a *simple task* in isolation from any other task(s).

Representation: Task resources are graphically represented by the arcs that connect a role vertex to a simple task vertex.

Collaborative Resource

Definition: These are resources used by the actors (at least a pair of actors) in order to perform certain simple task in collaboration with another actor(s) who perform a related simple task.

Representation: Collaborative resources are shown by the arcs that connect two related simple task vertices together.

ERP Process

Definition: A set of roles, task resources, simple tasks, and collaborative resources that are linked together in order to achieve certain ERP-related goal.

Representation: ERP Process is graphically represented by a connected graph similar to the one in *Figure 1*. An ERP Process is *collaborative* if at least one *collaborative task* exists in it. It seems that ERP Processes are always collaborative.

Awareness

Definition: Awareness is specialised knowledge about the objects that lead an actor to an understanding of various aspects of the ERP process. This specialised knowledge is defined in terms of various roles, simple tasks, collaborative tasks, task resources and collaborative resources.

Representation: Graphical representation of various levels of awareness of an actor includes a set of the objects (above collaborative semantic concepts) that constitute various paths from the actor's role vertices to each other vertices of the ERP Process MaP.

Actual Awareness

Actual Awareness is the awareness that an actor actually possesses within the ERP process. Actual awareness is represented by an integer number, ranging from zero to six, representing various levels of awareness.

Required Awareness

Required Awareness is an awareness that is attached to (and is an attribute of) each *task* and represents the expected level of awareness from the actor who performs the task. Its representation is the same as actual awareness.

The Awareness Model

It provides a new definition for *process awareness* for ERP processes in general, and for VCs in particular. The sharing of the contextual knowledge in VCs occurs at various levels depending on both focus and nimbus of the semantic concepts involved. Seven levels are identified in this chapter and are discussed below:

Level-0 Awareness

An actor is at level-0 if s/he possesses contextual knowledge about the objects that lead the actor to an understanding of the tasks that the actor performs within the VC. This knowledge is the sum of the actor's focus (his visibility and eyesight), as well as the tasks' nimbus (how clearly the tasks are presented to, and then conceived by, the actor). An example of level-0 awareness for an accountant includes: "I, the accountant (*role*) use a kind of dollarised forecast (*role artefact*) for cash planning purposes (*task*)." The role's accounting knowledge is his/her focus; whereas how clearly the task of "planning" is presented to the accountant (e.g., proper on-line help facilities, floor-control issues of the VC's chat rooms, etc.) is the nimbus that evaporates from the task object. An actor's level-0 awareness is sum of contextual knowledge about the objects that lead the actor to knowledge about all the *simple tasks* that the actor performs within the process.

Level-1 Awareness

Level-0 awareness is a prerequisite for level-1. An actor that reaches level-1 awareness will possess a specialised knowledge about all the objects that leads the actor to awareness about some of the actors within the VC. These are the actors with whom the actor has a direct task dependency.

Level-2 Awareness

An actor at level-2 awareness will have a knowledge about the objects that lead the actor to an understanding of every (other) role within the VC.

Level-3 Awareness

An actor at level-3 awareness has the knowledge about the objects that lead that actor to an understanding of all the interactions that occur between any pair of roles within the VC. Attaining level-3 awareness enables an actor to initiate level-3 context-sharing transactions with others within the VC.

Level-4 Awareness

An actor at level-4 awareness has a specialised knowledge about the objects that lead that actor to an understanding of how everything within the VC fit together to make up the ERP Process Map. Graphically, this level can be represented by the whole of the ERP Process Map. At this level, the actor has adequate contextual knowledge about what everyone does within the VC and how (using what resources, etc.) they perform their tasks (that is, the sum of everybody's level-0 awareness), who directly collaborates with whom and how (sum of all the level-1 awareness), who indirectly collaborates with whom and how (sum of all the level-2 awareness), and finally, how other actors collaborate with one another (sum of all the level-3 awareness).

Level-5 Awareness

Level-5 awareness is a knowledge about the objects that lead the actor to an understanding of the actual relationship between the ERP process and the overall context of the VC. At this stage, no graphical representation model exists for this level of awareness. This level represents the theoretical limit of the proposed framework, and its appearance in this chapter is simply due to its fitness to the overall evolutionary nature of the awareness. No further discussion will be given regarding this and the next level of awareness.

Level-6 Awareness

Level-6 awareness is a knowledge about the objects that lead the actor to an understanding of the history of the ERP process at different times as well as in similar communities at present time.

IMPLEMENTATION ISSUES OF THE PROPOSED FRAMEWORK

On the basis of this framework, the writer is in the process of developing an expert system that provides expert advice for answering the following two main questions:

(i)   In terms of awareness requirements, is an actor capable of performing a certain task within the ERP process?

(ii) If not, what objects need to be put within his/her focus in order to enable the actor to perform the task properly?

In the example of *Figure 1*, the ERP process has four subprocesses (that is, Financial Accounting FA, Order Processing OP, Customer Service CS and Financial Reporting FR). The notion of a subprocess is encapsulated within the individual tasks and its relevant resources. Each task possesses a set of attributes and relevant actions/steps. These attributes will indicate to which subprocess the task belongs. This will enable an actor to play various roles within different subprocesses without being permanently linked to a specific subprocess, a factor that can remove some complexities in existing ERP implementations. The interdependency that exist between various subprocesses is also simplified by encapsulating them within the task objects and their related resources in such a way that each task has equal opportunity (or follows same standard) to be linked to any other task within the ERP process, including to those tasks within the same subprocess. This will also reduce much of complexities that may exist in process-oriented ERP systems where the system must permanently maintain such linkages.

CONCLUSION AND FUTURE WORK

This chapter introduced a conceptual object-oriented framework based on process awareness for analysis and design of ERP systems for VCs, and its advantages over the process-oriented systems were also discussed. It was shown that knowledge space can be expanded by identifying the awareness gaps for various actors within the community. It was further suggested that these objects can either be put within the focus of the actors, or can be encouraged/ motivated to evaporate appropriate nimbus to automatically attract the attention of the actors who need to be aware of the object, or both. From a CSCW (Computer-Supported Cooperative Work) perspective these can be done by the means of effective interfaces that, among other things, encourage *articulation work* (Gerson, 1986), explicification of *situated actions* (Allen, 1984), identification of *mutual influence* (Robinson, 1991a), facilitation of *shared views/*

shared materials (Robinson, 1991b), and provision of a *double-level language* that allows both ambiguity and clarity (Robinson, 1991a). These fundamental concepts have been selected and are being investigated by the author from the CSCW literature as an initial effort for addressing the process of effective management of the contextual knowledge in ERP processes of VCs.

REFERENCES

Allen, T. J. (1984). *Managing the flow of technology.* Cambridge: MIT Press.

Daneshgar, F. (2000). *An awareness framework for business environments.* PhD Thesis. School of Computer Science. University of Technology, Sydney (UTS), Australia.

Daneshgar, F. (2001). An object-oriented awareness-based methodology for ERP. In L. Hossain & J. Patrick (Eds.), *Enterprise resource planning: Opportunities and challenge.* Hershey, PA: Idea Group Publications.

Gerson, E., & Star, S. (1986). Analysing due process in the workplace. *ACM Transactions on Office Information Systems, 4* (3).

Jacobs, F.R., & Whybark, D.C. (2000). *Why ERP?: A primer on SAP implementation.* New York: McGraw-Hill Higher Education.

Nonaka, I. (1991, November-December). The knowledge-creating company. *Harvard Business Review*, pp. 96-104.

Robinson, M. (1991a). Double level languages and cooperative working. *AI & Society, 5*, 34-60.

Robinson, M. (1991b). Computer supported cooperative work: Cases and concepts. *Proceedings of Groupware 91, SERC.* Utrecht, The Netherlands.

Snowden, D. (2002). Complex acts of knowledge: Paradox and descriptive self-awareness. *Special Issue of the Journal of Knowledge Management, 6* (2).

Part II

Data Warehousing and Data Utilization

Chapter VIII

Distributed Data Warehouse for Geo-spatial Services

Iftikhar U. Sikder
University of Maryland, Baltimore, USA

Aryya Gangopadhyay
University of Maryland, Baltimore, USA

ABSTRACT

This chapter introduces the research issues on spatial decision-making in the context of distributed geo-spatial data warehouse. Spatial decision-making in a distributed environment involves access to data and models from heterogeneous sources and composing disparate services into a meaningful integration. The chapter reviews system integration and interoperability issues of spatial data and models in a distributed computing environment. We present a prototype system to illustrate the collaborative access to data and as a model for supporting spatial decision-making.

INTRODUCTION

Distributed access to data and services brings closer involvement of different communities, regardless of geographic locations and social orientations. Diverse tools and Web services are now available to extract data and models from online repositories. The vision of geo-spatial data warehouse challenges the fundamental criticism directed against Geographic Information

Systems (GIS): being an "elitist" tool that harbors the gap between system users and non-users (Pickles, 1995). A unique advantage of having a distributed geo-spatial data warehouse is that access to geospatial information and services for decision makers and planners will promote Collaborative Spatial Decision Making (CSDM, NCGIA, 1995). Hence, many complex environmental problems can be resolved through collaboration, which would have been difficult to resolve otherwise. This chapter reviews the research issues of distributed GIS services and geospatial data warehouses in the context of collaborative decision-making. In the following sections, we identify some essential features of a distributed spatial data warehouse relevant to spatial decision-making, with respect different standards and protocols. Then, we discuss system integration and interoperability issues of spatial data and models. A prototype collaborative decision support system is presented to illustrate collaborative access to data, and model for supporting spatial decision. Finally, we identify the future research trends of distributed data warehouse in the framework of emerging research trends of semantic Web.

BACKGROUND

It has been reported that as much as 80% of general information contains spatial components (OGC, 2001). Typically, these include spatial data or geo-referenced information, such as digital or analog map, network, GPS data and satellite-based imagery. As spatial data and services are increasingly becoming available, there is a growing demand for robust information processing for explorative analysis, where a user is empowered to extract multiple services from different repositories. The use of spatial data cuts across many disciplines, ranging from ecosystem modeling to location commerce. This has resulted in many stand-alone native spatial data structures and domain models. The challenge is, however, to enable interoperability of the heterogeneous systems to communicate in a distributed computing environment.

Standards and Protocols

Serving spatial data from disparate sources and disseminating them to target users is also the vision of NSDI (National Spatial Data Infrastructure), ex-pressed by the Mapping Science Committee (NRC, 1993). However, the vision of NSDI could not conceive of the enormous growth of Internet, which underemphasizes the importance of effective processes of dissemination to users (NRC, 1999). At the object level, the Open GIS Consortium (OGC) is developing a number of specifications. The Open Geodata Interoperability Specification (OGIS) defines types and methods required for an interoperable system. The notable feature of OGIS is Abstract Specification. It includes the Essential Model and Abstract Model, which form the basis for development of Implementation Specifications (OGC, 2002a). The specification promises to provide interoperability of geospatial data and modeling system, through the use of common language for sharing geo-data and standardized definitions of interfaces. However, OGIS is an operational model, not a data standard (Gardels, 1995). Systems developed in compliance with the operational model will be interoperable, otherwise they will not. The specification does not explicitly provide any interoperability mechanism to link with legacy systems to allow geo-processing function. In addition, at the conceptual level, semantic conversion or mapping with existing systems with OGIS is still very difficult (Camara, 1997). A higher level of semantic modeling is still required before the actual mapping of OpenGIS and existing system could take place (Yuan, 1997).

Conventional approaches to interoperate different data warehouses rely on metadata or data dictionary (Inmon, 2001). This method is essentially dependent on catalog interoperability through standardization. In the case of geospatial data, the metadata standard developed by the Federal Geographic Data Committee (FGDC, 1999) emphasizes the content standard of geospatial database, rather than the database itself. For example, the standard does not specify how the two different geometric representations of a real world feature can be semantically mapped, rather it specifies how to document each representation in a standard protocol. Therefore, we still need another layer of semantic translator to communicate with them.

ISSUES IN DECISION MAKING AND SPATIAL DATA INTEROPERABILITY

One of the main functionalities of a distributed data warehouse is to provide the building blocks of decision support systems. The system should be able to combine heterogeneous spatial and non-spatial components provided by the data warehouse. The level of support may extend to:
i)   data input
ii)   combining model components
iii) spatial analysis, and
iv)   system output.

In order to support these features from distributed data warehouse, a DSS should have access to scalable and reusable components, which can be assembled in a modular fashion at different level of representation. This leads to the fundamental problem of system integration and interoperability issues in GIS.

Characteristics of Distributed Geospatial Data Warehouse

A distributed spatial data warehouse framework for decision support needs to address various complex research issues ranging from technical, social and institutional aspects. In this chapter, we will mainly focus on the technical issues on how distributed geospatial services can be effectively utilized in decision making or planning. Needless to mention, the institutional and social aspects are of no less importance in realizing the spatial services; these aspects have been dealt with separately (Sikder et al., 2002). We need to explore how the classical decision support framework fits with the emerging distributed autonomous services, and whether these new developments can cope with the arrangements of new standards, protocol, institutional regulations and so forth. The emerging emphasis on the decentralization of resources and services might need a novel approach to tailor decision models from disparate sources and customize them for user groups.

Unlike any alphanumeric data, spatial data require a complex organization of geometry, feature, theme, topology, projection and referencing systems (Adam et al., 1997; Worboys, 1999). Different level of abstraction of real world objects and geographic entities gives rise to different representation schemes. At the implementation level, the domain specific data models can hardly communicate to realize user request. The proliferation of different data types and model limits common geo-processing services, such as spatial selection, intersect, union, buffer and overlay, which are essential modules for selecting subset from data space of a warehouse. Some of the desirable characteristics of a distributed geospatial data warehouse are:

- Interoperable application environment to allow application developers to access and configure a specific service to solve a problem.
- Provide catalog and schema services to request and retrieve data in a user-defined storage and format.
- Access to the fundamental set of query and geo-processing functions to facilitate identification and integration of resources in a distributed environment.
- Semantic translation of community specific schema, vocabulary, taxonomy, and abstractions.
- Interface for collaborative interaction of user through spatial analysis and visualization.

These characteristics call for an interoperable architecture where application domains, such as environmental modeling or resource optimization tools, become a part of the data processing services of the warehouse. Distributed data warehouse research should be directed towards the spatial interoperability aspect of distributed data brokering and spatial decision-making.

Distributed Model Management

An essential feature of spatial decision support system is the integration of geographic data and geo-processing function or services in a distributed environment. Often, GIS models are developed for a specialized purpose, tightly woven with the data model, without regards to system interoperability. In the past, many integration frameworks have been proposed (Chou & Ding, 1992; Nyerges, 1993; Abel et al., 1994). However, these approaches do not support a model management system to support dynamic processing in a different spatio-temporal scale. Additionally, these approaches include lower level simple data transfer to high-level complex coupling. As far as software reusability is concerned, in a distributed environment, where there is little agreement on different components and modeling paradigms, lower level integration does not add much benefit when diverse models are to be communicated at a higher level. Moreover, there is an inherent dichotomy of the GIS model and environmental model. While the former focuses on representation of space-time relationship and spatial features, the latter is concerned with dynamic processes. Such space-process dichotomy determines the distinction in abstract models and languages used by GIS and models (Maidmet, 1996). To get around this problem, a unified conceptual model of the problem domain is essential prior to system development. In high performance distributed computing environments, modularizing model components calls for an object-oriented approach, which can accommodate flexible and iterative model processes, incorporating prototyping, use of class libraries, reuse and re-engineering of other application code, and late configuration to changing requirements.

Such object oriented modeling tools could be regarded as a generic decision model for problems of a certain class that can be customized through an instantiation process. Model formulation, from the user point of view, becomes the simple process of choosing and applying a set of special purpose domain oriented concepts for describing the problem domain. As far as the semantic contents of the models are concerned, a meta-model ontology would be necessary to describe spatial data and services in a modeling language. This aspect is discussed later in detail.

BROKERING SPATIAL SERVICES FOR GEO-PROCESSING

The middleware approach to access spatial services through a broker relies on a standard definition of "interfaces." The interface allows communication with legacy systems, regardless of native implementation language. Broker-based solutions, such as COM (Component Object Model) or CORBA (Common

Object Broker Architecture), offer an Interface Definition Language (IDL) to communicate different tiers of a solution. CORBA's naming service provides a mechanism to locate and register objects in an ORB (Object Request Broker)-based system. Through an encapsulating interface, the requesters of services (clients) are separated from the provider of services (server). ORB core delivers clients' requests for object implementation and gets the request back from the server to the client. This is initiated in a client's IDL stub and their IDL skeleton delivers the request to object implementation. This allows the client to have access, not only to remote methods (e.g., geo processing functions), but also provide a mechanism to instantiate spatial objects as if the system is running on a local machine. In the Internet, these services can be communicated through IIOP (Internet Inter-Orb Protocol). A distributed geospatial data warehouse can be created using the building block of CORBA, instead of developed from scratch. Typical problems associated with distributed computing, such as data replication, synchronization of operations at multiple sites, transaction management, and query optimization, can be efficiently executed in CORBA. Wang (2000) confirms this in an experimental CORBA-based system to facilitate geo-processing function as well as data retrieval.

Similarly, DCOM (Distributed Component Object Model) serves as the basis of Microsoft's solution for component interoperability across networks. In a DSS, COM compliant GIS can be use to create custom-tailored applications by making use of various components of different applications and returning the processing result to the native GIS. For instance, a user can create an instance of a component of a statistical package, which could then be used to process local GIS data, then the result is returned to the native GIS (Ungerer et al., 2002; Zhang et al., 2000). These embeddable components allow movement away from proprietary languages. In a distributed environment, coupling COM with GIS in an Internet map server allows clients to invoke various geo-processing functions through a Web browser, and the map server processes the request and returns the result to the client browser through a Web server. These tools are now commercially available, e.g., ESRI's MapObjects IMS, ArcIMS. In a somewhat homogenous environment (e.g., Java-to-Java), remote methods can be invoked from other Java virtual Machine (JVM). Although RMI (Remote Method Invocation) provides a simpler implementation model than CORBA and DCOM, a full-fledged distributed GIS in RMI is plausible. RMI has been reported to be less scaleable than RPC (Wang, 2000).

OpenGIS Simple Feature Specification (OGC, 2002b) outlines spatial data access for COM, CORBA and SQL with respect to "feature" — the basic unit of geospatial data — and "geometry." The specification emphasizes data access, rather than geo-processing (1998, Cuthbert). From the decision support point of view, having data access at the client's end without robust geo-processing capabilities amounts to little help. Moreover, in a middleware-based solution, the client has to pull a massive amount of data at his/her end and manage it locally. Such approaches assume the client's explicit ability to manipulate server connection and invoke remote objects. Thus, frequent spatial processes, such as spatial join between data from two different servers, needs to be coordinated at the client's end. Object level manipulations of spatial process often fail to provide high-level views to the application developer. In a DSS user or decision maker's view, spatial features or geometry need to be realized at a higher level of abstraction, while at the same time maintaining the transparency of system processes. Such systems are yet to be realized within the decision support framework and geospatial interoperability of data and models.

COLLABORATIVE DECISION MAKING IN DISTRIBUTED ENVIRONMENT

Collaborative decision-making and public GIS, often called GIS2 (Densham et al., 1995; Sheppard, 1995) involves a "bottom- up" planning, reflecting users' perspectives to explore the projected planning scenarios. Decision-making for environmental planning is inherently distributed in nature over space and time (Agnew, 1993; Craig et al., 1999). In a real life situation, it is often difficult to achieve the decision makers' view or an effective pattern of social interactions because of heterogeneous group behavior and undefined agendas (Mosvick et al., 1987). Also, the spatial nature of decision conflicts among the different users often needs to be resolved in real time. Equipped with transparent computing resources and visualization, decision makers can explore the multiple decision scenarios in a collaborative environment and converge to consensus through mediation.

There is growing interest on collaborative decision making over the Internet. Rao & Jarvenpaa (1991) outlined the theoretical aspect of the effectiveness of the group decision support system with regards to the theories of communication and human information processing capabilities. Dillenburg et al. (1992) put forward the idea of "distributed cognition," which acknowledges that group decision-making can be supported by tools to allow explicit representation and manipulation (visualization) of shared information. Lotov et al., (2001) illustrated implementation of the Point Associated Trade-Off techniques (PAT), Feasible Goals Method (FGM) and Interactive Decision Maps (IDM) techniques for visualization of the variety of feasible criterion vectors for group decision-making. In collaborative decision-making, a distributed data warehouse will provide users with these basic building block of model components and interactive simulation interfaces, which is informative and responsive to accommodate a newer approach to effective participation in decision-making.

Collaborative Spatial Decision Support System: GEO-ELCA

GEO-ELCA (Exploratory Land Use Change Analysis) is a collaborative spatial decision support system to support users to assess the non-point pollution impact of land use changes. Built in the framework of COM coupling strategy, the system makes use of local GIS data and geo-processing facilities, along with an external simulation model components — the non-point pollution model. GEO-ELCA implements a middleware component to allow for receiving a client's response as http requests through an active-X enabled browser to support GIS functionality through a customized Web browser. User requests are received and managed by a middleware component or Web server, which administers requests and transmission of response between client and middleware tiers. The request is processed in an Application Programming Interface (API), and the result is sent back to the Web browser in the form of images supported by the browser. Typical examples of requests are: change land use type, identify a feature, zoom in, database query, display different themes etc. The Web server is developed with MapObjects components and ESRI's Internet Map Server (IMS; ESRI, 2002). MapObjects is a set, lightweight COM, which comprises ActiveX controls and automation objects specifically for mapping purposes, which is used along with any ActiveX container.

Internet Map Server provides a mechanism for receiving and dispatching requests from a client Web browser to a MapObjects application, eliminating the

Figure 1: GEO-ELCA architecture for distributed access to process model and spatial data

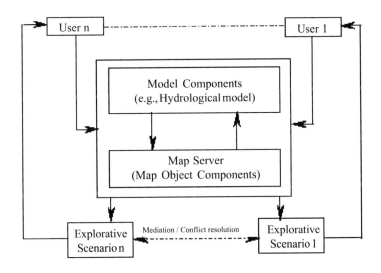

need for any Web server programming. Currently, the application implements the so-called "Simple Method" (Schueler, 1999) for estimating exports of various pollutants' runoff from different land uses. The open-end architecture of GEO-ELCA can be further customized using embeddable COM compliant external simulation models.

Exploring Decision Alternatives in GEO-ELCA

A key feature of GEO-ELCA is to provide users an exploratory tool to access the appropriate environmental data set and model base to visualize the consequences of a user decision. For example, a user can employ a visual query to find out a particular land use category. The query output can be further processed to a execute a simulation model.

Since the interaction process is in visual mode, a user need not have to have a prior idea of model components or parameters. A user can initiate a change in land use type by graphically selecting a polygon. The server side application processes the request and makes the necessary update in the database to reflect the corresponding the changes of the pollutant coefficients. Every request for change in land use type results in recalculation of the mass export of pollutant and corresponding statistics. The processed result is sent back to the Web server and then to the client side. GEO-ELCA allows the various features of GIS services on the Web. The system allows dynamic selection of a feature type (i.e., polygon – land use class) interactively, so that a user can change attribute items and

Figure 2: Visualization of collaborative explorative scenario

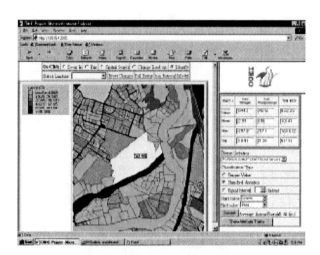

identify a feature property. The consequences of user decisions initiate the simulation model to estimate the yearly pollution load. The output can be visualized as pollutant distribution in terms of different classification schemes (e.g., standard deviation, plain break, quantile etc.), with modified map legend (both continuous and unique data type). The resulting pollution map can be visualized with multiple theme overlay. At its current stage of development, the system does not offer any mediating algorithm to resolve multiple scenarios. Such algorithm should involve a group consensus building mechanism through conflict resolution. Tools such as Analytic Hierarchic Process (Satty, 1990) or evolutionary search (e.g., genetic algorithm; Bennett, 1999) can be easily plugged in the system.

EMERGING TRENDS:
SPATIAL SERVICES IN SEMANTIC WEB

One of the shortcomings of the CORBA/DCOM and middleware-based approaches is that the client's application should have a prior understanding, to some extent, of the metadata of the responses of each object implementation. Any changes made to the services or to the data source requires a corresponding change in the object implementation. In a volatile Web environment, it is often difficult to keep track of each service and reflect the corresponding variations at the object implementation. This has necessitated the use of autonomous and reflexive objects, or so called "agents," to proxy different services. The agents communicate through a different level of ontology or well-specified domain vocabularies (Guarino, 1997). Through an URI (Uniform Resource Identifier) or a namespace, agents can register services. Since the namespaces are uniquely determined, there is no possibility of semantic mismatching of resources, regardless of their domain labels. These resources are formally described in RDF (Resource Description Framework) (Lassila & Swick, 1999), which provides a machine-readable metadata description through a triple (resource, property, value) to describe resource content in a Web page.

A distributed warehouse needs to express geometric primitives in an agent-understandable language. Open GIS's Abstract Specification provides such *simple features* in which geometric properties are defined. These features are encoded in a markup language released as GML (Geography Markup Language) (OGC, 2002c). Since GML has its root in RDF, using GML's core schema, one can define applications or domain schemas following RDF. For example, users can create new feature types or collection types from abstract feature types or collection types, which represents real world categories, such as "road," "bridges," etc. However, RDF lacks in inference and logical layer. In order to describe complex domain models, we need to specify data type and consistent expression for enumerations. Built on the top of RDF, DAML (DARPA Agent Markup Language) offers semantics of higher order relationships by including modeling constructs from descriptive logic. DAML based semantic translation and reasoning engine can be used in the local process to invoke generic procedures. DAML provides a declarative representation of Web service, model objects and user constraint in Web markup ontology to enable automated reasoning about declarative API (McIlraith, 2001). In a collaborative environment, multiple agents (both human or system automata) can specify different modeling parameters and constraints with different degree of preference, so that the resulting models conforms to the semantics of the model developer, expressible in a universally accepted ontology. Sikder et al. (2002) have proposed a multi-agent-mediated approach (OSIRIS-Ontology based Spatial Information and Resource Integration Scheme) to provide semantic interoperability and model composition.

CONCLUSION

We have addressed some of the issues relevant to distributed data warehouse and collaborative spatial decision-making. The heterogeneity of spatial object and geo-processing model components are discussed with respect to system integration framework. We have noted that currently there is no standard for re-use specification of existing spatial models at higher levels of abstraction, which would allow effective communication in the distributed spatial data warehouse architecture. There is a strong need for a generic model formalism to link models to the domain-specific knowledge. A formal description of the spatial data component and process model will allow better interoperation among heterogeneous systems. User or decision maker's views on spatial features or geometry needs to be realized at a higher level of abstraction without sacrificing object level interaction. The design of GEO-ELCA integrates GIS application models with a component-based framework, and serves complex analysis and simulation models by providing a mechanism for exploratory decision scenario. We have also noted that future development of distributed systems should comply with the emerging semantic Web framework in an agent-assisted environment. In terms of collaborative decision-making, the added advantage is that community based geo-spatial vocabulary, and the corresponding modeling semantics, can be communicated effectively. This will eventually allow multiple representations of spatial features at a different level of hierarchy in compliance with decision issues.

REFERENCES

Abel, D.J., & Kilby, P.J. (1994). The systems integration problem. *International Journal of Geographical Information Systems, 8* (1), 1-12.

Adam, N. & Gangopadhyay, A. (1997). *Database issues in Geographic Information Systems.* Kluwer International.

Agnew, J. (1993). Representing space: Space, scale and culture in social science. In J. Duncan & D. Ley, (Eds.), *Place/Culture/Representation* (pp. 251–71). London and New York: Routledge.

Bennett, D.A., Wade, G.A., & Armstrong M.P. (1999). Exploring the solution space of semi-structured geographical problems using genetic algorithms. *Transactions in GIS, 3* (1), 89-109.

Camara, G., Thome R., Freitas, U., & Miguel, A. (1999). Interoperability in practice: Problem in semantic conversion from current technology to OpenGIS. In A. Vckovski, K. Brassel & H. Schek (Eds.), *Interoperating Geographic Information Systems, (Eds.) Second International Conference.*

Chou, H. C., & Ding, Y. (1992). Methodology of integrating spatial analysis/ modeling and GIS. *Proceedings, 5th International Symposium on Spatial Data Handling,* (pp. 514-523). Charleston, SC.

Craig, W., & Elwood, S. (1998). How and why community groups use maps and geographic information. *Cartography and Geographic Information Systems, 25* (2), 95–104.

Cuthbert, A. (1999). OpenGIS: Tales from a Small Market Town. In A. Vckovski, K. Brassel and H. Schek (eds.), *Interoperating Geographic Information Systems) Second International Conference.*

Densham, P. J., Armstrong, M. P., & Kemp, K. (1995, September 17-21). *Report from the specialist meeting on collaborative spatial decision making, Initiative 17.* U. C., Santa Barbara: National Center for Geographic Information and Analysis.

Dillenburg, P., & Grimshaw, J.A. (1992). A computational approach to socially distributed cognition: Interaction learning situations with computers. *European Journal of Psychology of Education, 7* (4), 353-372.

ESRI. (2002). http://www.esri.com.

FGDC. (1999). http://www.fgdc.gov/.

Gardels, K. (1995, April). Open Geodata — CERES and ELIB. *Geo Info Systems.*

Guarino, N. (1997). Semantic matching: Formal ontological distinctions for information organization, extraction, and integration. In M. Pazienza, (Ed.), Information Extraction: A Multidisciplinary Approach to an Emerging Information *Technology* (pp. 139-170). Frascati, Italy: International Summer School, SCIE-97.

Inmon, W. (2001). A brief history of metadata: From master files to distributed metadata. Retrieved from http://www.billinmon.com/library/whiteprs/Metadata.pdf.

Lassila, O., & Swick, R. (2001). Resource Description Framework (RDF) Model and Syntax Specification, W3C (World-Wide Web Consortium). Retrieved from http://www.w3.org/TR/REC-rdf-syntax/.

Lotov, A., Bushenkov, V., Chernov, A., & Kistanov, A. (2001). Feasible goals method. Search for smart decisions. Retrieved from http://www.ccas.ru/mmes/mmeda/book5.htm.

Maidment, D.R. (1996). Environmental modeling with GIS. In Goodchild, M. F. et al (eds.), *GIS and Environmental Modeling: Progress and Research Issues* (pp. 315-323). Fort Collins, Colorado: GIS World, Inc.

McIlraith, S., Son, T. C., & Zeng, H. (2001, March/April). Semantic web services. *IEEE Intelligent Systems, 16* (2), 46-53.

Mosvick, R., & Nelson, R. (1987). *We've got to start meeting like this: A guide to successful business meeting management.* Glenview, IL: Scott, Foreman.

National Research Council. (1999). Distributed geolibraries: Spatial information resources, workshop summary. *Commission on Geosciences, Environment and Resources.* Washington, D.C.: National Academy Press.

National Research Council. (1993). Towards a coordinated spatial data infrastructure for the nation. Washington, D.C.: Mapping Science Committee, National Academy Press.

NCGIA. (1995, September). Collaborative Spatial Decision Support. *Specialist Meeting of NCGIA Research Initiative 17.* Santa Barbara, CA.

Nyerges, T. (1993). Understanding the scope of GIS: its relationship to environmental modeling. In M. F. Goodchild, B. O. Parks & L. T. Steyaert (eds.), *Environmental Modeling with GIS* (pp. 75-93). New York: Oxford University Press.

Open GIS Consortium. (2001). http://www.opengis.org.

Open GIS Consortium. (2002a). OpenGIS Abstract Specification. Retrieved from http://www.opengis.org/public/abstract.html.

Open GIS Consortium. (2002b). OpenGIS. *Simple Features Specification for CORBA/SQL/OLE/COM.* Retrieved from http://www.opengis.org/techno/specs.htm.

Open GIS Consortium. (2002c). OpenGIS. Geography Markup Language. (GML) *Implementation Specification.* Retrieved from http://www.opengis.org/techno/specs.htm.

Pickles, J. (1995). *Ground truth: The social implications of Geographic Information Systems.* New York: Guildford Press.

Rao, V.S., & Jarvenpaa, S.L. (1991). Computer support of groups: Theory-based models for SDSS research. *Management Science, 37* (10), 1347-1362.

Saaty, T. L. (1990). *Multicriteria Decision Making: The Analytic Hierarchy Process*. Pittsburgh: Expert Choice Inc/RWS Publications.

Schueler, T. (1999). Microbes and urban watersheds. *Watershed Protection Techniques*, 3 (1), 551-596.

Sheppard, E. (1995). GIS and society: Towards a research agenda. *Cartography and Geographic Information Systems*, *22* (1), 251-317.

Sikder, I., & Gangopadhyay, A. (2002a, October-December). Design and implementation of a web-based collaborative spatial decision support system: Organizational and managerial implications. *Information Resources Management Journal*, *15* (4).

Sikder, I., & Yoon, V. (2002 b). Software agent oriented framework for ontology driven interoperability of geo-spatial models. *Proceedings of the Decision Sciences Institute 2002 Annual Meeting*. San Diego.

Ungerer, M., & Goodchild, M. (2002). Integrating spatial data analysis and GIS: A new implementation using the COM. *International Journal of Geographical Information Science*, *16*, (1), 44-53.

Wang, F. (2000). A distributed geographic information system on the Common Object Request Broker Architecture (CORBA). *GeoInformatica*, pp. 89-115.

Worboys, M. (1995). *GIS: A computing perspective*. Taylor and Francis.

Yuan, M. (1997). Development of a global conceptual schema for interoperable geographic information. *Inerop '97*. Santa Barbara: UCSB.

Zhang, Z., & Griffith, D. (2000). Integrating GIS components and spatial statistical analysis in DBMS's. *International Journal of Geographical Science*, *14*, 543-556.

Chapter IX

Data Mining for Business Process Reengineering

Ted E. Lee
The University of Memphis, USA

Robert Otondo
The University of Memphis, USA

Bonn-Oh Kim
Seattle University, USA

Pattarawan Prasarnphanich
The University of Memphis, USA

Ernest L. Nichols, Jr.
The University of Memphis, USA

ABSTRACT

Transitioning from a mining to meaning perspective in organization data mining can be a crucial step in the successful application of data mining technologies. The purpose of this paper is to examine more fully the implications of that shift. The use of data mining technology was part of our cycle time study of the Poplar County Criminal Justice System (a fictitious name). In this paper we will report on the use of data mining in the Poplar County Criminal Justice System (PCCJS) study in an attempt to speed up their case handling processes. Marketing and finance researchers are more involved with "simple" (i.e., direct) relationships, whereas BPR researchers are more concerned with long chains of interacting processes.

This difference appears in the tools these researchers use: marketing and finance researchers are more interested in set-theoretic problems, BPR researchers, in graph-theoretic problems. Yet data mining technologies incorporate graph-theoretic algorithms. Consequently, they should be able to support hypothesis generation in BPR activities. We were able to come up with relevant and meaningful hypotheses for BPR in the PCCJS system by using data mining technology, specifically sequential pattern analysis: "Which areas we should look into in order to speed up the case handling process?" This valuable outcome would have not been possible without data mining technology, considering the large volume of data on hand. It is hoped that this study will contribute to broadening the scope of applicability of data mining technology.

INTRODUCTION

The terms *data mining* and *knowledge discovery* conjure up images of miners searching for gold or explorers seeking an unknown continent. Those images can be powerful, yet misleading, in that they strongly suggest that those using data mining tools have a clear picture of where and for what they are looking. More explicitly, those images of knowledgeable searchers imply the existence of two types of knowledge, which may not necessarily be true for data mining tool users: 1) a set of clues or "signs" that act as inputs to 2) a set of decision rules that process the clues into desired outcomes. For example, expert gold miners have a knowledge base of important signs and rules that allow them to distinguish gold ore from pyrite ("fool's gold").

Data mining in organizational environments, on the other hand, is conducted in human social contexts. This environment is vastly more complex and subtle than the mechanistic, engineered world of the miner. This difference is significant, in that many of the signs encountered in the human world of data mining activities are often equivocal, and the decision rules are more heuristic. "Mining" for patterns in organizational databases is thus more like mineralogical, or, better yet, archeological research, in which the relationships between data are fuzzy, messy, equivocal, or unknown.

Transitioning from a mining to meaning perspective in organization data mining can be a crucial step in the successful application of data mining technologies. The purpose of this paper is to examine more fully the implications of that shift. The use of data mining technology was part of our cycle time study of the Poplar County Criminal Justice System (a fictitious name). In this paper we will report on the use of data mining in the Poplar County Criminal Justice System (PCCJS) study.

THE POPLAR COUNTY CRIMINAL JUSTICE SYSTEM STUDY

Located in the southeastern United States, Poplar County (fictitious) contains a large metropolitan area of roughly one million people. Recent growth patterns have created problems with the county's infrastructure. One of — if not *the* most problematic infrastructure — has been the County Jail. The jail is constantly overcrowded. Originally built for a population of about 1,500 inmates, the jail now regularly houses about 2,300-2,500 inmates. This overcrowding has created a number of problems, some of which have prompted lawsuits from inmates as well as from the Federal Courts.

The Poplar County Commissioners have taken steps to increase the Jail's capacity; however, it has also determined that some of the overcrowding was associated with the length of time required to bring cases to trial and adjudicate them. Consequently, the Commissioners asked the researchers for their help in resolving some of these issues. The study began with interviews of County Jail personnel. Those interviews revealed many problems with which the Jail had responsibility but little control. For example, they had no control over who came into the Jail and who went out. They could not tell law enforcement officers that they could not take in prisoners, nor could they force the Courts to release more prisoners to make room. The interviews revealed the systematic interrelationships between the Jail and other agencies within the Poplar County Criminal Justice System (PCCJS).

To gain a better understanding of the PCCJS and the determinants of jail overcrowding, three intelligent strategies were employed. The first two strategies involved interviewing important PCCJS personnel, including, but not limited to, the County Sheriff's Office, General Sessions Court Clerk's Office, Pretrial Services, District Attorney's Office, local police departments, and so on. The first strategy involved objective questioning aimed at better understanding the effects of formal PCCJS workflows on jail overcrowding. This line of questioning led to the development of a PCCJS workflow process chart. That diagram provided a map to explain how the actions of one group impacted jail overcrowding. The second strategy involved subjective questioning aimed at eliciting beliefs as to how effectively and efficiently the formal workflow process worked. This second line of questioning was intended to "breath life" into the workflow diagram by ascertaining trouble spots and bottlenecks, as well as pinpointing possible solutions. Because of limited space, only the general process diagram for PCCJS is presented in Appendix I.

The third strategy was to analyze PCCJS transaction data to ascertain the system's overall performance. This data, which was drawn from almost all agencies within the PCCJS, was stored in Poplar County's Information Systems Services database. Unfortunately, the database was designed for tracking, but not for performance evaluation; that is, the database could report where and when a case was supposed to go next, but not how long it took to process an incoming jail inmate.

However, the researchers faced a dilemma in integrating the three types of data. On the one hand, the objective and subjective data gleaned from the interviews was used to construct a *graph-theoretic* workflow process diagram. On the other hand, the relational structure of the County's PCCJS relational database was set-theoretic. At issue was how to analyze set-theoretic data to support graph-theoretic BPR in a cost and time effective manner.

METHOD

Officials in a Criminal Justice system were interviewed to elicit their understandings and beliefs of the workflow operations. Members of the County Jail, County Sheriff's Office, Local Police Department, Pretrial Services, County Clerk, Public Defender's Office, and other agencies were interviewed. Based on those interviews, a workflow diagram was generated. The interviewees were then asked to engage in two rounds of double-checking.

Random sets of transaction data for the Criminal Justice System was collected over a period of three years. To account for seasonal variations in caseloads, one week was selected randomly from every quarter between summer 1997 to spring 2000. All cases from those weeks were selected. Any transaction associated with those cases was then selected and stored in the study's database. In this way, the start times of the cases were spread in a randomized fashion across the time study, but the transactions were drawn from anytime. The data was then analyzed using the two methods in data mining: association rules analysis and sequential pattern analysis.

DATA MINING

A major difficulty with the dataset was its internal relational structure. Like all relational databases, the PCCJS database was build upon a set theory foundation. That foundation gives relational database management systems wide applicability to those problems that can be conceived in and resolved through sets. For example, large numbers of customer-based transactions have long been successfully stored and analyzed through set-theoretic relational database systems.

However, many of the problems faced in BPR in general—and in the PCCJS study in particular—are often better understood in a graph-theoretic framework. (e.g., path analysis). Under these circumstances, traditional set-theoretic relational database capabilities have limited usefulness. Newer capabilities, particularly those based on data mining technologies, have built upon traditional relational database systems by incorporating graph-theoretic tools. The power of data mining technologies has been widely applied and investigated in the marketing and financial domains.

The problems facing BPR are different in many ways from those faced by marketing and financial organizations. One of the most evident is that marketing and finance researchers are more involved with "simple" (i.e., direct) relationships, whereas BPR researchers are more concerned with long chains of interacting processes (i.e., "hidden information"). This difference appears in the tools these researchers use: marketing and finance researchers are more interested in set-theoretic problems, BPR researchers, in graph-theoretic problems. Yet data mining technologies incorporate graph-theoretic algorithms. Consequently, they should at first glance be able to support hypothesis generation in BPR activities. The purpose of this paper is to investigate the extent to which graph-theoretic data mining algorithms can generate BPR hypotheses.

We started with the following two questions:

- Whether the presence of a type of reset reason is associated with another type of reset reason — Association Rules analysis
- Whether the presence of a type of reset reason is followed by another type of reset reason over a period of time, showing a sequential pattern — Sequential Pattern Analysis

The layout of the study's data set is provided in Appendix II. For example, whenever there is a status change in the case (#9749904), the change is recorded into the PCCJS system with a specific reason. The sequence of the reset reasons in the order of time is AR =>AT =>AT =>FA =>AT =>FF =>BW =>AT. If a case goes well as scheduled, there will be a smaller number of reset reasons for the case in that sequence. By using the technique of sequential pattern analysis, it is hoped that we could identify potentially problematic and/or meaningful sequential patterns of reset reasons in the cases under consideration.

Analysis of Association Rules Using Clementine

The data set used for our analysis is randomly select from 1997 to 2000: 09/28/97-10/04/97, 11/23/97-11/29/97, 02/22/98-02/28/98, 06/14/98-06/20/98, 07/26/98-08/01/98, 10/04/98-10/10/98, 02/28/99-03/06/99, 04/18/99-04/24/99, 07/11/99-07/17/99, 10/17/99-10/23/99, 02/06/00-02/12/00, and 04/16/00-04/22/00. The SPSS, a statistical software package, is used to detect missing value, invalid data, and outliers. The data cleaning process should be conducted at first, before performing further analysis, because the problem of missing data, incorrect or invalid data, and outliers could have a significantly destructive impact on final results. Fortunately, there are no missing values, incorrect data, and outliers in this data set; as a result, all observations are used for data mining analysis.

To conduct an analysis for association rules, the interested items, which are the reset reasons for our study, need to be recorded in a binary format (yes or no; 1 or 0). Since our original data set is in a different format (refer to Appendix I), data conversion process is required. SAS is used for this data conversion. There are 28 possible reset reasons resulting in 28 fields in the converted version. An example of data conversion can be shown as below:

Original format

Booking No.	. . . .	Reset Reasons	. . . .
97049600	. . . .	AR	. . . .
97049600	. . . .	AT	. . . .
97049600	. . . .	VR	. . . .
97049700	. . . .	AT	. . . .
97049700	. . . .	VP	. . . .

Converted format

Booking No.	. . . .	AR	AT	. . .	VP	VR	. . . . .
97049600	. . . .	1	1	. . .	0	1	. . . . .
97049700	. . . .	1	0	. . .	1	0	. . . . .

After the conversion, there are a total of 10,319 records to be used to perform data mining analysis. Clementine version 5.01, one of several commercial data mining tools, is selected to discover any association rules for reset reasons. The result of this analysis appears in *Appendix III*. Unfortunately, we were not able to find out any relevant or meaningful association rules among reset reasons.

Analysis of Sequential Patterns of Reset Reasons Using IntelligentMiner

The sequential pattern technique is used to search for any meaningful sequential patterns of the reset reasons. The potential findings would hopefully contribute to any reduction in cycle time of the jailing processes. For the sequential pattern analysis type, we had to use IntelligentMiner version 6.1 by IBM because Clementine version 5.01 did not support this type of analysis, which we overlooked at the outset of this project. So, we ended up doing data preparation again for this new data mining tool. Prior to conducting data mining analysis with the IntelligentMiner, data preparation, such as data cleaning and combining files into a single file, was performed with SAS and a new data file based on our original data set was produced as a flat file. The IntelligentMiner accepts input data in the form of either flat file format or database table/view. The data file produced from SAS is inputted into the IntelligentMiner under Data Wizard in the IntelligentMiner. Before performing mining or any analysis, a data object must be created and specified as input data through Data Wizard. Then, sequential pattern analysis for reset reason can be conducted. There are three input fields specified for the analysis:

- Transaction group field: Booking Number
- Transaction field: Create Date (Date the record was created or date the reset occurred)
- Item field: Reset Reason

The result of this analysis appears in *Appendix IV*. The result is somewhat interesting in the sense that there are many sequential patterns with consecutive AT reset reasons in the data set: AT=>AT (38%), AT=>AT=>AR (27%), RP=>AT=>AT(25%), RP=>AT=>AT=>AR (19%), and AT=>AT=>AT (16%). Especially, existence of the last sequential pattern with three consecutive AT reset reasons calls for further analysis. This result gives a clue as to which area the PCCJS Commissioners should look into to speed up the handling of the cases on their system.

DISCUSSION

The result of association rules analysis does not help us answer the first question we had at the beginning. After careful evaluation on the all identified association rules, it is concluded that there is no relevant or meaningful association rule among the reset reasons in cases. This interpretation might make sense, because most algorithms implementing association rules analysis are based on a simple counting algorithm. However, the result of sequential pattern analysis help us generate several BPR hypotheses, i.e., which areas we should look into to possibly reduce the number of reset reasons in cases, and, in turn, speed up the overall jail processing time for cases in the PCCJS system. As pointed out earlier, there are five significant sequential patterns in the reset reasons:

1.   AT=>AT (38%)
2.   AT=>AT=>AR (27%)
3.   RP=>AT=>AT(25%)
4.   RP=>AT=>AT=>AR (19%)
5.   AT=>AT=>AT (16%)

The first identified sequential pattern tells that 38% of the total cases under consideration involve two reset reasons of AT that is either reassignment of a defending attorney or request for determent of case by defending attorney. The next three sequential patterns are more specialized ones that are already factored into the first pattern. One of the most interesting and significant is the last sequential pattern: 16% of the total cases under consideration involve three reset reasons of AT. The next phase of this study will be to further investigate such cases that have these identified sequential patterns.

As in any IS project, selection of a right data software tool is important, especially when a given project needs to meet a tight deadline. We started with Clementine 5.01 by SPSS for association rules analysis because of easy access to this data mining tool. Since the sequential pattern analysis is one of the most typical data mining techniques discussed in the literature, we inadvertently assumed that this feature would be supported in Clementine. Even if there were some features available in Clementine to identify possible sequence patterns, we could not find a feature that specifically implements sequential pattern analysis. After switching to IntelligentMiner for sequential pattern analysis, we also ran the same data set for association rules analysis in IntelligentMiner for performance comparison. The result of association rules analysis from Intelligent Miner was same as that from Clementine, but there was a significant difference in processing time (20 to 30 min in Clementine vs. five to 10 min in IntelligentMiner). The IntelligentMiner provides both descriptive result and visualized result, unlike Clementine, which provides only the descriptive result.   With the Intelligent Miner, the conversion of data to be represented in a binary format is not required (refer to the subsection of "analysis of association rules using Clementine"). Hence, the same data format can be used to perform both association rule analysis and sequential pattern analysis. Based on our observation, IntelligentMiner is a more comprehensive data mining tool and can handle more complicated analysis than Clementine. However, it seems that Clementine is easier to understand and use than IntelligentMiner.

CONCLUSION

So far, we demonstrate how data mining technology can provide a support for analyzing business processes in the PCCJS system. The power of data mining technologies has been widely applied and investigated in the marketing and financial domains. One of the most evident is that marketing and finance researchers are more involved with simple relationships, whereas BPR researchers are more concerned with long chains of interacting processes. However, an appropriate application of data mining technology to BPR effort can be beneficial. We were able to come up with relevant and meaningful hypotheses for BPR in the PCCJS system by using data mining technology, specifically sequential pattern analysis: "Which areas we should look into in order to speed up the case handling process?" This valuable outcome would have not been possible without data mining technology considering the large volume of data on hand. It is hoped that this study will contribute to broadening the scope of applicability of data miming technology.

APPENDIX I:
GENERAL PROCESS DIAGRAM
(W/TIMES FROM INITIAL ARREST)

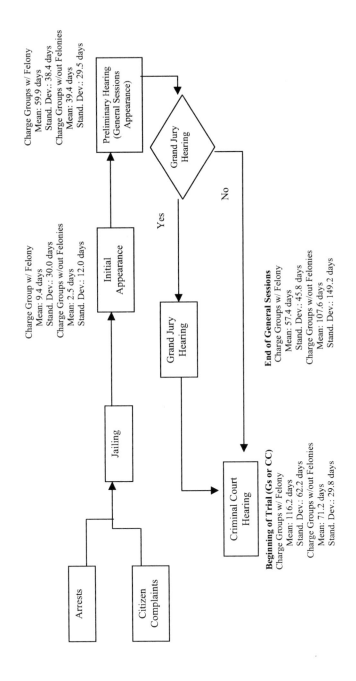

APPENDIX II:
DATA LAYOUT FOR PCCJS STUDY

RNI#	Booking number	Charge Code	Court Code	Arrest Agency	Officer ID	Arrest Date & Time	Charge Time	Charge Group Disposed Date	Charge Group Disposed Indicator	Probation Start Date	Court Division	Court Date	Court Session	Reset Reason	Creation date
162905	97049904	1	GS	SO	S2529	9/30/97 09:27	9/6/00 8:45	8/6/1998	Y	8/6/1998	7	8/6/98	1	AR	09/30/97 4:39
162905	97049904	1	GS	SO	S2529	9/30/97 09:27	9/6/00 8:45	8/6/1998	Y	8/6/1998	7	8/6/98	1	AT	10/01/97 14:03
162905	97049904	1	GS	SO	S2529	9/30/97 09:27	9/6/00 8:45	8/6/1998	Y	8/6/1998	7	8/6/98	1	AT	10/29/97 14:51
162905	97049904	1	GS	SO	S2529	9/30/97 09:27	9/6/00 8:45	8/6/1998	Y	8/6/1998	7	8/6/98	1	FA	11/12/97 11:49
162905	97049904	1	GS	SO	S2529	9/30/97 09:27	9/6/00 8:45	8/6/1998	Y	8/6/1998	7	8/6/98	1	AT	12/03/97 13:59
162905	97049904	1	GS	SO	S2529	9/30/97 09:27	9/6/00 8:45	8/6/1998	Y	8/6/1998	7	8/6/98	1	FF	01/07/98 17:48
162905	97049904	1	GS	SO	S2529	9/30/97 09:27	9/6/00 8:45	8/6/1998	Y	8/6/1998	7	8/6/98	1	BW	07/26/98 12:54
162905	97049904	1	GS	SO	S2529	9/30/97 09:27	9/6/00 8:45	8/6/1998	Y	8/6/1998	7	8/6/98	1	AT	07/27/98 10:58

1. RNI #: Number assigned to a criminal by Sheriff's department for identification.
2. Booking #: Number assign by courts system for grouping all charges against a defendant.
3. Charge Code: Code identifying the crime.
4. Court Code: GS for General Sessions.
5. Arrest Agency: Code of arresting agency. MP = Local Police, SO = Sheriff's Department.
6. Officer ID: Officer's assign number.
7. Arrest Date and Time: Date and Time of the arrest.
8. Charge Time: Date and time the inmate was entered into the system in the sally port.
9. Charge Group Disposed Date: Self-explanatory.
10. Charge Group Disposed Indicator: Y = all charges disposed. N = All charges not disposed. D = Case on Diversion.
11. Probation Start Date: Self-explanatory.
12. Court Division: Self-explanatory.
13. Court Date: Date assign for defendant to be in court.
14. Court Session: 1 = 9AM, 2 = 1PM, 3 = 10:30AM, 4 = 4PM
15. Reset Reason:
    AR: Arraignment; AT: Attorney; BW: Bench Warrant; D1: Application for Diversion;
    D2: End of Diversion; DP: Disposition; FA: Final Settings for Attorney;
    FF: Final Forfeiture; PH: Preliminary Hearing; RP: Report to Court; TR: Trial;
    VR: Video Arraignment; TT: Total Time.
16. Create Date: Date the record was created.

APPENDIX III

Support(%)	Confidence(%)	Rule Body		Rule Head
16.2225	92.0300	[AR]+[AT]+[DP]	==>	[RP]
18.6452	91.6600	[AR]+[DP]	==>	[RP]
20.2539	89.2400	[DP]	==>	[RP]
17.5308	89.1100 .	[AT]+[DP]	==>	[RP]
18.7809	90.5600	[VR]	==>	[AT]
11.4740	88.5600	[PH]	==>	[AT]
11.7841	88.0500	[VR]+[RP]	==>	[AT]
16.2225	87.0100 .	[RP]+[AR]+[DP]	==>	[AT]
10.3111	87.0000	[FF]	==>	[AT]
19.6724	86.6800	[DP]	==>	[AT]
17.6277	86.6600	[AR]+[DP]	==>	[AT]
17.5308	86.5600 .	[RP]+[DP]	==>	[AT]
11.4740	96.8100	[FF]	==>	[AR]
10.1173	96.4000	[BW]	==>	[AR]
48.7063	82.9100	[RP]	==>	[AT]
37.7847	81.8600	[RP]+[AR]	==>	[AT]
16.2225	92.5400	[RP]+[AT]+[DP]	==>	[AR]
18.6452	92.0600	[RP]+[DP]	==>	[AR]
20.3411	89.6200	[DP]	==>	[AR]
17.6277	89.6100	[AT]+[DP]	==>	[AR]

APPENDIX IV:
RESULT OF SEQUENTIAL PATTERN ANALYSIS

Sequence Support	Item sets	Sequence Support	Item sets	Sequence Support	Item sets	Sequence Support	Item sets
51.72	AT	20.002	DP	14.042	AT	11.668	RP
	AR		RP		RP		AT
							VR
40.406	RP	19.76	RP	13.577	RP		
	AT		AT		RP	11.474	PH
			AT		AT		AT
46.138	RP		AR		AT		
	AR					11.455	FF
		19.508	DP	13.364	RP		AR
38.085	AT		AT		RP		
	AT				RP	11.154	RP
		18.762	AT		AR		AT
37.475	RP		VR				AT
	AT			13.306	RP		AT
	AR	18.413	DP		VR		
			RP			11.086	RP
32.804	RP		AR	13.218	AT		AR
	RP				RP		AR
		17.463	DP		AT		
27.406	AT		AT			10.96	AT
	AT		AR	13.005	RP		AT
	AR				RP		VR
		17.153	DP		RP		
26.514	RP		RP		AT	10.922	RP
	RP		AT				RP
	AT			12.899	RP		AT
		16.223	RP		AT		AT
26.156	RP		RP		RP		AR
	RP		RP				
	AR			12.501	AT	10.902	AR
		16.038	AT		AT		AT
25.254	RP		AT		AT		
	AT		AT		AR	10.747	AR
	AT						AT
		15.99	AR	12.249	RP		AR
20.709	RP		AR		AT		
	RP				RP	10.534	AT
	AT	15.874	DP		AT		AR
	AR		RP				AT
			AT	12.23	AT		
20.341	DP		AR		AR		
	AR				AR		

Chapter X

Intrinsic and Contextual Data Quality: The Effect of Media and Personal Involvement

Andrew S. Borchers
Kettering University, USA

ABSTRACT

This chapter introduces the concepts of intrinsic and contextual data quality and presents research results on how individual perceptions of data quality are impacted by media (World Wide Web versus print) and personal involvement with the topic. The author advances four hypotheses, which are tested with a randomized experiment (n=127), dealing with information on cancer. First, subjects perceive reputable information sources as having higher data quality than non-reputable sources. Second, subjects perceive web-based material to be more timely, but less believable and of lower reputation, accuracy and objectivity than printed material. Third, individuals with greater personal involvement will be better discriminators of data quality in viewing reputable and non-reputable cancer information. Fourth, women are better discriminators of data quality in viewing reputable and non-reputable information than men. The first hypothesis was supported and limited support was provided for the second hypothesis.

INTRODUCTION

This chapter introduces the concepts of intrinsic and contextual data quality as described in the literature and presents research results on how individual perceptions of data quality are impacted by media (World Wide Web versus print) and personal involvement with the topic. There is a rich base of literature, both in Information Systems and Journalism, on "data quality" and "media creditability." While developed separately, these streams of research provide a consistent picture of how people view the quality of information they receive from different sources. Research results shed further light on the topic.

The impact of the Internet revolution on information sharing is widely acknowledged. But this access comes with a challenge as stated by Gilster (as cited in Flanigan, 2000). "One of the challenges of Internet publishing is that it turns our conventional expectations, built upon years of experience with newspapers and magazines, on their head. We can no longer assume that the appearance of a publication is necessarily relevant to the quality of its information."

BACKGROUND

The importance of data quality has been echoed among practitioners for many years. Redman (1998) summarizes the practical implications of poor quality. He points out the negative consequences of data quality problems on decision making, organizational mistrust, strategic planning and implementation, and customer satisfaction. In carefully studied situations, Redman finds increased cost of 8-12% due to poor data quality. Service organizations can find increased expenses of 40-60% (Redman, 1998). Strong, Yang & Wang (1997) support the seriousness of this issue in their study of 42 data quality projects in three organizations. Research by other authors note data quality issues in a number of settings, including airlines, health care (Strong, 1997), accounting (Xu, 2000; Kaplan, 1998), data warehousing (Ballou, 1999), and criminal justice (Laudon, 1986)

Over the years a number of authors have written conceptual articles on "data quality" (Wand, 1996; Wang, 1995, 1996; Strong, 1997). In these studies, it has become clear that data quality is a multidimensional concept (Wand, 1996) that can be viewed from a number of different perspectives. A panel discussion in 2000 (Lee, Bowen, Funk, Jarke, Madnick & Wand) found five different perspectives to discuss data quality. These included:

1.   Ontological perspective – This perspective deals with different views of reality that one can have based on actual observation, compared to what information systems tell a user is true. In Wand's work (1996), he identifies

the potential for incomplete, ambiguous and meaningless representation between the real world and the information system representation of the real world.

2. Architectural perspective – This view focuses in on system infrastructure (such as data warehouses, ERP systems, etc.), and how it refines and improves data quality.

3. Context Mediation perspective – In this view, the focus is on how to connect heterogeneous databases and achieve communication across space and time.

4. Time Based E-Commerce perspective – This perspective notes the impact that time has in the real-time world of the Internet. When firms use B2B e-commerce to closely couple supply chains, there is a real danger that time based data quality issues may arise.

5. Information Product perspective – This perspective notes that for many organizations today, data is their product. The quality of data from an end user perspective is the key focus in this perspective.

In talking about "data quality," a key starting point is to determine just what one means by the term. Wang (1996) provides what is perhaps the definitive work in developing a conceptual framework for data quality. Using a two-stage survey and sorting process, Wang develops a hierarchical framework for data quality that includes four major areas: intrinsic, contextual, representational and accessibility.

Intrinsic data quality refers to the concept that "data have quality in their own right" (Wang, 1996). Intrinsic dimensions include accuracy, objectivity, believability and reputation. Contextual data quality is based on the idea that data does not exist in a vacuum – it is driven by context. Contextual dimensions include relevancy, timeliness and appropriate amount of data. Representational data quality relates to the "format of the data (concise and consistent representation) and meaning of data (interpretability and ease of understanding)." Accessibility refers to the ease with which one can get to data (Wang, 1996).

This study focuses on intrinsic and contextual data quality for two reasons. First, the attributes studied were found to be significantly different between WWW and print media by a prior researcher (Klein, 1999, 2001). In one study, Klein (1999) found web based material to be more timely, but less believable and of lower reputation, accuracy and objectivity than printed material. In a more formal result (2001), Klein found traditional text sources to be perceived as more accurate, objective and to have higher reputation and representational consistency. Internet sources were found to be stronger in timeliness and appropriate amount.

The second reason for focusing on intrinsic and contextual data quality comes from a different literature base. Beyond the information systems literature, there is a body of literature among journalism scholars about the perceptions of Internet credibility (Flanagin, 2000; Johnson, 1998). The major thrust of this literature is in comparing the Internet to traditional sources with respect to credibility. Note that when referring to "credibility," these authors say, "the most consistent dimension of media credibility is believability, but accuracy, trustworthiness, bias and completeness of information are other dimensions commonly used by researchers" (Flanagin, 2000, p. 521). Hence, there is a rough correspondence of thinking about "credibility" in the journalism literature to the concept of "intrinsic" and "contextual" data quality in the information systems literature. Flanagin's work focuses in three areas. First, he looks at the perceived credibility of television, newspapers, radio and magazines compared to the Internet. The major finding, unlike Klein, is that there is little difference in credibility between media. Second, Flanagin looks at the extent to which Internet users verify what they receive. Third, and most important to this work, Flanagin looks at whether perceived credibility varies depending on the type of information being sought. Flanagin cites Gunther in suggesting that "greater involvement with the message results in, first, a wider latitude of rejection."

Finally, health care literature forms a final basis for this work. Bates (2000) notes the role of "word of mouth," and the Internet in particular, in providing consumers with health care information. Others have noted gender differences within many families when it comes to health information. Women are most often the conduit through which health care information is filtered, with men less involved. Further, they are the chief decision maker in health care matters in many families (Looker, 2001).

RESEARCH APPROACH AND HYPOTHESIS

The literature cited above suggests a number of interesting hypotheses. The author set out to investigate the topic using an experimental approach, where subjects were shown information about cancer from a "reputable" and a "disreputable" source using traditional print and the Internet as media. In this study the "reputable" source was a well-known national organization devoted to fighting cancer. The "disreputable" source was a WWW site that recommended alternative cancer treatments and abandoning traditional cancer treatment by doctors. Using this vehicle to study these relationships, the author posits the following hypotheses:

H1: Subjects will perceive web based material to be more timely, but less believable and of lower reputation, accuracy and objectivity than printed material.

H2: Individuals with greater personal involvement in cancer will be better discriminators of data quality in viewing reputable and non-reputable cancer information.

H3: Women are better discriminators of data quality in viewing reputable and non-reputable cancer information than men.

Further, since the experiment is premised on a source being "reputable" and "disreputable," the author tested an initial hypothesis (H0) that posits the "reputable" source has significantly greater intrinsic and contextual data quality than the "disreputable" source.

Figure 1 below demonstrates what the author hoped to find. H0, the initial hypothesis, is that the perception of low creditable sources is significantly less than high creditable sources. Hence, the two lines for Internet based and print based text should have a positive slope. H1 suggests a significant gap between the lines for Internet based sources and text based sources on the timeliness, believability, reputation, accuracy and objectivity dimensions. This assertion was based on prior literature by Klein (1999). H2 would suggest that the slope of the lines should vary based on one's personal involvement in cancer. Finally, H3 suggests that women are better able to differentiate credible from non-credible sources. Hence, the slope of the lines should vary based on gender.

Figure 1: Research Design

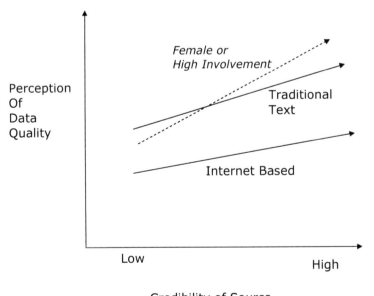

METHODOLOGY

In this research, subjects (n=127) reviewed information on cancer and answered a questionnaire. Subjects were drawn from mid-career students in MBA and MSIS classes at a Mid-western university. The sample is strongly multi-cultural with significant U.S., Indian and Chinese representation. Subjects were randomly assigned to one of four groups.

These four groups were shown cancer information based on two sources of information presented in two different formats. As noted, one source was a website of a highly credible national cancer organization. The second source of cancer information was a website of low creditability, a site that touted alternative medical treatments. The third and fourth sources were identical to the first two, with the exception that they were presented in printed form by way of a color document. Subjects were then asked about their perceptions of the data that they have viewed using Wang's intrinsic data quality dimensions (accuracy, objectivity, believability and reputation), as well as contextual dimensions (timeliness, relevancy and appropriate amount of information) and ease of use. Further, subjects were asked about their personal and family experience with cancer as well as demographic questions (gender, age and country of birth).

FINDINGS

After the data was collected, the author analyzed it in two different ways. First, the reliability of the four multi-item dimensions was appraised using Cronbach Alpha. *Table 1* below shows the result. Note that each dimension has an Alpha value of at least .80.

Table 1: Reliability estimates

Dimension	Cronbach's Alpha for Internet Sources	Cronbach's Alpha for Text Sources
Relevant (relevant, interesting and usable)	.8453	.8349
Accuracy (error-free, reliable and precise)	.9044	.8402
Objectivity (unbiased and objective)	.8933	.9141
Ease of Understanding (easily understood and readable)	.8218	.9106

The author generated a second set of statistics using a univariate ANOVA procedure to test each of the research hypotheses. H0 was tested for all eight measured data quality dimensions, using the source reputation (high or low) and media (print or WWW) as fixed factors. In testing H2 and H3, cancer involvement or gender were added as random factors. The hypotheses were tested by looking at the product term for source reputation and cancer involvement (H2) or Gender (H3). *Table 2* below summarizes the findings:

Table 2: Hypothesis testing results

Hypothesis	Dimension	F ratio	Significance
H0 – Initial difference due to reputation	Believable, Accuracy, Reputation, Objectivity and Appropriate Amount	10.526 to 24.489	.000 to .002
H0 – Initial difference due to reputation	Timeliness, Relevance, Ease of Use	< 1.4	> .35
H1 – WWW compared to print	Timeliness Believable Reputation Accuracy Objectivity Appropriate Amount Relevance Ease Of Use	2.587 1.036 .340 .483 1.132 .617 .030 .620	.110 .311 .561 .489 .290 .484 .865 .484
H2 – Personal involvement with cancer	Timeliness Believable Reputation Accuracy Objectivity Appropriate Amount Relevance Ease of Use	With all respondents F ratio < 4 US-only respondents had significant interaction on believability and reputation	With all respondents F > .05 US-only respondents were significant on believability and reputation
H3 – Gender	Believable Accuracy Reputation Objectivity Appropriate Amount Relevance Ease of Use	All < 4	All > .05

CONCLUSIONS AND FUTURE TRENDS

This research begins a line of work that seeks to understand the underlying factors behind different dimensions of perceived data quality. The experimental design appears to work reasonably. Note that the first hypothesis (H0) is supported for all four of the intrinsic data quality dimensions (believability, accuracy, objectivity and reputation) and one contextual dimension, appropriate amount. It did not hold for two contextual dimensions (relevancy and timeliness) and a representational dimension (ease of use). The researcher observed that these findings held true for all respondents, but that by limiting the sample to U.S. born respondents, the F ratios were significantly higher.

Do people perceive data quality differently depending on the media that data is presented in? The results of this paper suggest, as Flanigan (2000) did, that media is not a significant factor. This comes in contrast to Klein's work (1999; 2001), which suggested the contrary on five dimensions studied here: accuracy, objectivity, reputation, timeliness, and appropriate amount. It should be noted that there are differences in research approach in this paper and Klein's work. Here subjects saw exactly the same material in both Internet and text formats. In Klein's work, subjects were asked in general about Internet and text based sources used for a course project.

Do people become more discriminating of data quality for topics that they are personally involved in? This study provides, at least for cancer information, only limited support. When working with the full dataset, no interactions were found. When limited to U.S. born and raised subjects, there was an interaction effect on believability and reputation between media, reputation and cancer experience. However, family experience with cancer was not significant by itself. Finally, does gender play a role in one's ability to discriminate between reputable and non-reputable sources? This study would suggest that this is not so.

There are several limitations in this study and further areas for research. First, the author intended this work as only a first study and a vehicle to begin to understand the issues. Second, the personal involvement with cancer concept bears rework. The subject population included mostly younger adults. Fully half of the sample was in the age range of 26-35. It may be that their "involvement" in cancer is so remote that it has little impact on their perception of data quality. Further, the questions employed here focused only on one's family experience with cancer and did not elicit subjects' experience with cancer among friends or work associates.

Third, the author needs to revisit the data collection instrument used here (including the cancer literature). Although it was created using the terminology of Wang (1996), it may have lost some of its meaning with the multinational sample used in this work. Finally, this research data was collected in tandem with another survey instrument. The resulting form was four pages long and may have fatigued the participants.

Having noted these limitations and future areas of work, this line of research is important for several reasons. First, the Internet has become a de facto standard source of information for younger generations. Their perceptions of data quality, particularly compared to print, are a key factor in understanding how people will interpret what they see. The question of personal involvement in another interesting topic – do people become more discriminating in evaluating data quality on topics that have significant impact on them? Finally, there does appear to be an intersection of research in data quality that crosses between the information systems and journalism disciplines.

REFERENCES

Bates, D.W., & Gawande, A.A. (2000). The impact of the Internet on quality measurement. *Health Affairs, 19* (6), 104-114.

Flanagin, A. J., & Metzger, M. J. (2000). Perceptions of Internet information credibility. *Journalism and Mass Communications Quarterly, 77* (3), 515-540.

Looker, P.A., & Stichler, J. F. (2001). Getting to know the women's health care segment. *Marketing Health Services, 21* (3), 33-34.

Johnson, T. J., & Kaye, B. K. Cruising is Believing?: Comparing Internet and Traditional Sources on Media Credibility Measures. *Journalism and Mass Communications Quarterly, 75* (2), 325-340.

Kaplan, D., Krishnan, R., Padman, R., & Peters, J. (1998). Assessing data quality in accounting information systems. *Communications of the ACM, 41* (2).

Klein, B. D. (1999, October). Information quality and the WWW. *Applied Business in Technology Conference.* Rochester, MI: Oakland University.

Klein, B. D. (2001, Summer). User perceptions of data quality: Internet and traditional text sources. *Journal of Computer Information Systems, 41* (4).

Laudon, K. C. (1986, January). Data quality and due process in large inter-organizational record systems. *Communications of the ACM, 29* (1).

Smith, S. E. (1998). Reliable cancer resources on the Internet. *Information Today, 15* (6), 23, 28+.

Strong, D. M., Lee, Y. W., & Wang, R. Y. (1997). Data quality in context. *Communications of the ACM, 40* (5), 103-110.

Wand, Y., & Wang, R. Y. (1996). Anchoring data quality dimensions in ontological foundations. *Communications of the ACM, 39* (11), 86-95.

Wang, R., Reddy, M.P., & Kon, H.B. (1995). Towards quality data: An attribute-based approach. *Decision Support Systems, 13* (3/4), 349-372.

Wang, R. Y., & Strong, D. M. (1996). Beyond accuracy: What data quality means to data consumers. *Journal of Management Information Systems, 12* (4), 5-33.

Xu, H. (2000, December). Managing accounting information quality. *Proceedings of the 21st International Conference on Information Systems.*

Yang (Chair). (2000, December). Data quality in Internet time, space, and communities. *Proceedings of the 21st International Conference on Information Systems.*

Chapter XI

Healthcare Information: From Administrative to Practice Databases

M. R. Kraft
VA Hospital-Hines, Illinois and Loyola University, Chicago, USA

K. C. Desouza
University of Illinois at Chicago, USA

I. Androwich
Loyola University, Chicago, USA

ABSTRACT

This chapter defines and discusses healthcare data and various healthcare databases as resources for knowledge discovery that can support effectiveness research, quality improvement, and resource allocation. Privacy and confidentiality of health records are addressed along with the dimensions and complexity of information retrieval from healthcare databases and patient health records. The Veterans' Health Administration (VHA) data and databases are specifically addressed. Issues and methods of data preparation for a data mining exploration of a VHA Spinal Cord Injury (SCI) clinical database are presented from a nursing perspective. The potential of using healthcare databases for research is noted.

INTRODUCTION

The healthcare industry faces contradictory pressures of lowering cost and increasing quality of service, both of which require efficient decision-making. These business challenges of healthcare delivery require greater operational efficiencies and the tools necessary to provide real-time access to information. Healthcare facilities have at their disposal vast amounts of data from administrative and clinical databases. Capabilities for data storage have created databases of immense size that can be tapped to generate knowledge. However, the challenge is to extract relevant information from this data and act upon it in a timely manner (Desouza, 2002). Efficient decision-making is a by-product of thorough analysis of available data on a given problem. This chapter discusses the kinds of healthcare databases currently available, including claims, administrative and practice databases. Their potential for use in database research, designed to determine effectiveness of care, improve the quality of care delivered, and improve resource allocation, is presented. The Veterans' Health Administration (VHA) data is specifically addressed, and the issues and methods related to data preparation for a data mining exploration of a VHA Spinal Cord Injury (SCI) clinical database are presented from a nursing perspective.

BACKGROUND

With the movement of healthcare reimbursement from fee-for-service toward capitation models, healthcare information systems need to be able to detect developing cost, quality and access problems. Payers demand better documentation of care and outcomes. A subtle yet critical issue facing the healthcare industry is the documentation of professional practice and the ability to provide such information across the continuum of care (Orsolits, Davis & Gross, 1988). With the current healthcare system's emphasis on a business model, the application of the four diagnostic information categories identified by Drucker (1999) is appropriate. He identifies foundation information as the basic standard measurements within the industry; productivity information as the measurement of knowledge-based and service work; competence information, which looks at the core competencies of the industry; and resource allocation information, which addresses how both capital and people are allocated throughout the enterprise. These four kinds of information are seen as telling about the current state of the business and directing business tactics, and can all be related directly to healthcare information.

Healthcare providers are confronted daily with constantly changing information needs to manage care. Hersh (1999) indicates that in two of every three patient encounters, the average clinician has unmet information needs, even though managed care and other healthcare system innovations mandate that providers be knowledgeable about the details of patient care (Lewis, 1997). As practice data are computerized, the ability to capture, store, retrieve, organize, and analyze the information of clinical practice can provide information for decision support, enhancement of documentation, and identification of care trends and costs, with the ultimate goal of improved patient care. Generating information and knowledge calls for organizing data into a useful form. For purposes of this paper and within the framework of systems theory, information is defined as organized and processed data that can be communicated, and/or received, and when received, is meaningful and useful to the recipient. The capture and management of healthcare data has developed into the field of medical informatics.

Informatics

The title, *Informatics*, is derived from the French word, informatique, and is defined as computer and information science. Informatics consists of a set of technologies that facilitates the representation, management, and manipulation of data, information, and knowledge (Ball, Hannah, Newbold & Douglas, 1995). The field of information science concerned with analysis and dissemination of data through the application of information systems to various aspects of healthcare is known as medical informatics. Seelos (1993) defines the field as, "the science of information processing and the creating of information processing systems in medicine and healthcare delivery." The management component of informatics is the collection, aggregation, organization, movement and representation of information in an efficient, economical, and useful way. The processing component of informatics is the transformation of data or information, usually to a more complex state of organization.

Originally, the term medical informatics was thought adequate to cover all healthcare professions. With progress in the field of healthcare informatics, nursing began to recognize a discreet and unique body of knowledge related to nursing, information processing and information science separate from medicine. This has also occurred in other health disciplines, and it has been suggested that the phrase health informatics should replace medical informatics as the more appropriate umbrella term encompassing all disciplines in the health field (Hannah, Ball & Edwards, 1995).

Healthcare Information

Healthcare information is extraordinarily complex. "It often contains implicit attributes, internal intricacies, intentional ambiguities and inaccuracies" (Cimino, 1995. p.780). Southon, Braithewaite& Lorenzi (1997) outline three dimensions in health information: management information, professional information and patient information. They identify overlap and commonalties, but feel that fundamental differences exist in the types of information required for each dimension, the way the information is used, and the way standards are maintained. The achievement of a comprehensive and integrated data structure that can serve the multiple needs of each of these three dimensions is a goal in most healthcare information system development.

The cost of information is usually not stated or, indeed, even known (Blois, 1987), but information represents a large percentage of the healthcare cost structure. The healthcare industry is approaching the same level of investment in information systems found in the banking and finance industry. About 1/3 of the cost of healthcare in the United States — some 300 billion dollars — represents the cost of capturing, storing, and processing such information as patient's records, physicians' notes, test results, and insurance claims (Evans & Wurster, 1997). The cost of information technology is definitely high, but the cost of manual information handling is also expensive (Appleby, 1997). It has been estimated that 25% of hospital cost is spent on information handling, primarily as a means of communication. It is now much easier to access more information at a substantially lower cost. This ability should facilitate more informed choices and better decisions, but with all the increases in "cheaper information," little progress has been made in deriving knowledge from this information. Unfortunately, healthcare faces what Fransman (1996) has described as the "information paradox." Currently, there is a glut of healthcare data, too much for one person to process. There is a cost to the collection of every piece of data, so data collection will require justification. The more precise the data, the more it will cost. Does the information requested increase our knowledge for the benefit of the patient? How much information will we need, want, and be able to afford?

There are indications that the most frequent problem with healthcare information is a lack of availability (Desouza, 2001). Too much information, information in the wrong place, incomplete, inaccurate, inconsistent, illegible or difficult to understand information is also noted.

Healthcare Records

Patient health records represent comprehensive documents of the continuity of healthcare and are a rich source of data for research. Such data are generally accessible, accurate and relatively inexpensive. The advantages of using healthcare records as a source of information are accurate and timely data, rich clinical detail and dates attached to data elements. Traditionally, the paper record is documented in a "diary" style (Gabrieli, 1990), and includes documentation that produces a defensive legal record. Documentation in health records is assumed to be legally and medically accurate and reliable. Historically, the nursing documentation in the patient's "chart" has been seen as a "transaction log rather than an evolving repository of practice based on nursing knowledge" (Bakken & Constantino, 2001, p. 52). As nursing diagnoses, interventions and patient outcomes are captured, the nursing record becomes a document that records actual nursing practice. This kind of nursing documentation offers the opportunity for study of actual nursing practice and its effects on patient outcomes.

The move to computerized patient record systems (CPRS) has radically changed the traditional healthcare record and how the data and information in the record is used.   Sinclair (1990) argues that the computer's assistance, in the form of memory support and decision support, introduces changes in the definition of professional expertise. With computers to filter and/or analyze data, a lack of knowledge of specific facts becomes less important.

There are disadvantages to using healthcare records as a data source. Concerns related to such data are that data are collected as a by-product of some other processes; data are probably collected and entered by many people without any quality check; data may have different structure even within the same database; and missing data may be common (Lange & Jacox, 1993). Too often the data are so disconnected that there is no useful information. Other disadvantages are related to the non-research purpose of the record, the presence of selective information, the need for interpretation of certain information in the record, and the difficulty with data verification (Krowchuk, Moore & Richardson, 1995).   Although concern has been expressed about the reliability and validity of health record data, most investigators operate on the premise that healthcare records provide fairly accurate information. Identified factors that influence reliability and validity of health record data include the clinical competence of the recorder, patient cooperation, the type of provider and setting of care, situational factors, and the type of data collected and recorded (Aaronson & Burman, 1994). These authors suggest that the reliability of health records can be assessed by the consistency with which a single recorder documents specific information, and by having the same data recorded by two different providers.

Privacy, Confidentiality, and Security

Confidentiality is an emerging problem in computerized clinical data sets. Technology has encouraged the accumulation of an unlimited quantity of healthcare data, but has also created a resurgence of controversy in the issues of privacy and confidentiality (Rittman & Gorman, 1992; Romano, 1987). The development of electronic databases has raised the concern of a patient's right to privacy as compared to potential societal benefits of the use of the data for quality improvement and effectiveness research (Gostin, 1997). Styffe (1997) addressed the unique meaning of privacy, confidentiality, and security as related to patient data in clinical information systems. Individuals are concerned with privacy as their right to determine when, how, where, and to what extent their information is transmitted. Confidentiality is the concern of healthcare providers and organizations and, according to Styffe (1997), is the "trust placed that information shared will be respected and used only for the purpose disclosed." It is based on the relationship between the person disclosing and the person receiving information. Security is built into clinical information systems and addresses the levels of authorization necessary for access to data and information. Computer security involves the protection of data against accidental or intentional disclosure to unauthorized persons.

Data ownership is a critical issue. Questions about when patient consent is necessary to access years of patient information need to be addressed. Must one freely consent to being included in a database? Historically, retrospective data access has not required patient consent, but as databases increase, the appropriate use of years of patient information raises ethical concerns (Peck et al., 1997). Permission to use data beyond the original intent has rarely been obtained explicitly (Wuerker, 1997). McArt & McDougal (1985) stated that, "permission by subjects to use data collected on them is generally not required in a secondary data analysis unless additional data are sought or subjects may be considered at risk because of the sensitivity of the data collected" (p. 56). Fiesta (1996) suggests that from a legal standpoint, widespread usage will eventually establish a uniform standard of database usage. Some advocates suggest that research access to patient information should be limited to "epidemiological data," but only if the linkage to individual records is removed (Wechsler, 1996).

New rules to protect the privacy of all medical records under the Health Insurance Portability and Accountability Act (HIPAA) become effective in December 2002, and will require written consent from patients before any disclosure of medical information, even for routine actions like insurance billing (Childs, 2001). HIPAA compliance will be mandatory and healthcare facilities, providers, and payers are currently developing implementation plans. Prior to HIPAA, permission to use data beyond the original intent has rarely been obtained explicitly. Human subject committees will have to determine whether use of data represents a threat to confidentiality and, if risk is high, subjects may have to be re-contacted to get permission to use their personal health data for research and quality improvement initiatives.

All healthcare professionals must face the issue of a possible breach in information security. Such an event is serious enough that in addition to legal liability, the healthcare professional may suffer a loss of information necessary for practice (Sardinas & Muldoon, 1998). The Code of Ethics for Nurses (ANA, 1985) stresses that when patient anonymity cannot be guaranteed, client consent for use of medical records must be obtained.

DATABASES

It has been estimated that the amount of data in the world doubles every twenty months (Frawley, Pietetsky-Shapiro & Mathaus, 1992). The information available on the Internet is thought to double in less than every nine months (Turban & Aronson, 2001).   Information gathering capacity has increased exponentially (Tan & Sheps, 1999) and, as a result, much transactional data are moved into databases for storage.   Currently, databases are measured in gigabytes and terabytes. A terabyte has been described as the equivalent of two million books (Hedberg, 1995). As the amount of collected data grows, the need to efficiently analyze data also increases. Massive amounts of data remain largely unexplored and may even be on the verge of being discarded.

A database can be defined as "any structured representation of data which describes a subset of the real world" (Newbold, 1993). A database is an organized repository of data: a collection of interrelated records; any set of files subject to manipulation by a common database management system (DBMS). A database must meet standards that ensure comprehensiveness through inclusion of core criteria and accuracy of data while avoiding redundancy. Data quality and integrity must be maintained and security must be provided. Databases must be planned to facilitate access to an integrated collection of data for multiple users and multiple applications and must also interface with future advances in technology. There are several kinds of databases that can be important in providing information for healthcare providers. They include claims databases used for billing, administrative databases that usually include some details of medical care, and practice databases built from patient records or data from specific clinical departments, such as radiology, laboratory, and pharmacy. Healthcare databases may also include disease specific information, such as cancer or SCI registries.

Claims Databases

Claims databases are compiled by third party payers, quality assurance organizations and the government, and are used primarily for billing Medicare and other third-party payers. Generally the claims databases are quite large, but lack the richness of detail found in practice databases (Tierney & McDonald, 1991).

Administrative Databases

Administrative databases store financial and administrative data used in facility/system management and include patient demographics, as well as coding for Diagnostic Related Groups (DRGs), International Classification of Diseases

(ICD9) and Current Procedural Terminology (CPT), which reflect some areas of medical care (Wray, Ashton, Kuykendall & Hollingsworth, 1995). The Medicare database is an administrative database containing information on the utilization of covered medical services, diagnoses, episodes of illness and the Medicare-covered costs of healthcare for more than 35 million beneficiaries (McPhillips, 1991). This database has been linked to several national surveys on aging and provides a valuable source of information on health services and aging (Lillard & Farmer, 1997). Cowper, Hynes, Kubal & Murphy (1999) recommend that outcomes researchers use administrative databases as either the principal source of data or as a supplement to other primary data collection. Ray (1997) suggests that administrative databases are a potentially useful source of data for retrospective studies. According to Palmer (1997), the increasing availability of clinical details in large healthcare databases makes comprehensive process-based measures of quality more possible. Such databases are now being used to measure quality of care over time and across institutions, and Davidoff (1997) predicts that databases will be powerful tools for quality improvement in healthcare. Currently most regional database explorations start with administrative databases built from reimbursement transactions. Disadvantages to using administrative databases are probably primarily related to the fact that these systems were not created for research purposes and there was no research input into the design and types of information to be collected. Historically, with few exceptions, developers of national data sets have not considered practice or operational systems as content sources for their data sets (McDonald, Overhage, Dexter, Takesue & Dwya., 1997). Iezzoni (1997) believes that in the future, administrative and clinical data will have less distinctive boundaries and both data types will be utilized in regional efforts to assess quality in healthcare services.

Practice Databases

Healthcare institutions compile practice databases with data generated from the delivery of care to patients. This data comes from a variety of institutional sources, such as the laboratory, pharmacy, radiology, and medical records. These practice databases may vary widely in content but are considered as representative of accurate and timely clinical data (Tierney & McDonald, 1991). Although most practice databases are established to augment clinical care through storage and transmission of data, they have significant potential for research. If stored properly and if accessible to the researcher, practice databases can provide input for data mining systems (Psomas, Schaufele & Madhaven, 2000). Practice databases have been seen as a valuable source in meeting the needs of healthcare systems for epidemiological information (Pringle & Hobbs, 1991). Because a database represents real world relationships, it may be used in a predictive way in health services research. Using primary care databases as research tools does identify the possibility of major problems with incomplete recording; data are of little use unless high quality data are collected.

Lazaridis (1997) presents the mantra of "reduce, reuse, and recycle" as appropriate for *reducing* the need for expensive and difficult clinical trials by *reusing* data already available in existing databases which can be *recycled* into products (information) not envisioned when data were initially collected. He adds the fourth R of *responsibility*, stressing the need to consider the legal and ethical implications of using data in ways not originally intended. Temple (1990) urges caution in using databases to assess effectiveness. He lists as an area of concern the fact that such evaluations are always retrospective and unblinded, with high potential for patient selection bias and analyst bias. Temple recommended that every "startling" finding in database effectiveness research should be subjected to a controlled trial. Rubin (1997) states that the presence of observational rather than experimental data is a complication of large data base research. Ray (1997) believes the gold standard for evidence of efficacy, safety, and cost-effectiveness is a randomized controlled trial, but recognizes that retrospective studies have been the primary tool used to evaluate policy and program changes. Hlatky et al. (1984) proposes the use of an observational database as complementary to the randomized controlled trial in assessing the efficacy of therapy. They present the primary purpose of an observational database as the collection and distillation of "accumulated clinical experience to make accurate predictions for individual patients" (p. 375).

Potential Database Problems

Threats to validity inherent in large databases include sampling and measurement errors. Sampling errors are the result of the selection of cases, and measurement errors develop as the result of problems with operational definitions of concepts. Because data bases exist over long periods of time, reliability threats are created by such things as clerical error, subtle changes in data collection techniques with improved diagnostic skills, and the instrumentation used to collect data. Appraisal of data includes consideration of accuracy, representativeness, authorship and authenticity (Reed, 1992). The validity of conclusions in research depends partly on the completeness and accuracy of the data. Incomplete data is meaningless. Both random and systematic errors can occur in data collection and management. Such errors may be identified with measures of frequency, central tendency, range, and dispersion. Knowing the data well can help in the identification and resolution of potential errors (Roberts, Anthony, Madigan & Chen, 1997). Rather than accepting data at face value, the researcher must consider all potential limitations. Ray (1997) identifies the major problems with retrospective data studies as poor data quality, lack of concurrent controls, an inability to ascertain essential study outcomes, and incomplete or missing data. Data problems are seen as the primary explanation for outliers. Another identified problem is related to the potential for coding errors (Cowper, Hynes, Kubal & Murphy, 1999).

Database Research

Databases have been used in research for observational studies to improve the conduct of research through protocol adherence, subgroup targeting, collaboration, data collection and methodology; and in process research studies and hypothesis research studies (Pryor et al., 1985). Databases are ideally suited for observational descriptions. These descriptions can be as simple as frequencies or as complex as statistical analyses of co-variates. Lange & Jacox (1993) identified interest in using clinical and administrative healthcare databases for health policy research because of national concern about the quality, cost, and outcomes of healthcare. In reviewing the possibilities of research using large databases, they list several policy-related issues that could be addressed by nurse researchers:

1.   What is the standard practice in various settings?
2.   What is the relationship between variations in practice and patient outcomes?
3.   What are the effects of different staff mixes on patient outcomes and costs?
4.   What are the total costs for episodes of treatment of specific conditions and what part of those costs is attributable to nursing care? (p. 202)

"A large database represents a resource in which the behavior of analytic techniques can be studied and compared with alternative strategies" (Pryor et al., 1985, p. 639). The Cardiovascular Disease Databank at Duke University Medical Center with information on over 9,000 patients is the observational databank discussed by these researchers. This databank is structured through four essential elements: complete prospective data collection; regular follow-up of patients; close collaboration among clinicians, researchers and other multidisciplinary team members; and careful use of multivariable statistical methods. The Duke Cardiovascular Databank has been used to determine factors that influence the prognosis of patients with coronary artery disease and to develop a prognostic model for prediction of outcomes. Another example of database research is the use of the American Rheumatism Association Medical Information system (ARAMIS) to study patients with rheumatoid arthritis resulting in an increased understanding of the clinical course of the disease, frequency of hospital admissions, causes of morbidity, risk factors for morbidity, and variations in treatment costs (Tierney & McDonald, 1991). Other database studies include the use of artificial intelligence (AI) for managed care modeling

(Borok, 1997), hospital infection control (Brossette et al., 1998), the development of a prediction model for premature birth (Goodwin et al., 1997) and Medicare fraud (Milley, 2000).

When the Omnibus Budget Reconciliation Act (OBRA) (Public Law 101-239) created the Agency for Healthcare Policy and Research (AHCPR) in 1989, the bill mandated a report on the feasibility of linking research related data with data collected by both Federal and non-Federal agencies as the basis for medical effectiveness research (U.S. DHHS, 1991). Effectiveness research uses epidemiological methods to examine large databases. Such research requires databases with large numbers of cases and standardized reliable data elements. Potential data sources identified were Department of Defense (DOD) data, Veterans' Health Administration (VHA) data, and data collected by individual states in the Uniform Hospital Discharge Data Set (UHDDS). Areas of concern identified in moving to database linkages included data accessibility, data standards, vocabulary standards, data processing standards, security standards, and the maintenance of confidentiality. A recent partnership between the Agency for Healthcare Research and Quality (AHRQ), formerly the AHCPR, and public and private statewide data organizations has led to the Healthcare Cost and Utilization Project (HCUP) which is the development of a "family of databases" that include multi-state inpatient and outpatient discharge records with data elements that include demographics, clinical, diagnostic, and procedural information (Steiner, Elizhauser, & Schnaier, 2002). This project is seen as the largest collection of all-payer, administrative data that allows longitudinal population-based studies. The research potential of HCUP is enhanced with linkages to other databases such as the American Hospital Association (AHA) annual survey.

Veterans Health Administration Data

The Veterans Health Administration (VHA), part of the Department of Veterans Affairs (DVA), represents the largest healthcare system in the United States. VHA utilizes an internally developed health information system (HIS), originally called the Decentralized Hospital Computerized Program (DHCP), which has evolved into the current Veterans Integrated Systems and Technology Architecture (VistA). Since the beginning of electronic data collection in 1980 (Kolodner, 1997), VHA data, stored in a centralized repository, now represents "fairly comprehensive, patient-level inpatient and outpatient data on healthcare utilization of all patients receiving care in the VHA" (Murphy, Cowper, Seppala, Stroupe, & Hynes, 2002, p. 7-8). Data elements have been added and subtracted over this time period, and some elements are not available for every year, but years of data collection and the use of encrypted patient identifiers do allow for longitudinal studies. The Quality Enhancement Research Initiative (QUERI) within the VA health system has identified data needs, data weaknesses, and data availability as part of their quality improvement program that has a disease-management approach (Hynes, Cowper, Kerr, Kubal & Murphy, 2000). In 1998, the VHA founded the VA Information Resource Center (VIReC) to serve as a database and informatics resource and referral center to researchers and others who use VA information systems for research concerning the care needs of veterans served in the VHA. VIReC staff provide consultation about access to and utilization of both VA and non-VA databases for research, management, and quality improvement applications.

It should be noted that all transactional data captured in VistA is not stored in the central repository. Patient acuity from nursing files is stored, but other nursing data elements such as nursing diagnoses and interventions are not.

Data Warehouses

The collection of data into large databases has led to the creation of data warehouses for the storage of multiple databases and the recognition that potentially valuable data warehouse contents should be analyzed. Thus, the need for data mining is demonstrated. The data warehouse is a composite of hardware, middleware, databases, warehousing tools, and software (Marietti, 1997). Data warehousing is a process and the data warehouse is the location in which the process takes place. Typically, in a data warehouse, data input comes from a variety of sources in a variety of formats (DeJesus, 1999). Within the warehouse, data is cleansed of extraneous and erroneous material and then transformed into a common format for availability to the end user. There are three different functional areas in a data warehouse, and each is customized to meet specific business or facility needs. First is data acquisition or the handling of data from a variety of sources that must be identified, copied, formatted, cleansed, normalized, audited, and prepared for loading. Second is data storage and archiving. The third component of a warehouse is that of data access. Data access requires an assortment of products including intelligent agents, query capability, statistical analysis, data dictionaries, data discovery, on-line analytical processing (OLAP), and data visualization (Fletcher, 1997; Mattison, 1996). Marietti (1997) considers the heart of the data warehouse to be the analytical database. The benefits of data warehousing include immediate information delivery, the ability to do trend and outcome analysis, query and report capabilities, and the ability to integrate data from multiple sources (Shams & Farishta, 2001). DeJesus (1999) suggests the data warehouse as a useful tool for healthcare in disease management and the prediction of at-risk populations, if warehouse contents are analyzed and used in decision-making.

KNOWLEDGE DISCOVERY IN DATABASES

Large databases have emerged as attractive but controversial sources of information (Johnson, 1999; Matchar, et al., 1997; Wuerker, 1997). As the body of data collected grows in size and complexity, there is a resulting consensus that significant untapped knowledge lies hidden in many large databases. Data mining and knowledge discovery in databases (KDD) relate to the process of extracting valid, previously unknown and potentially useful patterns and information from raw data in large databases (Biswas, Weinberg & Fisher, 1998; Frawley, Piatetsky-Shapiro & Matheus, 1992; Kiel, 2000; Lingras & Yao, 1998; Simoudis, 1998). KDD shares much with statistical and exploratory data analysis in terms of statistical procedures for modeling data and handling noise. The extraction of information or knowledge from large databases is closely related to exploratory data analysis. Often, data mining and KDD are treated as synonyms and refer to the whole process in moving from data to knowledge (Raghavan, Deogun & Sever, 1998). "A primary goal of knowledge discovery is the interpretation of discovered concepts in the context of domain knowledge" (Biswas, et al., 1998, p. 224.) The explosion of data and the development of large databases have led to the creation of data warehouses and recognition of the need for data mining. Surviving the information explosion means not only knowing how to classify and access information, but also how to apply it. Neural networks have become one way to organize the increased information in a way that makes it relevant in the context in which decisions are made (Tan & Sheps, 1998).

Data Mining

Data mining is "an interdisciplinary field bringing techniques of machine learning, pattern recognition, statistics, databases, and data visualization to address the issues of information extraction from large databases" (Cabena, Hadjinian, Stadler, Verhees & Zanasi, 1998, p. ix). The analogy of "mining" suggests the sifting through of large amounts of low-grade ore (data) to find something valuable — information (Psomus, Schaufele & Madhaven, 2000). Data mining is a multi-step, iterative inductive process (Cabena, et al., 1998; Gerber, 1998) useful in deriving useful knowledge from real-world databases through the application of pattern extraction techniques (Raghaven, et al., 1998, p. 402). It includes such tasks as problem analysis, data extraction, data preparation and cleaning, data reduction, rule development, output analysis and review (Darling, 1998; Gilman, 1997; McDonald, Brossette & Moser, 1998). Data mining is the process of discovering meaningful new correlations, patterns and trends by sifting through large amounts of data stored in repositories, using pattern recognition technologies as well as statistical and mathematical techniques (Gartner Group, 1999).

Data mining has emerged as one of the powerful techniques for extraction of useful information from databases (Kostoff & Geisler, 1999). Large amounts of data can be explored to uncover previously unknown patterns that may include surprising patterns of relationship that might not have been otherwise found. Initial applications of data mining were in business and industry and data mining is seen as an essential analytical skill in the business community (SPSS, 2000). However, a number of published studies now address the value of data mining within the healthcare industry. These studies have looked at such varied issues as infection patterns (Brossette, et al., 1998), Medicare fraud (Milley, 2000), the prediction of premature births (Goodwin, et al., 1997) and the prediction of hospitalization of long-term care patients (Abbot, Quirolgico, Marchand, Canfield & Adya, 1998).

Database mining has been called the "confluence of machine learning techniques and the performance emphasis of database technology" (Agrawal, Tmielinski & Swami, 1998, p.16). Because data mining involves retrospective analyses of data, experimental design is considered outside the scope of data mining. Data mining looks through an entire database to find trends, patterns, and relationships that may not have otherwise been noticed (Rudin, 1996). The process of implementing data mining generally begins with the selection and preparation of data to be mined. Data is then qualified using cluster and/or feature analysis to reduce the complexity of data management. Next is the selection and application of a a data mining tool. After the data has been mined, analysis is done, and the final step of the data mining process is the application of knowledge discovered (Gerber, 1998). "The greatest obstacle in locating potentially useful patterns in data is the likelihood that the database wasn't constructed with discovery processes in mind" (Norton, 2000).

Steps for KDD are goal setting, selection of data, preprocessing (cleansing data of noise and errors, developing procedures to account for missing data, developing naming conventions), transformation (reducing data by finding features that can represent several elements of the data), mining, and interpretation/evaluation (data visualization). Data visualization is an invaluable counterpart to data mining. Visualization includes displays of trends, clusters and differences (Gray et al., 1996). Data mining algorithms allow for interpretation and prediction analysis based on information in databases (Schulman, 1998). Data mining has the ability to take information and go beyond stating what was into the realm of predicting what could be.

John (1997) suggests that two types of patterns are discovered with data mining: predictive and informative. Predictive patterns represent an educated guess about the value of an unknown attribute, given the values of other known attributes. Pattern analysis can be defined as the examination of the configuration of relationships of the elements of phenomena. Informative patterns present interesting patterns that provide new insight to a domain expert. The value of informative patterns lies in whether actions are suggested to the domain expert and whether suggested actions are effective. Interestingness of a pattern is a measure used to determine whether to discard, or keep and explore a pattern further. "Data miners are often more interested in understandability than accuracy of predictability" (Glymour, Madigan, Pregibon & Smyth, 1996, p. 15). Mills (1991) suggests that patterns may reveal enabling predictions and thus generate hypotheses for further investigation.

Four factors leading to the accessibility of data for decision-making are: the incredible increase in computing power with expanded computational speed; the accumulation of large amounts of data; the advancement of methods to benefit from data modeling, without requiring a detailed knowledge of statistical concepts; and the visual nature of current generation data modeling software (Danziger, 1997). Computerization of data does not make up for bad data, but once data has been cleaned, the analysis of vast amounts of data may identify potentially important relationships that do not emerge from sparse data. The analyst must formulate a query to extract data from a database, extract the aggregated data, visualize the results in a graphical way, and analyze the results. The process of analysis requires domain knowledge.

Requests to perform pattern extraction tasks are queries. There are several classes of queries in data mining: hypothesis testing, generalization, classification, characterization, association, and clustering (Raghavan, et al., 1998). Classification, e.g., discrimination, identification, recognition, implies decision making or response selection of some kind based on a system of rules that partitions data into groups (Balakrishnan & Ratcliff, 1996, p.615). Hypothesis testing queries do not explicitly discover patterns within data, but receive as input a stated hypothesis that is then evaluated against a selected database. The hypothesis is a conjecture about the existence of a specific pattern within the database and the goal is verification of the hypothesis being tested. Data mining without a preconceived hypothesis is discovery driven. Operations of discovery-driven data mining include creating prediction and classification models, analyzing links, segmenting databases, and detecting deviation (Simoudis, 1998). These operations are supported by a variety of techniques, including predictive modeling, supervised induction, association discovery, sequence discovery, conceptual clustering, and visualization.

Commonly used techniques in data mining are artificial neural networks, decision trees, genetic algorithms, the "nearest neighbor" method, and rule induction. Classification queries use decision variables or examples to partition data into subclasses. Characterization queries derive common features of a class regardless of the characteristics of other classes. An association query discovers associations among values grouped by selection phrase with a user specified minimum support requirement. Combinations of rules are found within a pre-set confidence factor that specific associations occur. Clustering queries partition data of a relational table with members of each cluster sharing a number of properties. Five common types of information yielded by data mining are: association, sequences, classifications, clusters, and forecasting. Associations happen when occurrences are linked to a single event. Sequences are events linked over time. Classification recognizes patterns that describe the group to which an item belongs. Clustering is related to classification but differs in that no groups have yet been defined and mining discovers different groupings within data. Data mining is almost always used in conjunction with traditional data analysis techniques. Themes of modern statistics of fundamental importance to data miners are clarity about goals, appropriate reliability assessment and accounting for sources of uncertainty. The convergence of statistics and data mining is developing a promising research area.

DATA MINING AND SPINAL CORD INJURY

There is little evidence that nurse researchers seek aggregate patient data that might reveal trends and patterns among patients with similar situations or treatments. Such information can be useful in understanding patterns and in predicting patients' responses to conditions and interventions. Information systems can be designed to aggregate such data and present it in a variety of formats. Exploration of nursing data elements within a spinal cord injury (SCI) database was proposed as a mechanism to help in the identification of major phenomena basic to SCI nursing care. Utilization of information in SCI databases may be a means of bringing more focused and appropriate care to SCI individuals who, as consumers of significant costly care resources, are "outliers" in the healthcare system (Lincoln & Builder, 1999). Patients identified as outliers are those whose annual care costs far exceed normally expected healthcare costs. In our rapidly changing healthcare system, it is important to know aggregate costs of SCI to ensure that adequate funds are allotted for care of the SCI population. Although SCI occurs much less frequently than other types of injury and debilitating disease, the cost of SCI to individuals and to society is staggering. Berkowitz, O'Leary, Kruse & Harvey (1998) estimate that SCI costs the nation more than 9.7 billion dollars per year. Direct care costs within the first year of injury average $223,261, with an additional annual cost for SCI care of at least $26,000. Equipment, supplies, medications, and environmental modification costs increase both figures. Indirect costs related to loss of income and productivity are more difficult to compute, with consideration given to age at injury and earning potential. but indirect cost estimates can be projected as significant. The aggregate annual direct and indirect costs of new cases of SCI may be between 7.2 and 9.5 billion dollars (Berkowitz et al., 1998).

This database analysis uses data mining techniques to determine if there are patterns of patient needs, nursing diagnoses, nursing interventions, and patient outcomes that can contribute information that can improve the efficiency and effectiveness of the delivery of SCI nursing care. Analysis may demonstrate that information patterns related to the presence of specific nursing diagnoses and the choice of specific nursing interventions that promote desired outcomes can be used to allocate resources for SCI care delivery. The application of the data mining process to this SCI clinical database may determine that this research method can lead to a better understanding of how to use data to improve SCI nursing practice.

Study Setting

The setting for this study is a large tertiary care Veteran's Health Administration (VHA) Hospital located on a 62-acre campus within the metropolitan Chicago area. The Veterans Administration (VA) is involved in the full continuum of SCI care and has the largest single network of SCI care in the nation (DVA, 2000). This hospital has two acute rehabilitation/continuing care inpatient SCI units with a total of 68 beds, a hospital-based SCI home care program, and a 30 bed residential SCI unit. The hospital uses the national VA hospital information system (HIS) known as the Veterans Health Information Systems and Technology Architecture (VistA). VistA, one of the most extensive hospital information systems in the world, is an internally developed, comprehensive integrated system that provides for both administrative and clinical support and documentation of care. Over a 20-year period, VistA has evolved to include over 70 applications, as well as numerous links to commercial products. VA software is written in MUMPS (Mass General Utility Multi-Programming System), an ANSI (American National Standards Institute) programming language now call "M" (Kolodner, 1997).

The modular design of the VA nursing software within VistA allows computerization of data for clinical, administrative, research, and educational purposes, as well as quality improvement (Vance, Gillian-Storm, Kraft, Lang & Mead, 1997; Vance, Kraft & Lang, 1998). The data collection system of the VA nursing software incorporates the elements of the nursing minimum data set (NMDS) as defined by Werley and others (Werley, Devine & Zorn, 1990). The NMDS standardizes the items of essential core nursing data for collection, storage, and retrieval. It includes 16 elements categorized into three broad groups: nursing care, client demographics, and service (Werley & Leske, 1991). These elements represent data used on a regular basis by nurses in any setting where nursing care is provided, and are considered necessary for the analysis of nursing practice and its impact on outcomes and cost effective care. The goal of the NMDS is to provide for comparability of nursing data across clinical populations, settings, and geographic areas. The specific nursing care elements in the NMDS are nursing diagnoses, nursing interventions, outcomes and intensity of nursing care. Most computerized nursing information systems (NISs) now utilize the NMDS as the framework for data capture.

The VA nursing database for patient health problems is built on the North American Nursing Diagnosis (NANDA) taxonomy and the care planning process of diagnosis, intervention, and outcome reflects the nursing process. Nursing diagnoses provide a common language within the profession, which can enhance communication between nursing clinicians, improve continuity of care, help formulate expected outcomes, assist in addressing cost-effectiveness of care, and allow emphasis on clinical nursing research. Nursing diagnoses have been recognized as the nursing equivalent of Diagnostic Related Groups (DRGs). The use of nursing diagnosis increases the possibility of giving comprehensive care by identification, validation, and documentation of response to specific health concerns. Nursing diagnosis allows clinicians to describe nursing practice within a shared framework.

Permission to use the VHA SCI database for this study was obtained from the facility's institutional review board (IRB) which includes the Human Studies Subcommittee (HSS) of the Research and Development (R&D) Committee and the R&D Committee itself. Since there were no interventions and no direct contact with patients, the facility IRB gave an expedited review approval. IRB approval for the study was also obtained from the Institutional Review Board of Loyola University. Confidentiality for this study was maintained by using the internal VA patient coding to download data. This data was immediately re-recoded by the investigator to remove all possibility of patient identification.

PROCESSES AND ISSUES

Data Gathering

The 525 patients with 1,107 admissions to the study unit between July 1989 and June 2000 became the study sample. The list of admissions to the study unit was downloaded from an ORACLE mainframe database built through nightly data extracts from VistA. After identification of the study population, nursing diagnoses and interventions selected for these patient encounters were identified using an identification and ranking query that is part of the VistA nursing software. Since the nursing data elements of interest in this study are not included in the VA national data warehouse, this data was downloaded directly from the operational database to a P.C. Data related to age, date of injury and level of injury was obtained directly from the mainframe SCI Registry database that is another VistA software package.

Data Cleaning

Typically, data preparation is the lengthiest part of the data mining process. It is estimated that 80% of the time spent in a data mining project is spent in data preparation and cleaning (Desouza, 2001; Gerber, 1998). Erroneous data can be a significant problem in real world databases. Data may be redundant or insignificant to the problem. Data preparation includes data selection (identification and extraction of data), data preprocessing (sampling and quality testing), and data transformation (conversion into an analytical model) (Cabena, Hadjinian, Stadler, Verhees & Zanasi, 1998). Goodwin et al. (1997) identify the issues obstructing progress in data mining for improved health outcomes as "data quality, data redundancy, data inconsistency, repeated measures, temporal (time-contextual) measures, and data volume" (p.291). Computerization of data does not make up for bad data, but once data has been cleaned, the analysis of vast amounts of data may identify potentially important relationships that do not emerge from sparse data. The analyst must formulate a query to extract data from a database, extract the aggregated data, visualize the results in a graphical way, and analyze the results. Invariably, routinely collected data is full of errors and incompleteness. Much of the data collected from this computerized database was found to be non-standardized and at a nominal level of measurement. As a result, data were visually inspected, structured, and checked for accuracy, reliability, and redundancy. Data "noise" included redundant, insignificant, erroneous, and missing data. Differences in punctuation and case or changes in word sequence were recognized by the computer software as new terms, new labels, or new variables. This required the researcher to make a visual inspection of all diagnostic and interventional labels and create a structure of labels that represent label clusters with a common or shared meaning. Data visualization is an invaluable counterpart to data mining. Visualization includes displays of trends, clusters, and differences. The visual review of all eleven years of data in this study took approximately 500 hours of time.

Data Categorization

There were 4,750 different diagnostic labels in the cumulative eleven-year database that, after visual inspection, were determined to represent 161 unique nursing diagnoses. Through further inspection, these were clustered into 20 diagnostic categories. Two domain experts with significant SCI knowledge and experience reviewed the categories to reach a consensus on the labels for the diagnostic categories. The selected diagnostic categories for the cumulative data were: Skin Care; Elimination; Self Care Deficit; Infection Prevention/Control; Mobility; Respiratory Function; Psychosocial Adaptation; Pain Management; Knowledge Deficit; Nutrition; Fluid Volume Maintenance; Acute Problem Management; Safety/Prevention of Injury; Activity/Rest; Cognitive

Table 1: Ranking of nursing diagnosis clusters

Years	89-90	90-91	91-92	92-93	93-94	94-95	95-96	96-97	97-98	98-99	99-00
Skin Care	1	1	1	1	1	1	1	1	1	1	1
Elimination	3	2	2	2	2	2	2	2	2	2	2
Self Care Deficit	2	3	4	3	3	4	3	4	4	5	5
Infection Prevention	5	4	3	4	4	3	4	3	3	3	3
Mobility	7	5	10	6	5	5	5	5	7	6	6
Psychosocial Adapt.	4	6	6	5	7	7	6	6	5	7	7
Respiratory Function	6	7	5	7	6	6	8	7	6	4	4
Comm. Reintegration	N/A	8	11	9	N/A	8	10	8	8	9	9
Pain Mgmt.	8	9	9	8	8	9	9	10	12	8	8
Knowledge Deficit	9	10	7	12	10	10	7	9	9	10	10
Fluid Volume Maint.	11	11	12	13	14	14	14	13	13	14	16
Nutrition	10	12	8	10	9	13	12	11	14	15	15
Miscellaneous	13	13	13	15	17	16	17	16	17	11	13.
Acute Medical Mgmt.	12	14	15	14	11	11	13	14	15	16.	14
Activity/Rest	13	15	14	11	12	15	16	15	11	13	11
Prevention of Injury	N/A	16	16	16	13	12	11	12	10	12	12
Temperature Control	N/A	17	19	19	N/A	N/A	N/A	N/A	N/A	N/A	17
Cognitive Functioning	N/A	18	18	17	16	17	15	17	16	17	18
Sexual Health	N/A	19	17	18	15	19	19	18	N/A	N/A	N/A
Sensory/Perceptual Deficit	N/A	N/A	N/A	N/A	N/A	18	18	N/A	N/A	N/A	N/A

Functioning; Temperature Control; Sexual Health; Communication, and Miscellaneous. Any diagnostic label within the cumulative database that did not appear at least eleven times during the eleven-year study period was assigned to the category of "Miscellaneous." A map of the annual diagnostic rankings for each of the eleven years in the study was developed to determine if there were significant changes in nursing diagnosis over the study time frame (see *Table 1*). The data set is currently being examined using data mining methodology.

Ongoing and Future Research

The potential for original research with pre-collected data is tremendous. The better acquainted the researcher is with the database, the greater the potential for creative new research. Secondary analysis is described as "extremely versatile in that it can be applied to studies designed to understand the present and the past; to understand change; and to examine phenomena comparatively" (Kiecolt & Nathan, 1985, p. 47). Advantages of such data analysis include larger samples, elimination of instrument development, sample selection, and data collection (Abel & Sherman, 1991). Aggregated data may provide insight and information that is useful in patient care delivery, program planning, and policy development. Lange & Jacox (1993) have identified interest in using clinical and administrative healthcare databases for health policy research because of national concern about the quality, cost, and outcomes of healthcare.

The use of data mining, by definition, excludes the possibility of testing preconceived hypotheses. Data miners do not pose a question, as much as ask the system to discover data patterns that may be predictive. The process of data mining may result in the identification of hypotheses for future research. Of specific interest is a predictive model using artificial neural networks for hospital length of stay based on nurse diagnosis. Care must be taken in the evaluation and analysis of data sets since data set variables may not adequately reflect the secondary analyst's concepts of interest. The task of designing a study using available data can be challenging.

CONCLUSIONS

The identification of patient outcomes sensitive to nursing care is a priority for nursing research. Research related to SCI nursing diagnoses and SCI nursing interventions may demonstrate under which particular circumstances specific interventions promote the most effective outcomes for SCI patients. The need to capture outcomes has been recognized by providers, payers, and policy makers. Knowledge discovery in clinical databases is a step toward the identification of outcomes and the measurement of effectiveness. Outcomes may be classified as "generic" or pertinent to all healthcare consumers, or "condition-related" and pertinent to sub-populations of patients with specific diseases or conditions. In addition, time becomes a dimension of outcome measurement. Outcome related data might come from multiple sources, such as the patient, families and caregivers, healthcare professionals, and biomedical instrumentation (Zielstorff, 1995). Assessment of effectiveness of care, according to Ozbolt (1996), requires standardized data aggregated in databases for comparison across times, conditions, and institutions. To analyze healthcare data, it is critical that data are stored in a retrievable format according to standards that will allow for data sharing and data queries while patient privacy and confidentiality is protected. There must also be a way to link outcome data to all influencing factors such as co-morbidities, procedures, treatments, interventions, patient demographics, etc.

Ozbolt (1991) has suggested that the failure of nursing to agree upon and offer a valid defined and standardized data set for inclusion in healthcare databases has created the problem of the lack of nursing inclusion. The inclusion of nursing data is absolutely necessary for nursing research on effectiveness. Nursing data are not included in many healthcare databases including the UHDDS (Uniform Hospital Discharge Data Set). There are several reasons why nursing is invisible in most existing healthcare datasets. Nursing data has not been required for regulatory reporting and reimbursement. In addition, the lack of a widely accepted nursing structured terminology supports the "non-capture" of nursing data. The issues identified by the work from AHCPR regarding data accessibility, data standards, and vocabulary standards are all identified in the study of SCI nursing data. The application of data mining techniques to the databases found in healthcare does have the potential to discovery of undetected patterns of practice and outcomes, and may also generate practice hypotheses for further research.

REFERENCES

Aaronson, L., & Burman, M. (1994). Use of health records in research: Reliability and validity issues. *Research in Nursing & Health, 17*, 67-73.

Abbot, P., Quirolgico, S., Marchand, R., Canfield, K., & Adya, M. (1998). Can the U.S. minimum data set be used to predict admissions to acute care? *Medinfo 9. Pt2* (13), 18-21.

Abel, E., & Sherman, J. (1991). Use of national data sets to teach graduate students research skills. *Western Journal of Nursing Research, 13* (6): 794-797.

Agrawal,R., Tmielenski, T., & Svami, A. (1998). Database mining: A performance perspective. San Jose, CA.: IBM Almaden Research Center.

American Nurses Association. (1985). *Code of ethics for nurses*. Kansas City, MO: American Nurses Association.

Appleby, C. (1997, March 5). Cyberspaced. *Hospitals and Health Networks*, pp. 30-32.

Bakken, S., & Costantio, M. (2001). Standardized terminologies and integrated information systems: Building blocks for transforming data into nursing knowledge. In J. M. Dochterman & H. Grace, (Eds.), *Current issues in nursing* (pp. 52-59). St. Louis: Mosby.

Balakrishnan, J., & Ratcliff, R. (1996). Testing models of decision making using confidence ratings in classification. *Journal of Experimental Psychology, 22* (3), 615-633.

Ball, M., Hannah, K., Newbold, S., & Douglas, J. (1995). *Nursing informatics: Where caring and technology meet* (2nd ed.). New York: Springer.

Berkowitz, M., O'Leary, P., Kruse, D., & Harvey, C. (1998). *Spinal cord injury: An analysis of medical and social costs*. New York: Demos Medical Publishing, Inc.

Biswas, G., Weinberg, J., & Fisher, D. (1998). ITERATE: A conceptual clustering algorithm for data mining. *IEEE Transactions on Systems, Man, and Cybernetics, 28* (2), 219-230.

Blois, M. (1987). What is it that computers compute? *M.D. Computing*, 4 (3), 31-33, 56.

Borok, L. (1997). Data mining: Sophisticated forms of managed care modeling through artificial intelligence. *Journal of Health Care Finance*, 23 (3), 20-36.

Brosette, S., Sprague, A., Hardin, M., Waites, K., Jones, W., & Moser, S. (1998). Association rules and data mining in hospital infection control and surveillance. *Journal of the American Medical Informatics Association*, 5 (4), 273-281.

Cabena, P., Hadjinian, P., Stadler, R., Verhees, J., & Zanasi, A. (1998). *Discovering data mining: From concept to implementation.* Upper Saddle River, NJ: Prentice Hall, Inc.

Childs, N. (2001, February). Health agency releases medical data privacy standard. *Provider*, p. 12.

Cimino, J. (1995). Vocabulary and healthcare information technology: State of the art. *Journal of the American Society for Information Sciences*, 48 (10), 777-782.

Cowper, D., Hynes, D., Kubal, J., & Murphy, P. (1999). Using administrative databases for outcomes research: Select examples from VA health services research and development. *Journal of Medical Systems*, 23 (3), 240-259.

Danziger, D. (1997). Data mining—It's not just for statisticians anymore. Retrieved from http://www.tgc.com/dsstar/9710.

Darling, C. (1998). Data mining for the masses. Retrieved from http://www.datamation.com/plugIn/workbench/dataming.

Davidoff, F. (1997). Databases in the next millennium. *Annals of Internal Medicine*, 127 (8), 770-774.

DeJesus, E. (1999, October). State of the art/Data mining. *BYTE.* Retrieved from http://byte.com/art/950/sec8/sec8.htm.

Desouza, K. (2001). Artificial intelligence for healthcare management. In *Proceedings of the First International Conference on Management of Healthcare and Medical Technology*. Enschede, The Netherlands: Institute for Healthcare Technology Management.

Desouza, K. (2002). *Knowledge management with artificial intelligence.* Westport, CT: Quorum Books.

Drucker, P. (1999). *Management challenges for the 21st century.* New York: HarperCollins Books.

Evans, P., & Wurster, T. (1997, September-October). Strategy and the new economics of information. *Harvard Business Review*, pp. 71-82.

Fiesta. (1996). Legal issues in the information age—Part 2. *Nursing Management*, 27 (9), 12-13.

Fletcher, D. (1997). No fool's gold: Guarantee riches from your data mine. *Healthcare Informatics*, pp. 115-118.

Fransman, M. (1996, July). Information regarding the information superhighway and interpretive ambiguity. *IEEE Communications Magazine*, 34 (7), 76-80.

Frawley, W., Piatetsky-Shapiro, G., & Matheus, C. (1992). Knowledge discovery in databases: An overview. *AI Magazine,* pp. 213-228.

Gabrieli, E. (1990). Electronic healthcare records: A discourse. *Journal of Clinical Computing*. 18 (5&6), 130-143.

Gartner Group. (2000). Retrieved from http://www.gartner.com.

Gerber, C. (1998). Excavate your data. Retrieved from http://www.PlugIn/workvench/datamine/exacv.htm.

Gilman, M. (1997). Nuggets™ and data mining. White paper. Melville, NY: Data Mining Technologies, Inc.

Glymour, C., Madigan, D., Pregibon, D., & Smyth, P. (1997). Statistical themes and lessons for data mining. *Data Mining and Knowledge Discovery*, 1, 11-28.

Goodwin, L., Prather, J., Schlitz, K., Iannacchione, M., Hage, M., Hammond, W., & Grzymala-Busse, J. (1997). Data mining issues for improved birth outcomes. *Biomedical Sciences Instrumentation*, 34, 291-296

Gostin, L. (1997). Health care information and the protection of personal privacy: Ethical and legal considerations. *Annals of Internal Medicine*, 127 (8), 683-690.

Graves, J., & Corcoran, S. (1989). The study of nursing informatics. *Image*, 21 (4), 227-231.

Gray, J., Chaudhuri, S., Bosworth, A., Layman, A., Reichart, D., Venkatrao, M., Pellow, F., & Pirahesh, H. (1997). Data Cube: A relational aggregation operator generalizing group-by, cross-tab, and sub-totals. *Data Mining and Knowledge Discovery*, 1, 29-53.

Hannah, K., Ball, M., & Edwards, M. (1994). *Introduction to nursing informatics*. New York: Springer-Verlag.

Hedberg, S. (1995, October). State of the art/The data mining gold rush. *BYTE*. Retrieved from http://www.byte.com/art95/sec8/art2.html.

Hersh, W. (1999). A world of knowledge at your fingertips: The promise, reality, and future directions of on-line information retrieval. *Academic Medicine*, 74 (3), 240-243.

Hlatky, M., Lee, K., Harrell, F., Califf, R., Pryor, D., Mark D., & Rosati, R. (1984). Tying clinical research to patient care by use of an observational database. Statistics in Medicine, 3, 375-384.

Hynes, D., Cowpere, D., Kerr, M., Kubal, J., & Murphy, P. (2000). Database and informatics support for QUERI: Current systems and future needs. *Medical Care*, 38 (6), 114-128.

Iezzoni, L. (1997). Assessing quality using administrative data. *Annals of Internal Medicine, 127* (8), 666-674.

John, G. (1997). *Enhancements to the data mining process.* Stanford University Doctoral Dissertation. Ann Arbor, MI: UMI Dissertation Services. UMI Number: 9723376.

Johnson, N. (1999). Evaluating the quality and applicability of database-derived outcomes studies. *Formulary, 34,* 603-606.

Kiecolt, K., & Nathan, L. (1985). *Secondary analysis of survey data.* Thousand Oaks, CA: Sage Publications.

Kiel, J. (2000). Data mining and modeling: Power tools for physician practices. *MD Computing: Computers in Medical Practice, 17* (3), 33-34.

Kolodner, R. (ed.). (1997). *Computerizing large integrated health networks: The VA success.* New York: Springer Verlag.

Kostoff, R., & Geisler, E. (1999). Strategic management and implication of textual data mining in government organizations. *Technology Analysis & Strategic Management, 11* (4), 493-525.

Krowchuk, H., Moore, M., & Richardson, L. (1995). Using health care records as sources of data for research. *Journal of Nursing Measurement, 3* (1), 3-12.

Lange, L., & Jacox, A. (1993). Using large data bases in nursing and health policy research. *Journal of Professional Nursing, 9* (4), 204-211.

Lazaridis, E. (1997). Database standardization, linkage and the protection of privacy. *Annals of Internal Medicine, 127* (8), 696.

Lewis, E. (1997, Spring). Guest editorial. *Nursing Administration Quarterly,* viii-x.

Lillard, L., & Farmer, M. (1997). Linking medicare and national survey data. *Annals of Internal Medicine, 127* (8), 691-695.

Lincoln, T., & Builder, C. (1999). Global healthcare and the flux of technology. *International Journal of Medical Informatics, 53,* 213-224.

Lingras, P., & Yao, Y. (1998). Data mining using extensions of the rough set model. *Journal of the American Society for Information Science, 49* (5), 415-422.

Marietti, C. (1997). The data warehouse. *Healthcare Informatics,* pp. 93-102.

Matchar, D., Samsa, G., Matthews, J., Ancukiewicz, M., Parmigiani, G., Hasselblad, V., Wold, P., D"Agostino, R., & Lipscomb, J. (1997). The stroke prevention policy model: Linking evidence and clinical decisions. *Annals of Internal Medicine, 127* (8), 704-711.

Mattison, R. (1996). State of the art: Warehousing wherewithal. Retrieved from http://www.cio.com/archive/040196_soa_content.html.

McArt, E., & McDougal, L. (1985). Secondary data analysis: A new approach in nursing research. *Image, 17* (2), 54-57.

McDonald, C., Brossette, S., & Moser, S. (1998). Pathology information systems: Data mining leads to knowledge discovery. *Archives of Pathology & Laboratory Medicine. 122*, 409-411.

McDonald, C., Overhage, J., Dexter, P., Takesue, B., & Dwya., D. (1997). A framework for capturing clinical data sets from computerized sources. *Annals of Internal Medicine, 127* (8), 675-682.

McPhillips, R. (1991). *National and regional databases: The big picture. In Patient outcomes research: Examining the effectiveness of nursing practice. Proceedings of the State of the Science Conference.* NCNR, DHHS, NIH Publication # 93-3411.

Milley, A. (2000). Health care and data mining. *Health Management Technology, 21* (8), 44-45.

Mills, W. (1991). Why a classification system? In R. Carroll-Johnson, (Ed.), *Classification of nursing diagnoses: Proceedings of the 9th conference* (pp. 3-5). Philadelphia, PA: Lippincott.

Murphy, P., Cowper, D., Seppala, G., Stroupe, K., & Hynes, D. (2002). Veterans Health Administration inpatient and outpatient care data: An overview. *Effective Clinical Practice.* Retrieved from www.acponline.org/journals/ecp/May/June02/Murphy.

Newbold, D. (1993). Deciding data. *Nursing Times, 89* (48), 64-65.

Norton, M. (2000). Knowledge discovery with a little perspective. *Bulletin American Society for Information Science,* pp. 21-23.

Orsolits, M., Davis, C., & Gross, M. (1988). Nursing informatics and the future: The twenty-first century. In M. Ball, K. Hannah, U. Jelger, & H. Peterson, (Eds.), *Nursing informatics: Where caring and technology meet.* New York: Springer-Verlag.

Ozbolt, J. (1991). Strategies for building nursing data bases for effectiveness research. In *Patient outcomes research: Examining the effectiveness of nursing practice. Proceedings of the State of the Science Conference.* DHHS, NIH Publication # 93-3411.

Ozbolt, J. (1996). From minimum data to maximum impact: Using clinical data to strengthen patient care. *Advanced Practice Nursing Quarterly, 1* (4), 62-69.

Palmer, R. (1997). Process-based measures of quality: The need for detailed clinical data in large health care databases. *Annals of Internal Medicine, 127* (8), 733-738.

Peck, M., Nelson, N., Buxton, R., Bushnell, J., Dahle, M., Rosebrock, B., & Ashton, C. (1997, Spring). LDS hospital, a facility of intermountain health care. *Nursing Administration Quarterly,* 29-49.

Pringle, M., & Hobbs, R. (1991). Large computer databases in general practice. *British Medical Journal, 302,* 741-742.

Pryor, D., Califf, R., Harrell, F., Hlatsky, M., Lee, K., Mard, D., & Rosati, R. (1985). Clinical databases: accomplishments and unrealized potential. *Medical Care, 23* (5), 623-647.

Psomas, J., Schaufele, M., & Madhaven, G. (2000). Data mining overview and select vendor tools. Unpublished manuscript.

Raghavan, V., Deogun, J., & Server, H. (1998). Knowledge discovery and data mining. *Journal of the American Society for Information, 49* (5), 397-402.

Ray, W. (1997). Policy and program analysis using administrative databases. *Annals of Internal Medicine, 127* (8), 712-718.

Reed, J. (1992). Secondary data in nursing research. *Journal of Advanced Nursing, 17,* 877-883.

Rittman, M., & Gorman, R. (1992). Computerized databases: Privacy issues in the development of the nursing minimum data set. *Computers in Nursing, 10* (1), 14-17.

Roberts, B., Anthony, M., Madigan, E., & Chen, Y. (1997). Data management: Cleaning and checking. *Nursing Research, 46* (6), 350-352.

Romano, C. (1987). Privacy, confidentiality, and security of computerized systems: The nursing responsibility. *Computers In Nursing, 5* (3), 99-104.

Romano, C., & Brennen, P. (1991). Computerizing the documentation of patient care. In C. D'Argenio, (Ed.), *Implementing Nursing Diagnosis-based Practice.* St. Louis: Mosby.

Rubin, D. (1997). Estimating causal effects from large data sets using propensity scores. *Annals of Internal Medicine, 127* (8), 757-763.

Rudin, K. (1996.) What's new in data warehousing? *DBMS Data Warehouse Supplement.* Retrieved from http://www.dbmsmag.com/9708.htm.

Sardinas, J., & Muldoon, J. (1998). Securing the transmission and storage of medical information. *Computers in Nursing, 16* (3), 162-168.

Schulman, S. (1998). Data mining: Life after report generators. *Information Today, 15* (3), 52.

Seelos, H. (1993). The empirical object of medical information. *Journal of Medical Systems, 7* (2), 87-96.

Shams, K., & Fareshta, M. (2001). Data warehousing: toward knowledge management. *Topics in Health Information Management, 21* (3), 24-32.

Simoudis, E. (1998). Data mining: A technology comes of age. Retrieved from http://www.software.ibm.com/sq/issues/vol24/datatch.htm.

Sinclair, V. (1990). Potential effects of decision support systems on the role of the nurse. *Computers in Nursing, 8* (2), 60-65.

Southon, F., Braithwaite, J., & Lorenzi, N. (1997). Strategic constraints in health informatics: Are expectations realistic? *International Journal of Health Planning and Management,12,* 3-13.

SPSS. (2000). Build leading-edge e-commerce and business intelligence curricula. Retrieved from www.spss.com/education.

Steiner, C., Elizhauser, A., & Schnaier, J. (2002, May/June). The healthcare cost and utilization project: An overview. *Effective Clinical Practice.* Retrieved from http://www.acponline.org/journals/ecp/mayjun02/steiner.htm.

Styffe, E. (1997, Spring). Privacy, confidentiality, and security in clinical information systems: Dilemmas and opportunities for the nurse executive. *Nursing Administration Quarterly,* 21-28.

Tan, J., & Sheps, S. (Eds.) (1999). *Health decsion support systems.* Gaithersburg, MD: Aspen Publishers, Inc.

Temple, R. (1990). Problems in the use of large data sets to assess effectiveness. *International Journal of Technology Assessment in Health Care, 8,* 211-219.

The American Nurse. (1999). New nursing recognition criteria announced. *The American Nurse, 9.* Washington: American Nurses Association.

Tierney, W., & McDonald, C. (1991). Practice databases and their uses in clinical research. *Statistics in Medicine, 10,* 541-557.

Turban, E., & Aronson, J. (2001). *Decision support systems and intelligent systems.* Upper Saddle River, NJ: Prentice Hall.

U.S. Department of Health and Human Services. (1991). *The feasibility of linking research-related data bases to federal and non-federal medical administrative data bases* (AHCPR Publication No. 91-0003). Rockville, MD: U.S. Department of Health and Human Services.

Vance, B., Gilleran-Strom, J., Kraft, M., Lang, B., & Mead, M. (1997). Nursing use of systems. In R. Kolodner, (Ed), *Computerizing large integrated health networks.* New York: Springer-Verlag.

Vance, B., Kraft, M. R., & Lang, B. (1998). Nursing software development and implementation: An integral aspect of the Veterans Health Administration information system infrastructure. In S. Moorhead & C. Delaney, (Eds.), *Information systems innovations for nursing: New visions and ventures.* Thousand Oaks, CA: Sage Publications.

Werley, H., & Leske, J. (1991). Standardized comparable, essential data available through the nursing minimum data set. In J. Turley & S. Newbold, (Eds). *Nursing Informatics 91: Pre-conference proceedings.* Heidelberg-Berlin: Springer-Verlag.

Werley, H., Devine, E., & Zorn, C. (1990). *Nursing minimum data set: Data collection manual.* Milwaukee, WI: University of Wisconsin School of Nursing.

Weschler, J. (1996). Electronic transmission, sharing of health information raising patient privacy concerns. *Formulary, 31,* 990-991.

Wray, N., Ashton, C., Kuykendall, D., & Hollingsworth, J. (1995). Using administrative databases to evaluate the quality of medical care: A conceptual framework. *Social Sciences in Medicine, 40* (12), 707-715.

Wuerker, A. (1997). Longitudinal research using computerized clinical databases: Caveats and constraints. *Nursing Research, 46* (6), 353-358.

Zielstorff, R. (1995). Capturing and using clinical outcome data: Implications for information systems design. *Journal of the American Medical Informatics Association, 2,* 191-196.

Chapter XII

A Hybrid Clustering Technique to Improve Patient Data Quality

Narasimhaiah Gorla
Wayne State University, USA

Chow Y. K. Bennon
Hong Kong Polytechnic University, Hong Kong

ABSTRACT

The demographic and clinical description of each patient is recorded in the databases of various hospital information systems. The errors in patient data are: wrong data entry, absence of information provided by the patient, improper identity of the patients (in case of tourists in Hong Kong), etc. These data errors will lead to a phenomenon that records of the same patient will be shown as records of different patients. In order to solve this problem, we use "clustering," a data mining technique, to group "similar" patients together. We used three algorithms: hierarchical clustering, partitioned clustering, and hybrid algorithm combining these two, and applied on the patient data using a C program. We used six attributes of patient data: Sex, DOB, Name, Marital status, District, and Telephone number as the basis for computing similarity, with some weights to the attributes. We found that the Hybrid algorithm gave more accurate grouping compared to the other algorithms, had smaller mean square error, and executed faster. Due to the privacy ordinance, the true data of patients is not shown, but only simulated data is used.

INTRODUCTION

The establishment of the Hospital Authority marked the milestone for all public hospitals in Hong Kong. Under the management of the Hospital Authority, the daily operations of the public hospitals are linked and are under the centralized control of Hospital Authority Head Office (HAHO). Whenever a person uses any service of any one of the public hospitals, his/her personal information will be entered into a corresponding clinical information system. All the clinical information systems are linked and share a master database system that is known as the Patient Master Index (PMI). The main function of PMI is to maintain and control the demographic data of patients. Each patient record is identified by his/her Hong Kong Identification Card (HKID) number or Birth Certificate number. The personal data in PMI can be accessed by any linked clinical information system. Whenever the detail of a patient is updated by any linked clinical information system, PMI is updated automatically. Ideally, each patient should have a unique master record in PMI. However, a patient may contain two or more records in the PMI due to reasons, such as: a patient comes to a hospital without his/her HKID, the information of the patient is wrongly reported by a second party; a patient cannot be identified by any valid document, the patient is a non-Hong Kong resident, such as tourist, a baby is born without a Birth Certificate, data entry operators make typing errors.

If any of the above cases occur, a unique pseudo-identification number will be generated by the clinical information system to identify the patient temporarily. Once the HKID or Birth Certificate number is provided by the patient during hospitalization, the personal information will be updated and the pseudo-identification number will be discarded. However, many patients cannot provide their identification documents before they leave the hospital. More temporary records may be generated for the same patient when a patient attends a hospital several times, thus more and more "duplicate" records will be generated in the PMI database.

The objective is to develop a methodology to cluster records in the PMI database based on the similarity of attributes of the patients and to validate the methodology using experiments. Those records with high similarity, presumably belonging to the same patient, will be clustered and reported. Hospital staff can make use of the reports to study the identity of "similar" records and merge them as necessary. The benefits of this study to the hospital are: i) time can be reduced on producing accurate patient records, ii) searching for data can be speeded up since dummy records are reduced, iii) the historical data of a patient becomes more complete and accurate, and iv) the quality of patient records is improved in general. The following section provides background to the study. The next two sections provide the data model and representation respectively. Later sections describe clustering methodology and give the results of the application of methodology on sample data. Finally, the last two sections provide future trends and conclusions.

BACKGROUND

Cluster analysis is the formal study of algorithms and methods for grouping, or classifying similar objects, and has been practiced for many years. Cluster analysis is one component of exploratory data analysis (EDA) (Gordon, 1981). Cluster analysis is a modern statistical method of partitioning an observed sample population into disjoint or overlapping homogeneous classes. This classification may help to optimize a functional process (Willett, 1987). A cluster is comprised of a number of similar objects collected or grouped together. "A cluster is an aggregation of points in the test space such that the distance between any two points in the cluster is less than the distance between any point in the cluster and any point not in it" (Everitt, 1974).

Cluster analysis is a tool of exploratory data analysis (EDA). The major steps to be considered are shown in *Figure 1* (Baker, 1995). The process is an endless loop in which new insights are obtained and new ideas are generated each time through the loop. The major steps in clustering methodology are:
1.   Data collection: The careful recording of relevant data is captured.
2.   Initial screening: Raw data from the database undergoes some massaging before it is ready for formal analysis (for example, normalization).

Figure 1: Clustering methodology

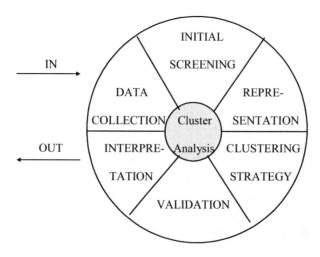

3. Representation: Here the data is put into a form suitable for analysis. In our research, we use the form of proximity index.
4. Clustering strategy: We choose three strategies: hierarchical clustering, partitional clustering, and hybrid clustering.
5. Validation: Simulated patient data will be used to test the algorithms. The result of cluster analysis will be compared with the known duplicates in the simulated data.
6. Interpretation: we integrate the results of cluster analysis with previous studies and draw conclusions.

DATA MODEL
Selection of Patient Attributes
In this research, the goal is to group together the records with similar attributes. A large number of variables (attributes) is not desirable to find the similarity-reduction, and selection of variables is a fundamental step in cluster analysis (Hand, 1981). In systems, i.e., PMI database, a patient is characterized by the following variables:
a) HKID number / Birth Certificate number
b) Name in English
c) Name in Chinese
d) Marital status
e) Sex
f) Date of birth
g) Age
h) Address / District code
i) Telephone number
j) Nationality
k) Religion

The values of some of these variables may change considerably over time, or they are not filled in the database. In order to determine which variables are to be chosen, three basic criteria are used: stability of the variable, accuracy of the variable, and importance of the variable. It is important to reduce the number of variables, since computer time increases dramatically with an increase in the number of variables (Anderberg, 1973). Since the HKID numbers of two records belonging to the same patient are different, or the HKIDs are missing, HKID is not a suitable variable for clustering purposes. The variables of nationality and religion are optional input to the hospital information system, and we find that over 80% of patients do not provide such information, hence nationality and religion are not suitable. The variable age is not suitable, since patients born in different months of same year may be grouped into the same age. We are left then with six variables for computing similarity:

1.   Sex
2.   Name in English
3.   Date of birth
4.   Marital status
5.   District code
6.   Telephone number

Furthermore, marital status, district code and telephone number are unstable variables. They often change because a patient may get married or change his/her residence and telephone number. However, these changes occur rarely, so the stability of these variables remain quite high. The variable Name in English may also be changed, but it is rare. The final variable, date of birth, will not change. Thus, we use the above six variables and use different combinations of these variables to obtain good clusters.

DATA REPRESENTATION, STANDARDIZATION, AND WEIGHTING

Data Representation

Clustering algorithms group objects based on indices of proximity between pairs of objects. Each object is represented by a pattern or d-place vector, which indicates the d-attributes of the object. The collection of each d-place pattern forms a pattern matrix. Each row of this matrix defines a pattern and each column denotes a feature or attribute (*Figure 2a*). The information of the pattern matrix can be used to build a proximity matrix (*Figure 2b*). A proximity matrix $[d(i,j)]$ gathers the pair-wise indices of proximity in a matrix, in which each row and column represents a pattern. A proximity index can represent either a similarity or dissimilarity. The more the ith and j^{th} objects resemble one another, the larger the similarity index or the smaller the dissimilarity index. Only the upper triangle of the proximity matrix needs to be considered, as it is symmetric. The properties of a proximity index between the ith and k^{th} pattern [denoted as $d(i,k)$] have been summarized as:

1)   (a) For a dissimilarity, $d(i,i) = 0$, for all i.
       (b) For a similarity, $d(i,i) >= \max d(i,k)$, for all i.
2) $d(i,k) = d(k,i)$, for all (i,k).
3) $d(i,k) > 0$, for all (i,k).

Figure 2: A pattern matrix and a proximity matrix

$$
\begin{bmatrix}
x_{11} & x_{12} & \cdots & x_{1d} \\
x_{21} & x_{22} & \cdots & x_{2d} \\
\cdot & \cdot & \cdots & \cdot \\
\cdot & \cdot & \cdots & \cdot \\
x_{n1} & x_{n2} & \cdots & x_{nd}
\end{bmatrix}
\qquad
\begin{bmatrix}
d(1,1) & d(1,2) & \cdots & d(1,n) \\
 & d(2,2) & \cdots & d(2,n) \\
 & & \cdot & \cdots & d(3,n) \\
 & & & \cdot & \cdot \\
 & & & & d(n,n)
\end{bmatrix}
$$

(a) Pattern matrix   (b) Proximity matrix

A C-program is written to perform the cluster analysis. As stated earlier, six attributes of each patient are used for our analysis: Sex, Date of birth, Name, Marital status, District code, and Telephone number. The HKID number is used internally for testing purposes, but not to compute clusters.

Dissimilarity Computation

Comparison between two objects can be expressed in either similarity or dissimilarity. The Euclidean distance, a mathematical function of the distance between two objects, is used for measurement. Let $[x_{ij}]$ be our pattern matrix, where x is the jth feature for the ith pattern. The ith pattern, which is the ith row of the pattern matrix, is denoted by the column vector x_i.

$$x_i = (x_{i1}, x_{i2}, \ldots \ldots x_{id})^T , \quad i = 1,2,\ldots\ldots,n$$

The Euclidean distance between object i and object k can then be expressed as:

$$d(i,k) = [\sum_{j=1}^{d} (x_{ij} - x_{kj})^2]^{1/2}$$

As our data file consists of both ordinal and binary values, we handle it in the following way. Let the attribute of a patient be $j = \{1,2,3,4,5,6\}$ equivalent to {sex, date of birth, name, marital status, district code, telephone number} respectively. For any object i or k, if j = 1,4,5,6, (i.e., attribute = sex, marital status, district code or telephone number),

$$(x_{ij} - x_{kj}) = \begin{cases} 0, & \text{if } x_{ij} = x_{kj} \\ 1, & \text{otherwise} \end{cases}$$

If j = 2 (i.e., attribute = date of birth),

$(x_{ij} - x_{kj})$ = the number of days between two dates of birth.

If j = 3 (i.e., attribute = name),

$(x_{ij} - x_{kj})$ = the percent of mismatched characters between two names.

The sum of these six individual values, by the definition of Euclidean distance, represents the overall dissimilarity between two objects, which forms the basic component in our proximity matrix. For example, consider the following two rows from the pattern matrix:

$$\begin{bmatrix} X_1 \\ X_2 \end{bmatrix} = \begin{bmatrix} M & 02071972 & \text{CHAN TAI MAN} & S & NP & 23121256 \\ F & 02081972 & \text{CHAN YEE MAN} & S & QRB & 27191928 \end{bmatrix}$$

for j=1,	$(d_{11} - d_{21}) = 1$	(Not the same sex)
for j=2,	$(d_{12} - d_{22}) = 31$	(No. of days between date of births)
for j=3,	$(d_{13} - d_{23}) = 1 - 9/12 = 0.25$	(% of no. of mismatch characters)
for j=4,	$(d_{14} - d_{24}) = 0$	(Both are single)
for j=5,	$(d_{15} - d_{25}) = 1$	(Not the same district code)
for j=6,	$(d_{16} - d_{26}) = 1$	(Different telephone no.)

By the definition of Euclidean distance, the dissimilarity between x_1 and x_2 is:

$$d(1,2) = [1^2 + 31^2 + 0.25^2 + 0^2 + 1^2 + 1^2]^{1/2} = 31.0494$$

Treatment of Missing Data

In practice, the pattern vectors can be incomplete because of errors, or unavailability of information. Jain (1988) described a simple and general technique for handling such missing values. The distance between two vectors x_i and

x_k containing missing values is computed as follows. First, define d_j between the two patterns along the jth feature:

$$d_j = \begin{cases} 0, & \text{if } x_{ij} \text{ or } x_{kj} \text{ is missing} \\ x_{ij} - x_{kj}, & \text{otherwise} \end{cases}$$

Then the distance between x_i and x_k is written as:

$$d(i,k) = [\frac{d}{d - d_o} \Sigma d_j^2]^{1/2}$$

where d_o is the number of features missing in x_i or x_k or both.

If there are no missing values, then $d(i,k)$ is the Euclidean distance. In this research, missing data is represented by "0" in the data file. Now, suppose the telephone number of patient 2 is missing (i.e., $x_{26} = 0$) in the previous example, $d_o = 1$

$$\Sigma d_j^2 = 1^2 + 31^2 + 0.25^2 + 0^2 + 1^2 + 0^2 = 963.0625$$

$$d(1,2) = [6 / (6 - 1)] \times 963.0625 = 33.9952$$

Data Standardization

The individual dissimilarity value for all attributes of a patient falls between 0 and 1, except the attribute of the date of birth, whose value varies from 0 to hundreds of thousands. This creates a bias in the cluster analysis towards date of birth. Normalization is performed so that the range of all measurements is 0 to 1. The standard normalization for a number, x_{ij}, can be expressed as:

$$x_{ij}^* = \frac{x_{ij} - m_j}{s_j}$$

where $$m_j = (\sum_{i=1}^{n} x_{ij}) / n$$

and $$s_j^2 = [\sum_{i=1}^{n} (x_{ij} - m_j)^2] / n$$

where

> x_{ij} is the actual magnitude of the variable,
> m_j is the mean of all x_{ij} for attribute j, and
> s_j is the standard deviation of all x_{ij} for attribute j.

Consider the previous example, let there be 100 patient records (i.e., n=100). x_{12} can be represented as the number of days between the date of birth and a standard date of 31121999. Therefore:

> x_{12} = days difference between 02071972 and 31121999 = 10039
> x_{22} = days difference between 02081972 and 31121999 = 10008

Now, suppose $m_2 = 18000$, $s_2 = 8000$, for 100 patient records:

> $x_{12}^* = (10039 - 18000) / 8000 = -0.9951$
> $x_{22}^* = (10008 - 18000) / 8000 = -0.9999$
> $(d_{12} - d_{22}) = (-0.9951) - (-0.9999) = 0.0039$
> $d(1,2) = [1^2+0.0039^2+0.25^2+0^2+1^2+1^2]^{1/2} = 1.7569$

Thus, dominance of a single attribute is avoided.

Weighting

As discussed before, some attributes change more often than others over a period of time, therefore it is necessary to give higher weight to more stable attributes. Different weightings will result in different clusters. Applying the weighting factors, the Euclidean distance between object i and object k becomes:

$$d(i,k) = [\sum_{j=1}^{d} w_j (x_{ij} - x_{kj})^2]^{1/2}$$

CLUSTERING ALGORITHMS

Hierarchical Clustering

A hierarchical clustering is a sequence of partitions in which each partition is nested into the next partition in the sequence (*Figure 3*). The algorithm for hierarchical clustering starts with the disjoint clustering, which places each of the *n* objects in an individual cluster. The procedure of hierarchical clustering is as follows:

Let the *nxn* proximity matrix be D=[d(i,j)].
L(k) is the level of the kth clustering.
A cluster with sequence number m is denoted as (m).
The proximity between clusters (r) and (s) is denoted as d[(r),(s)].

Step 1. Begin with the disjoint clustering having level L(0)=0 and sequence number m=0.

Step 2. Find the least dissimilar pair of cluster in the current clustering, say pair [(r),(s)], such that d[(r),(s)] = min {d[(i),(j)]}.

Step 3. Increment the sequence number : m ← m+1.
Merge clusters (r) and (s) into a single cluster to form the next level clustering m. Set the level of this clustering to L(m) = d[(r),(s)].

Step 4. Update the proximity matrix, D, by deleting the rows and columns corresponding to clusters (r) and (s), and adding a row and column corresponding to the newly formed cluster.
The proximity between the new cluster, denoted (r,s), and the old cluster (k) is defined as follows (Jain, 1988):

$$d[(k),(r,s)] = \alpha_r d[(k),(r)] + \alpha_s d[(k),(s)] + \beta d[(r),(s)] + \Upsilon \, | \, d[(k),(r)] - d[(k),(s)] \, |$$

where α_r, α_s, β, Υ are parameters that are based on the type of hierarchical clustering.

Step 5. If all objects are in one cluster, stop, or else go to Step 2.

Two methods for updating the proximity matrix are provided: Single-link and compete-link. The Single-link clusters are based on connectedness and are characterized by minimum path length among all pairs of objects in the cluster. The proximity matrix is updated with d[(k),(r,s)] = min {d[(k), (r)], d[(k),(s)]}, which corresponds to $\alpha_r = 0.5$, $\alpha_s = 0.5$, $\beta = 0$ and $\Upsilon = -0.5$. Complete-link clusters are based on complete sub-graphs where the diameter of a complete sub-graph is the largest proximity among all proximities for pairs of objects in the sub-graph. The update of the proximity is given by d[(k),(r,s)] = max {d[(k), (r)], d[(k),(s)]}, which corresponds to $\alpha_r = 0.5$, $\alpha_s = 0.5$, $\beta = 0$ and $\Upsilon = 0.5$. The following example illustrates how clusters are formed among five records, with equal weighting factor of 1. Let the pattern matrix be:

$$
\begin{array}{c|llllllll}
1 & M & 15121982 & \text{HO WAI CHI} & M & MK & 27191235 \\
2 & F & 02091952 & \text{TAI YUK YU} & S & TST & 27271111 \\
3 & M & 12111969 & \text{PON TAK HONG} & M & TST & 23401239 \\
4 & M & 15121982 & \text{HO WAI CHI} & M & MK & 27191235 \\
5 & F & 01031962 & \text{TAI YUK CHU} & S & TST & 27274300 \\
\end{array}
$$

The corresponding proximity matrix is:

$$
\begin{array}{c|ccccc}
 & 1 & 2 & 3 & 4 & 5 \\
\hline
1 & 0 & 2.5 & 2.0 & 0 & 2.4 \\
2 & & 0 & 2.2 & 2.5 & 1.4 \\
3 & & & 0 & 2.0 & 2.1 \\
4 & & & & 0 & 2.4 \\
5 & & & & & 0 \\
\end{array}
$$

(By single-link)   (By complete-link)

$$
\begin{array}{c|cccc}
 & 2 & 3 & 1,4 & 5 \\
\hline
2 & 0 & 2.2 & 2.5 & 1.4 \\
3 & & 0 & 2.0 & 2.1 \\
1,4 & & & 0 & 2.1 \\
5 & & & & 0 \\
\end{array}
\qquad
\begin{array}{c|cccc}
 & 2 & 3 & 1,4 & 5 \\
\hline
2 & 0 & 2.2 & 2.5 & 1.4 \\
3 & & 0 & 2.0 & 2.1 \\
1,4 & & & 0 & 2.4 \\
5 & & & & 0 \\
\end{array}
$$

The number of clusters formed depends on the value of a threshold level.

$$
\begin{array}{c|ccc}
 & 3 & 1,4 & 2,5 \\
\hline
3 & 0 & 2.0 & 2.1 \\
1,4 & & 0 & 2.1 \\
2,5 & & & 0 \\
\end{array}
\qquad
\begin{array}{c|ccc}
 & 3 & 1,4 & 2,5 \\
\hline
3 & 0 & 2.0 & 2.2 \\
1,4 & & 0 & 2.5 \\
2,5 & & & 0 \\
\end{array}
$$

$$
\begin{array}{c|cc}
 & 3,1,4 & 2,5 \\
\hline
3,1,4 & 0 & 2.1 \\
2,5 & & 0 \\
\end{array}
\qquad
\begin{array}{c|cc}
 & 3,1,4 & 2,5 \\
\hline
3,1,4 & 0 & 2.5 \\
2,5 & & 0 \\
\end{array}
$$

Figure 3: Hierarchical clustering

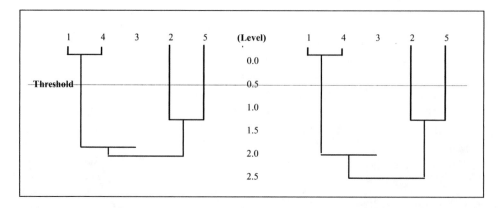

From the above graph, it can be seen that a small threshold will return a larger number of clusters, while a large threshold will return a smaller number of clusters. In this research, we would like to obtain the most similar patient records, which implies a large number of clusters; thus it requires a smaller threshold value.

Partitional Clustering

A partitional clustering determines a partition of the n patterns into k groups or clusters, such that the patterns in a cluster are more similar to each other than to patterns in other clusters. The value of k may or may not be specified. The most commonly used partitional clustering strategy is based on the square error criterion. The objective is to obtain the partitions, which minimizes the square error for a given number of clusters. Suppose that a given set of n patterns in d dimensions has been partitioned into K clusters $\{C_1, C_2, ...C_K\}$ such that cluster C_K has n_K patterns and each pattern is in exactly one cluster, so that:

$$\sum_{i=1}^{K} n_i = n$$

The mean vector, or centre, of cluster C_K is defined as the centroid of the cluster, or

$$m^{(K)} = \frac{1}{n_K} \sum_{i=1}^{n_K} x_i^{(K)}$$

where $x_i^{(K)}$ is the ith pattern belonging to cluster C_K. The square error for cluster C_K is the sum of the squared Euclidean distances between each pattern in C_K and its cluster centre $m^{(K)}$:

$$e_K^2 = \sum_{i=1}^{n_K} (x_i^{(K)} - m^{(K)})^T (x_i^{(K)} - m^{(K)})$$

This square error is the within-cluster variation. The square error for the entire clustering containing K clusters is the sum of the within-cluster variation:

$$\varphi_W = E_K^2 = \sum_{i=1}^{K} e_i^2$$

The pooled mean, *m*, is the grand mean vector for all the patterns:

$$m = \frac{1}{n} \sum_{i=1}^{K} n_i \, m^{(K)}$$

The between-cluster variation is defined as $f_K^2 = (m^{(K)} - m)^T (m^{(K)} - m)$,

and the sum of the between-cluster variation is $\varphi_B = F_K^2 = \sum_{i=1}^{K} f_i^2$.

The overall square error for the entire clustering is expressed as $\varphi = \varphi_w + \varphi_B$. The basic idea of an iterative clustering algorithm is to start with an initial partition and assign patterns to clusters, so as to reduce the overall square error. It is clear that increasing the between-cluster scatter j_B decreases the within-cluster scatter φ_w and vice verse. This general algorithm for iterative partitional clustering method is given by Gorden (1981). The partitional clustering proce-dure is as follows:

Step 1. Select an initial partition with K clusters. Repeat Steps 2-5 until the cluster membership stabilizes.

Step 2. Generate a new partition by assigning each pattern to its closest cluster centre.

Step 3. Compute new cluster centres as the centroids of the clusters.

Step 4. Repeat Steps 2 and 3 until an optimum value of the criterion function is formed or the total number of iteration is reached.

Step 5. Adjust the number of clusters by merging and splitting existing clusters or by removing small clusters, or outliers.

Hybrid Clustering

In this research, we develop and use a hybrid clustering, in which the hierarchical and partitional algorithms are combined and modified to produce clustering. We compare the results of the hybrid algorithm with the other two clustering algorithms. From the output of hierarchical clustering, we can obtain different cluster combinations for a different threshold. They serve as the initialization for the partitional clustering. The hybrid clustering algorithm can be described as follows:

Step 1. Select an initial partition from one of the results of hierarchical clustering by adjusting different threshold of the level.

Step 2. Generate a new partition by assigning each pattern to other clusters one by one.

Step 3. Compute new cluster centres as the centroids of the clusters, as well as the overall square error.

Step 4. Choose the partition with the lowest value of overall square error.

Step 5. Repeat Steps 2 - 4 for other patterns.

Step 6. Repeat Steps 2 - 5 until an optimum value of the criterion function is found or the specified number of iteration is reached.

Refinements

As discussed before, there are several factors that affect clustering, and these need to be adjusted to obtain better results. The number of attributes is one of the factors. The higher the number of attributes, the more accurate the results will be. However, the running time will increase. There should be a tradeoff between them. The second factor is weight assignment to attributes. An attribute should not be weighted too high, since it will dominate other attributes. There should be an appropriate weighting for each attribute. Thirdly, the number of clusters chosen for initialization in partitional clustering is another factor. If the number of clusters is too small, the overall square error will be too high. But if the number of clusters is too large, the records of the same patient may distribute into different clusters. Therefore, different combinations of these factors needed to be experimented with until satisfactory results are obtained.

RESULTS

In order to test the clustering algorithms, simulation studies involving the generation of artificial data set, for which the true structure of the data is known in advance, is used. The performance of the clustering method can then be assessed by determining the degree to which it can discover the true structure.

First Experiment

A simulated data set is used to compare the power of the three clustering algorithms. For an easy identification of duplicated records, 20 records are used, in which five of them are with repetitions. In hierarchical clustering, both the single-linkage method and the complete-linkage method are used to cluster the records. The corresponding dendrograms for both the single-linkage and complete-linkage are shown in Appendix 1. In both methods, the duplicated records are grouped, but with different subsequent formation of clusters. From the dendrograms, it can be seen that a small threshold will produce the same clustering result. The summarized results for the three algorithms are shown in *Figure 4*.

From *Figure 4*, it can be seen that the mean square error of hierarchical clustering is larger than that of partitional clustering. However, the percentage of error in hierarchical clustering is smaller than that of partitional clustering when the number of iteration is small. The result of partitional clustering can further be improved by increasing the number iteration so as to reduce the mean square error, and percentage of error. At the same time, it increases the time for convergence. Hybrid clustering combines the advantages from both the hierarchical clustering and partitional clustering. With a good choice of threshold, records are well structured into clusters by the initializing hierarchical clustering. Then the structure is further re-organized in order to reduce the mean square error by the following partitional clustering. As the choice of initial number of cluster is first determined by the hierarchical part, number of iteration can highly be reduced to get the local minimum or even the global minimum. The rate of convergence is much faster than that of partitional clustering.

Figure 4: The best results for the three clustering algorithms with 20 input records

Algorithm	No. of cluster	mean square error		% of error		No. of iteration
		iteration	iteration	iteration	iteration	for convergence
Hierarchical	5	1124	-	0	-	-
	10	60.4	-	0	-	-
	15	20	-	0	-	-
Partitional	5	101.9	91.55	40	40	>500000
	10	40.45	38.9	60	60	>500000
	15	33.4	30.25	100	80	>500000
Hybrid	5	227.05	201.55	0	0	<50000
	10	36.8	30.1	0	0	<50000
	15	20	20	0	0	<100

Second Experiment

A second simulation study is also performed, but with a much larger data set. 100 records are used in which 10% are with repetition. The summarized results from the hierarchical clustering, partitional clustering and hybrid clustering are shown in *Figures 5 to 7*, respectively.

As can be seen in *Figure 5*, the best solution is obtained without any error by the hierarchical clustering (number of cluster=90). It forms the initialization of number of clusters in hybrid clustering. The structure of the result can further be reduced with a decrease in mean square error by increasing the number of iteration (number of cluster=88 in *Figure 7*). In *Figure 6*, the best solution is obtained when the number of clusters is 93 with 10% of error. This solution is

Figure 5: Summarized result for the hierarchical clustering with 100 input records

Threshold	No. of cluster	Mean square error	% of error
0.5	90	100	0
1	90	100	0
1.5	25	. 865	0
2	2	71249	0
3.5	2	72215	0

Figure 6: Summarized result for the partitional clustering with 100 input records

No. of cluster	Within Error	Between Error	Mean sq. err
5	12006.2	3.8	12010.0
10	3075.9	8.1	3084.0
15	1411.8	11.8	1423.6
20	810.2	12.0	822.2
25	545.1	12.9	558.0
30	402.0	19.8	421.8
35	295.8	23.9	319.7
40	244.0	30.2	274.2
45	201.6	31.2	232.8
50	134.0	33.3	167.3
60	118.6	48.2	166.8
70	82.7	69.4	152.1
80	61.0	75.4	136.4
90	30.9	81.0	111.9
91	25.2	83.1	108.3
92	20.2	85.2	105.4
93	9.1	86.4	95.5
94	8.5	87.5	96.0
95	7.4	89.4	96.8
96	5.9	91.2	97.1
97	5.2	92.7	97.9
98	2.7	95.8	98.5
99	1.0	98.3	99.3
100	0.0	100.0	100.0

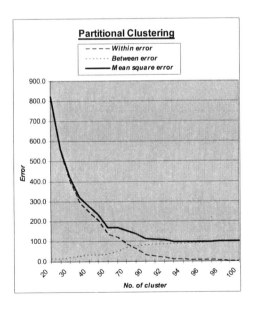

Figure 7: Summarized result for the hybrid clustering with 100 input records

Algorithm	Threshold	No. of cluster	Mean square error				
			No. of iteration				
			0	100	200	500	1000
Hybrid	0.5	90	100	95.2	94.4 (reduce to 88 clusters)	94.4 (reduce to 88 clusters)	94.4 (reduce to 88 clusters)
	1	90	100	95.2	94.4 (reduce to 88 clusters)	94.4 (reduce to 88 clusters)	94.4 (reduce to 88 clusters)
	1.5	25	865	824	806	794	794
	2	2	712 49	70867	70584	70151.9	70151.9
Partitional		90		132.01	132.01	132.01	111.88
		25		596.71	596.71	596.71	570.71
		2		72105.97	72105.97	72105.97	7274.97

only the local minimum with 1000 iterations. A global minimum appears when the number of iteration is increased so that there is no error. The rate of convergence is much lower in partitional clustering than the hybrid clustering. As seen in *Figure 7*, the hybrid clustering converges after 500 iterations, but the partitional clustering still oscillates.

Comparison

The primary step in hierarchical clustering is to group those records with high similarity. Once the records are grouped into any cluster, they will not be further considered individually. The similarity of the whole cluster will then be compared with other records to form a much larger cluster, if necessary. On the other hand, partitional clustering considers all the records every time and tries to group them into different clusters with the total least difference among the elements within clusters. It needs a very long time to re-structure the clustering before a fairly good result can be obtained. The combination of the two algorithm forms the hybrid clustering algorithm. It tries to reduce the time of iteration required in partitional clustering by constructing a quite good starting structure using hierarchical clustering first. The objective is then achieved by further searching the global minimum value of the overall mean square error.

FUTURE TRENDS

The present research has the following limitations, and thus the research can be extended to eliminate these limitations. The weights we used are somewhat arbitrary. More simulation studies may be needed to determine the appropriate weights on the training data set. Secondly, the threshold value was arbitrarily chosen in this research, since we are aware of the actual data. In a real life situation, we do not know what percentage of patients have multiple records. The threshold value can also be estimated based on the error history of patient records. Thus, future researchers may need to repeat the experiment with different threshold values in order to determine the best one. Finally, the selection of the attributes of patient records needs consideration. This research can be extended to determine the appropriate set of attributes, by considering the knowledge of the hospital staff and also by using other algorithms (such as genetic algorithms) that will help determine an optimal set of attributes. Genetic algorithms, developed based on biological evolution, are widely used to solve optimization problems in data mining techniques (Berson & Smith, 1997). By using genetic algorithms, various combinations of attributes will be considered and evaluated for superiority in identifying records of the same patient. In this research, we considered clustering algorithms as a data mining technique. Future research should consider other techniques, such as association rules, use of entropy, etc. (Han & Kamber, 2001), and compare the results with clustering. Entropy is an information-based concept that can be used to partition a data set based on an attribute, resulting in a hierarchical discretization. Another extension to the present research can be done by employing other clustering algorithms proposed, such as those by Guha et al. (2000, 2001), and comparing the results. These issues are left for future investigation.

CONCLUSION

In this research, we illustrated the use of data mining techniques, particularly clustering algorithms, to identify duplicate patient records in Hospital Information Systems. The reasons for errors in patient data are wrong data entry, insufficient information provided by the patient, improper identity of the patients (in the case of tourists in Hong Kong), etc. The clustering algorithms are used in this research to cluster all the records of each patient together, so that high quality data records of each patient can be maintained. The importance of this research cannot be over-emphasized because of the fact that wrongly grouped records or ungrouped records of a patient will give rise to inaccurate or missing information about the patient's medical history, which will further lead to erroneous conclusions by the doctors.

We used three clustering algorithms: hierarchical, partitioned, and hybrid that combines the other two. Our results show that Hybrid algorithm gave more accurate groupings compared to the other algorithms, and result was obtained faster (fewer iterations). In the hybrid algorithm, by minimizing the total squared error, we could obtain the best clustering. In this research, we demonstrated that data mining technique could be used to detect data duplications by experimenting on a smaller set of data. However, this procedure can be adapted to any size data set, since we observed in our research that the hybrid algorithm ran a thousand times faster than conventional partitional clustering algorithms. We used six attributes of patient data to cluster the patient records — Sex, Date of birth, Name, Marital status, District, and Telephone number — as the basis for computing similarity of patient records. We also used some weights to these variables in computing similarity, which were based on simulation.

REFERENCES

Anderberg, M. R. (1973). *Cluster analysis for applications*. New York: Academic Press.

Backer, E. (1995). *Computer-assisted reasoning in cluster analysis*. New York: Prentice Hall.

Berson, A., & Smith, S. (1997). *Data warehousing, data mining, & OLAP*. McGraw-Hill.

Diday, E. (1994). *New approaches in classification and data analysis*. New York: Springer-Verlag.

Everitt, B. S. (1974). *Cluster analysis*. London: E. Arnold.

Gordon, A.D. (1981). *Classification: Methods for the exploratory analysis of multivariate data*. London: Chapman and Hall.

Guha, S., Rastogi, R., & Shim, K. (2000). ROCK: a robust clustering algorithm for categorical attributes. *Information Systems, 25* (5), 345-66.

Guha, S., Rastogi, R., & Shim, K. (2001). CURE: An efficient clustering algorithm for large databases. *Information Systems, 26* (1), 35-58.

Han, J., & Kamber, M. (2001). *Data mining: Concepts and techniques*. Morgan Kaufmann Publishers.

Hand, D.J. (1981). *Discrimination and classification*. New York: J. Wiley.

Hubert, L.J. (1995). *Clustering and classification*. Singapore: World Scientific.

Jain, A.K. (1988). *Algorithms for clustering data*. NJ: Prentice Hall.

McLachlan, G. J, (1988), Mixture models: Inference and applications to clustering". NY: M. Dekker.

Modell, M.E. (1992). *Data analysis, Data modeling, and classification*. New York: McGraw-Hill.

Rencher, A.C. (1995). *Methods of multivariate analysis*. New York: Wiley.

Sholom, M. W. (1991). *Computer systems that learn*. CA: Morgan Kaufmann.

Spath, H.. (1980). *Cluster analysis algorithms for data reduction and classification of objects*. New York: Halsted Press.

Willett, P. (1987). *Similarity and clustering in chemical information systems*. New York: J. Wiley.

APPENDIX 1:
SIMULATION RESULT - DENDROGRAMS FOR SINGLE-LINK OUTPUT VS COMPLETE-LINK OUTPUT

(a) Single Linkage of Hierarchical Clustering

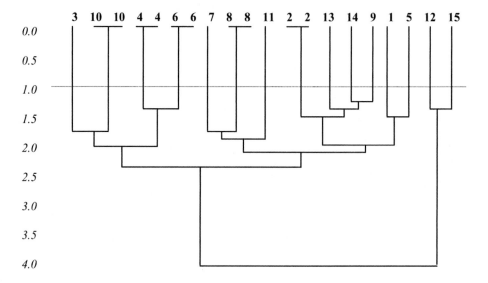

(b) Complete Linkage of Hierarchical Clustering

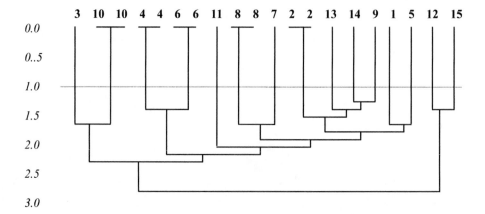

Chapter XIII

Relevance and Micro-Relevance for the Professional as Determinants of IT-Diffusion and IT-Use in Healthcare

Roel W. Schuring
University of Twente, The Netherlands

Ton A. M. Spil
University of Twente, The Netherlands

ABSTRACT

User-adoption of new IT-applications is the proof-of-the-pudding when it comes to IT-success in healthcare. As a consequence, many studies are made of the role of the users in the introduction of new IT in both theory and practice. This paper introduces relevance *and* micro-relevance *as key determinants of IT-diffusion and IT-use, respectively. Relevance is the degree to which the user expects that the IT-system will solve his problems or help to realize his actually relevant goals. Micro-relevance is the degree to which IT-use helps to solve the here-and-now problem of the user in his working process. Central to both concepts is the degree to which goals or problems that IT is related to are actually pressing in nature. Goals and problems that are less pressing do not result in relevance. Goals that are pressing may still not be micro-relevant on the level of executing work. A study amongst 56 general practitioners (GPs) on the introduction of an Electronic Prescription System (EPS) demonstrated the importance of relevance and micro-relevance. To these GPs, time-pressure and communication with pharmacy and hospitals were highest on the agenda. In that light, the innovation of EPS was not relevant. Lack of micro-relevance level obstructed intensive use of EPD by those who had introduced the innovation. As a consequence, those who adopted the EPD only used it sparsely.*

Every improvement is a change but not every change is an improvement. *(Heraclitus)*

INTRODUCTION

The central perspective of our approach is that user-adoption of new IT-applications is the proof-of-the-pudding when it comes to IT-success. This contribution will elaborate on two factors that determine the diffusion and the use of IT: relevance and micro-relevance. We will use an example in the healthcare sector to illustrate how these factors work. Healthcare is changing (Tange, 1997), and information and communication technology is a driving force for many of these changes (Suomi, 2001). At the same time, many authors report cases of failure of ICT innovations (Southon et al., 1999; Gelderman, 1998). The cause of these failures is often searched for in resistance and user participation (Ballantine et al., 2000; Offenbeek & Koopman, 1996). Professionals in healthcare organization get the blame for opposing changes in their working processes. But Pare & Elam (1999) state that they are positive about using information systems to access up-to-date knowledge, for continual medical education, for access to healthcare in rural and remote areas, for the quality of patient care and for the interaction within a healthcare team. Also, Timpka (1989) demonstrated the fundamentally positive attitude of physicians towards the use of IT. So, there is no resistance to change, there is only resistance to bad change (Barlow, 2001). Therefore, the assumption is made that there is more to IS success than resistance alone. While resistance is still important, there is an increasing awareness that there is a wide range of more complex organizational and people-related factors to be taken into consideration (Lorenzi & Riley, 1994). Southon et al. (1999) concludes that the capability to bring IS benefits is severely compromised by our inability to adequately address the problems of the healthcare working process. So, user-perspectives are by no means new to IT-evaluation in general, or in the healthcare sector specifically. Still there is a degree of "magic" in successful IT-introductions, as compared to the "disappointing surprise" after failures. We contribute to the topic by focusing on the relevance factor as an important success factor for ICT implementation in healthcare and probably beyond healthcare. Or as Whyte et al. (1997) sharply observes, "we must understand the attributes of information systems that users perceive to be important."

BACKGROUND

We can use a wide range of sources that discuss user-perspectives in IT-introduction. This section gives a short overview of intriguing literature. The aim is to demonstrate that relevance and micro-relevance are not *the* determinants of user-adoption. Rather, they are important determinants among other factors. One of the ultimate goals of our research project in this field is to propose a model that neatly balances the role of such factors.

First, such factors may be looked for in general literature on change and on the introduction of new technologies. For example, in the balance model of organizational change risks, Leavitt (1965) introduced four domains in which these risks will occur: tasks, structure, technology and people. People, at that time, were not the most important domain. Offenbeek & Koopman (1996) connect people with resistance potential because they can feel that the quality of their working life will be decreased. Mumford (1983) observed that user participation contributes to effective organizational change. Wissema (1987) defines resistance as willingness to change and the difference between results and expectations.

When we focus on IT introduction more specifically, we again see a number of interesting sources. Thong & Yap (1995) discuss the user-satisfaction approach to IT effectiveness. They mention the debatable operationalization, poor theoretical construct and misapplication as critics to the approach. On the basis of their review, they conclude that attitude is the construct that lies at the root of user-satisfaction, and suggest ways to improve operationalization and measurement of attitude. Paré & Elam (1999) studied attitudes, expectations and skills in relation to physicians' acceptance of IT systems. Physicians with formal training on computers were more knowledgeable about informatics concepts and reported that computers would be more beneficial to healthcare, although it is not clear whether the training causes this attitude. Also, it becomes clear that user-priorities regarding IT-innovations vary strongly. The functional uncertainty is often described in information systems literature. It occurs in the task domain of Leavitt. In each situation, the interpretation and the meaning can be different.

Therefore, it is necessary to establish a functional specification with user and providers of the information systems. Henry & Stone (1999) state this to be information quality. Within the healthcare sector, Walley & Davies (2001) conducted a study to the internal barriers to technological IT-advancement in the healthcare sector. The involvement of stakeholders is arguably one of the most distinctive characteristics of IT projects. There are instruments to identify user-needs, but they question whether they are actually used. Van der Pijl (1994) shows that there is more to say about people than just resistance or user participation. Both users and providers of information systems have their own targets, not necessarily going hand-in-hand. A central question is whether the provider intention is the same as the user interpretation (Sperber & Wilson, 1986). We will re-define relevance in the next section. Finally resources, (human, physical and monetary components, Ansoff, 1965) are needed to implement the new information system into the organization. The human resources can both be insufficient in time and in experience (risk of technology). Insufficient material resources (Offenbeek & Koopman, 1996) will have a limiting influence on the other three risk domains.

In this chapter, we will focus on a single determinant to user-adoption of IT in healthcare, i.e., relevance. We keep in mind that, although relevance plays a major role in determining IS success on user-level, it only plays its role within the context of other factors that were briefly mentioned in this section (Schuring & Spil, 2001). It is most important to elaborate the construction of a framework that brings these factors together. Saarinen & Sääksjärvi (1995) point out that different factors act as critical success factors under different circumstances. This will also apply when a framework of success factors is limited to user-related factors. However, in this chapter we will solely concentrate on relevance and the empirical findings in this area.

RELEVANCE AND MICRO-RELEVANCE: DEFINITION

Saracevic (1975) defines relevance is a measure of the effectiveness of a contact between a source and a destination in a communication process. This is a somewhat abstract wording of what we would define as: *"the degree to which the user expects that the IT-system will solve his problems or help to realize his actually relevant goals."* There are three dimensions that are kept implicit in Saracevic' definition that we altered. We use the word "expects," since we want to stress that relevance is a factor that is important in the course of the adoption process, not only in evaluation. Second, instead of effectiveness we use "solve problems and goals." By doing so, we imply that effectiveness has two dimensions: to take away existing negative consequences (problems), and to reward with positive consequences (reach goals). Third, the word *actual* is crucial in our view of relevance. Relevance is not to be confused with the degree to which the user considers outcomes as being positive. The set of outcome-dimensions that someone considers "positive" is larger than the set of outcome-dimensions that are relevant. Imagine a physician, who basically considers IT-outcomes of a computer decision support system, such as assistance in diagnosis, disease prevention, or more appropriate dosing of drugs (Thornett, 2001), as "positive." This does not automatically imply that the IT-adoption is relevant to him. We would say it is only relevant if these dimensions are high on his goal agenda. That is why we use the word actual. Again, this is a more explicit wording of a dimension that is implicitly included where Saracevic' uses the word effectiveness in his definition. The actually relevant goals may be a mix of short-term goals and long-term goals. If, for example, smooth communication with hospitals or pharmacy is his prime actual problem or goal, the user will only consider the IT-innovation as relevant when it actually helps to improve that communication, notwithstanding the fact that he might have a positive attitude towards that innovation as long as the innovation helps to solve other problems or other goals that are on the lower positions in his agenda-ranking. We discovered in our case studies that it is not sufficient for an innovation to effectuate a positive attitude amongst users. The IT-innovation should be relevant.

Micro-relevance is a related concept that can be used to describe a similar phenomenon once the new IT is installed. Micro-relevance is defined as *"the degree to which IT-use helps to solve the here-and-now problem of the user in his working process."* The use of new equipment or new IT-procedures is a conscious activity. In every conscious activity that is goal-oriented to a specific goal, there is a reason why that course of action is being chosen. Similar to what was discussed above on "relevance," not every course of action that a user basically considers as "positive" is "micro-relevant." Again, let's illustrate this with an example. Imagine a patient with virus infection visits a physician. The physician might notice the similarity to a number of other patients he has met that week and decide on diagnosis and treatment fairly quickly. To this doctor, the use of a decision support system to determine diagnosis is not micro-relevant. However, a colleague of his may not feel so confident and thus use the diagnostic support system. We discovered that micro-relevance is a key factor in explaining IT-use in our case studies. *Box 1* gives an overview of relevance as we propose to use it.

Relevance and micro-relevance are notable refinements of the way the role of the user is being discussed in the existing literature. Thornett (2001) implicitly refers to relevance and micro-relevance when he discusses limited adoption and use of DSS by primary physicians where "consultation time is lengthened by their

Box 1: Relevance and micro-relevance

FRAMEWORK OF IT RELEVANCE TO USERS

User Relevance
- Definition: degree to which the user expects the that the IT-system will solve his problems or help to realize his actually relevant goals
- (Co)determines: IT-diffusion
- Generic sub-dimensions
  - Reward:
    1) Positive dimensions, e.g., economic, social or functional improvement, that is high on the actual agenda of the user
    2) Negative dimensions: decrease of discomfort, savings of time or effort
  - Start-up barrier:
    1) low initial cost
    2) immediacy of the reward
- Point of confusion: many things that a user finds positive need not necessarily be relevant

Micro-relevance
- Definition: the degree to which IT-use helps to solve the here-and-now problems of the user in his working process
- (Co)determines: IT-use
- Generic sub-dimensions
  - Absolute value of relevance
  - Degree to which relevance complies with the micro-agenda, that is, the things that are considered most important for the next moment to spend.
  - Start-up barrier on activity level:
    1) low initial cost
    2) immediacy of the reward
- Point of confusion: things that are relevant need not necessarily be micro-relevant

use and there is no appreciable impact on patient satisfaction." It is an example where other outcomes that are basically considered as positive (as mentioned above: better diagnosis, more appropriate dosing of drugs, and other) are overruled by limited relevance and micro-relevance.

Saracevic (1975) provides a historic positioning of relevance. The roots lay in the 1930s and 40s, where the distinction between information and relevant information is made by Bradford (Saracevic, 1975, p. 324). In order to make the distinction between relevant and non-relevant information, he discusses the nature of communication. By doing so, he recognizes that relevance to a subject depends on specific dimensions, for example, the subject's knowledge, representation and values. He discusses a number of (philosophical) approaches to relevance. The elaboration we propose above builds on the radical pragmatism-perspective or, more specifically, Cooper's (1971) utility function: "Relevance is simply a cover term of whatever the user finds to be of value about the system output, whatever its usefulness, its entertainment, or aesthetic value, or anything else." Wilson (1973) adds to this that relevance is situational. Ballantine et al. (1999) put it in the following way: "Depending on the type of task, the information generated by the system may be more or less appropriate, which will affect its success or failure." Saracevic (1975) distinguishes various other approaches to relevance, of which a number focus on the basic source of relevance, such as logical relevance, the nature of interference and the pertinence view of relevance. We are very much aware of the fact that our elaboration of relevance does not, in full, retain the differences between those points of view. It is merely a practical elaboration that we use to predict user-adoption.

The pragmatic perspective of relevance that we choose resembles the notion of "relative advantage," as discussed in the Innovation Diffusion literature by Rogers. Rogers (1983, 1997) reserves a central role for "relative advantage," which is the user's view of "the degree to which an innovation is better than the idea it supersedes." Relative advantage can be economic or social. Rogers adds that, "The nature of the innovation largely determines what specific type of relative advantage is important to adopters, although the characteristics of the potential adopter also affect which dimensions of relative advantage are most important." Based on a review of hundreds of empirical studies, Rogers concludes that relative advantage explains 49% of the rate of adoption of innovations.

It is most notable that the organizational factors are not explicitly included in our user-relevance framework. It should be kept in mind that the user's agenda of problems and goals depends on his role in the society (Barnard, 1938). The influence of the organization on this agenda depends on many aspects, including the involvement with other organizations, on time and on place. As a consequence, our framework reflects the actual impact that organizational goals and preferences have on the user, and thus, on organizational behavior.

Also, other scholars have detailed relevance to levels or factors, for example, Saracevic (1996), Schamber (1994), and Cosijn & Ingwersen (2000). Our distinction between relevance and micro-relevance takes a different starting point, as it distinguishes between the situations where the user is or is not actually working in a process in which he may use the IT system as a major difference.

MULTIPLE CASE STUDY RESULTS
Case Study Method

Our research was set up to both assess the situation regarding the electronic prescription system "EVS" in the Netherlands and the theory that is described above that was set up to provide an instrument that could be used to unravel the diffusion-situation of the prescription system. This resulted in a case-study protocol that covers all the topics that are mentioned in the framework in open-ended questions. In line with the case-study approach by Yin (1984), we discerned different case-situations on the basis of our theoretical framework. Particularly, the network-situation of general practitioners and the degree of adoption of previous ideas served as a basis to make categories of general practitioners. A total of 56 case studies were conducted. Each general practitioner was visited in his/her own working situation and interviewed for over an hour. We had data available on the size of each category, which enabled us to quantify the qualitative data that we gathered.

Empirical Findings

Under the header relevance for the GP, questions were asked about problems or wishes that the GP experienced as important at the moment of asking, during implementation of the Electronic Prescription System. *Figure 1* gives an overview of all the situational relevance factors mentioned. Here we will summarize the results of the main seven:

1. Communication (with pharmacy, with colleagues when visiting each other's patients, with hospital about available capacity and about progress concerning specific patients).

    In more than half of the cases, improvements to communication with colleagues, pharmacists and hospitals were crucial. The EPS system does not deliver these features. Saarinen & Saaksjarvi (1992) measured the improved internal communication and improved inter-organizational communication under the header "impact of the IS on the organization." None of these success factors was satisfied in our cases.

2. Time (these GPs experience a very high time pressure: long working hours, always behind schedule).

    In 55% of the cases, and independently of each other (the term was not mentioned by the interviewee), the GPs stated that there should be a diminishing of the time pressure. Both in the description of the EPS, as well as in international literature, it is made assumable that EPS will not diminish the time of consult (Mitchell & Sullivan, 2001; Thornett, 2001).

3. Money (compensation is considered too low).

    Forty-five percent of the case studies reported that the GP expected a fee in return for going through the trouble of implementing and using EPS. At the moment of interviewing, it was not clear what financial profit the new system would deliver for the GP, although it was expected that the revenues for the government would be substantial by saving on expenses on drugs.

4. Software (is considered user-unfriendly, is old-fashioned, has limited capabilities, requires a lot of effort to maintain).

    In about 20 case studies, lack of trust in the existing software and in the software supplier were mentioned as a barrier for (wanting to) use the new EPS. They said that first things had to change in the GP-IS market and in the GP-IS itself before EPS could be a success.

5. Free Choice (... of treatment after setting the diagnosis. A prescription system should propose the full arrange of available pharmaceutical or non-pharmaceutical treatments and not a restricted pre-selection).

   About the same amount of GPs want to retain freedom of choice for medication of the patient. Although this seems to be a resistance matter, it is also a relevance matter because the EPS does not comprehend new ideas and new treatments, which are already known in the general practice.

6. International Code Primary Care (ICPC) (is said to be difficult to use, although its use is an absolute precondition to the use of the Electronic Prescription System. Also, the coding does not cover all diseases or relevant states the patient can be in. Certain codes have to much detail, other lack detail).

   Although the use of ICPC seems useful to many GPs (in structuring and communicating), the time that it will cost to find the right code and the omissions of some codes will form a barrier for EPS use.

7. Formulary (this is the record of available drugs for every disease. GPs that mention this point want to maintain autonomy to alter this record).

   Twenty percent of the GPs make use of a personal or regional formulary. The EPS makes use of a formulary of the Dutch council for GPs and often does not have the possibility to keep the own formulary when an update of the software is installed.

Finally, once the computer-system was installed, use of the system was mostly sparse. The way of working was relatively complicated and added relatively little value in most patient-doctor contacts.

Figure 1:   Case study results

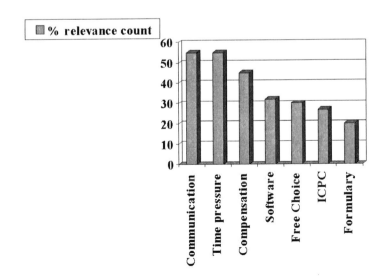

ANALYZED RELEVANCE AND MICRO-RELEVANCE

We analyzed the empirical results of the previous section with the characteristics of relevance and micro-relevance as described in *Box 1*. User relevance tells us more about the adoption of the system and micro-relevance shows improvements on the working process. The relevance of the EPS to general practitioners was, on the average, very low. The economic and social benefits were scarce, as the main problems on the agenda of general practitioners were (1) communication between practitioners, with the hospital and with the pharmacy and (2) time pressure. The EPS did not help to solve these problems. Also, the initial cost was high to many practitioners, as the IT-use in their starting-situation was by far not sufficient to be able to use the EPS system. About 27% of the general practitioners make sufficient professional use of the computer to be able to start right away with the EPS-use. The remainder first would have to further structure their electronic patient records, or would even have to start using the computer professionally at all. The economic benefits of the system are potentially substantial, but they do not appear for the user but for the ministry and for the healthcare insurance companies. The costs involved with updating the system are higher than the benefits. A promise is made on practical support, but not for every practice such service becomes available. The immediacy of the reward is therefore not recognizable. Socially, the new system is more seen as a threat than a benefit. The patient-GP interaction changes, as also noticed for micro-relevance, and this change is not for the good. The quality of the GP service can improve as Sullivan & Mitchell (2001) pointed out. Saving in time and effort is not to be expected, as the same authors point out, which is seen as most wanted by the GP's. This characteristic is most critical in our opinion.

Beside the general relevance of the new system we want to know if the system improves the working process of the user, the micro-relevance. Although GPs say double-checking prescriptions by use of the EPS would be relevant to them, it is more micro-relevant to stay in personal touch with his patient during the visit than to double-check if the intended prescription can be further optimized. Where the barrier to use the ICPC code was already high in general terms, we see that the micro-relevance is really problematic. There is a high start-up barrier to start to search for such coding during the prescription process for one specific patient (In fact, the initial use of any particular code takes learning-time since the codes were not sufficiently clear and accessible. The micro-relevance of that learning is negative, since it will take a lot more time and effort to complete the prescription for that initial patient). This also made the immediacy of the reward within the use process meager. During the study, we discovered that relatively many General Practitioners used the EPS system *after* the consult. We tend to conclude that the micro-relevance after the patients' consult is higher than during the consult. When GPs double-check their prescriptions after the consult, there is generally less time-pressure (as this will only be done for those few patients where the GP feels uncertain). Also, there are few other ways to double-check prescriptions afterwards. This also contributes to the micro-relevance.

CONCLUSIONS

Relevance has long since been a central notion to IT-theory. In our study, we monitored a great number of factors that (co) determine IT diffusion and use in 56 case studies. These cases provided us with enough evidence that, for this particular (electronic prescription) system in this particular (healthcare) branch, relevance and micro-relevance were by far the most important determinant for failure of diffusion and use of the system.

We agree with Wilson (1973) that, "relevance is not a single notion but many." We feel that the distinction between user relevance and micro-relevance follows the more philosophical thoughts of Schutz (1970) when he introduced motivational relevance (course of action to be adopted) and topical relevance (perception of something being problematic).

In terms of our framework new ICT innovations will not be adopted without relevance and micro-relevance to the user.

REFERENCES

Althuis, T. R., & Rikken, S. A. J. J. (2000, April). Electronic support for general practitioners in prescribing Drugs. *Health Information Developments in the Netherlands,* pp. 62-66.

Ballantine, J., Bonner, M., Levy, M., Martin, A., Munro, I., & Powell, P. L. (1998). Developing a 3D Model of IS Successs. In Garrity & Sanders, (eds.) *Information Systems Success Measurement.* Hershey, PA: Idea Group Publishing.

Barnard, C.I. (1938). *The Functions of the Executive.* Cambridge, MA: Harvard University Press.

Barlow, C. (2001). Following and accelerating the design evolution curve in healthcare. *First International Conference on Management and Healthcare and Medical Technology.* Enschede.

Bergeron, B. P., & Bailin, M. T. (1999). Medical Information Technology: a vehicle for change. *International Journal of Healthcare Technology and Management,* 1 (1), 29-45.

Cooper, W.S. (1971). A definition of relevance for information retrieval. *Information Storage and Retrieval, 7* (1), 19-37.

Cosijn, E., & Ingwersen, P. (2000). Dimensions of relevance. *Information Processing and Mangement, 36,* 533-550.

Delaney, B. C., Fitzmaurice, D. A., Riaz, A., & Hobbs, F. D. R. (1999). Can computerized DSS deliver improved quality in primary care? *British Medical Journal, 312,* 1008-1012.

Finley, P.N., & Forghani, M. (1998). A classification of success factors for decision support systems. *Strategic Information Systems, 7,* 53-70.

Garrity, & Sanders. (1999). *Information systems success measurement.* Hershey, PA: Idea Group Publishing.

Gelderman, M. (1998). The relation between user satisfaction, usage of is and performance. *Information & Management, 34,* 11-18.

Henry, J. W., & Stone, R. W. (1999). End user perception of the impacts of computer self-efficacy and outcome expectancy on job performance and patient care when using a medical information system. *IJHTM, Special issue on advances in the management of technology in Healthcare,* 1 (1/2), 103-124.

Lagendijk, P.J.B., Schuring, R. W., & Spil, A. A. M. (2001). *Het Elektronisch Voorschrijf Systeem, van kwaal to medicijn.* Universiteit Twente, Enschede.

Linnarson, R. (1993). Decision support for drug prescription integrated with computer-based patient records in primary care. *Medical Information, 18,* 131-142.

Lorenzi, N. M., & Riley, R. T. (1994). *Organizational aspects of health informatics.* New York: Springer-Verlag.

Mason, R. O. (1978). Measuring information output: A communication systems approach. *Information & Management, 1* (5), 219-234.

Mitchell, E., & Sullivan, F. (2001). A descriptive feast but an evaluative famine: systematic review of published articles on primary care computing during 1980-97. *British Medical Journal, 322,* 279-282.

Mumford, E. (1983). *Designing human systems for new technology.* Manchester Business School.

Offenbeek, M. van & Koopman, P. (1996). Interaction and decision making in project teams. In M.A. West, (ed.), *Handbook of Work Group Psychology.* New York: John Wiley & Sons, Ltd.

Pare, G., & Elam, J. J. (1999). Physicians' acceptance of clinical information systems: an empirical look at attitudes expectations and skills. *International journal of Healthcare Technology and Management, 1* (1), 46-61.

Pijl, P. G. J. van der (1994). Measuring the strategic dimensions of the quality of information. *Journal of Strategic Information Systems, 3* (3), 179-190.

Rogers, E. M. (1983). *Diffusion of innovations.* New York: The Free Press.

Rogers, E. M., & Scott, K. L. (1997). The diffusion of innovations model and outreach from the National Network of Libraries of Medicine to Native American Communities. Retrieved from http://www.nnlm.nlm.nih.gov/pnr/eval/rogers.html

Sperber, D., & Wilson, D. (1986). *RELEVANCE, communication and cognition.* Oxford: Basil Blackwell.

Saarinen, T., & Saaksjarvi. (1992). Process and product success in information system development. *Journal of Strategic Information Systems, 1* (5), 266-277.

Saracevic, T. (1975). Relevance: A review of and framework for the thinking on the notion in information science. *Journal of the American Society for Information Science, 26* (6), 321-343.

Saracevic, T. (1996, October 13-16). *Relevance reconsidered: '96 Proceedings of COLIS 2: Second International Conference on Conceptions of Library and information Science: Integration in Perspective* (pp. 201-218). Copenhagen, Denmark: The Royal School of Librarianship.

Schamber, L. (1994). Relevance and information behavior. *Annual Review of Information Science and Technology, 29,* 3-48

Schuring, R. W., & Spil, T. A. M. (2001). *Relevance as a major driver of Innovation and diffusion of ICT in Healthcare Organizations.* First international conference on management and healthcare and medical technology, Enschede.

Schutz, A. (1970). *Reflections on the problem of relevance.* New Haven, CT: Yale University Press.

Southon, G., Sauer, C., & Dampney, K. (1999). Lessons from a failed IS iniative: Issues for complex organisations. *Medical Informatics, 55,* 33-46.

Spil, T. A. M. (1996). *The effectiveness of strategic information systems planning in professional organizations.* PhD thesis, Enschede.

Sullivan, F., & Mitchell, E. (1995). Has general practitioner computing made a difference to patient care? *British Medical Journal, 311,* 848-852.

Suomi, R. (2001). Streamlining operations in healthcare with ICT. In R. A. Stegwee & T. A. M. Spil, (eds.), *Strategies for Healthcare Information Systems.* Hershey, PA: Idea Group Publishing.

Tange, H. (1997). *Medical narratives in the electronic medical record.* PhD Thesis, Maastricht.

Thornett, A. M. (2001). Computer decision support systems in general practice. *International Journal of Information Management, 21,* 39-47.

Timpka, T. (1989). Introducing hypertext in primary healthcare: A study on feasibility of decision support for practitioners. *Computational Methods and Programs in Biomedicine, 25,* 49-60.

Walley, P. & Davis, C. (2001). Implementation IT in NHS Hospitals: internal barriers to Technological Advancement." Paper presented on the 1st Hospital of the Future Conference, Enschede, The Netherlands.

Whyte, G., Bytheway, A., & Edwards, C. (1997). Understanding user perceptions of IS Success. *Journal of Strategic IS, 6,* 35-68.

Wilson, P. (1973). Situational relevance. *Information Storage and Retrieval, 9* (8), 457-471.

Wissema, J. G. (1987). *Angst om te veranderen? Een mythe!* Assen: Van Gorcum.

Yin, R.K. (1984). *Case study research, design and methods.* London: Sage Publications.

Zviran, M., & Armoni, A. (1999). Integrating hospital information systems: a bottom up approach. *IJHTM, Special issue on advances in the management of technology in Healthcare, 1* (1/2), 168-179.

Chapter XIV

Development of Interactive Web Sites to Enhance Police/Community Relations

Susan A. Baim
Miami University Middletown, USA

ABSTRACT

This chapter discusses research conducted to determine the feasibility of introducing police Web sites and virtual communities as new tools in the move toward community-oriented policing. Using citizen satisfaction surveys designed to evaluate police department performance in three Ohio cities, a profile of future citizen expectations regarding interactions with the police is constructed. Based on differences in the demographics of the cities' populations, probabilities of success in implementing online communications with the police are assigned. A model for establishing a virtual community for the Trenton, Ohio Police is explored in light of the survey results and established community-oriented policing theory.

INTRODUCTION

Imagine the following two scenarios, each of which could easily happen in any one of a thousand different city neighborhoods nationwide.

Scenario 1: After a long day at the office, Mrs. Sally Jones returns home after dark. Approaching her front door, she notices that it is ajar. As she gets closer, a man, covered head to toe in black, bursts from her home and runs past her into the night. Grabbing her cell phone, she dials 911 and reaches the police. Officers are dispatched promptly, but Mrs. Jones is afraid to go inside — in case someone else lurks in the shadows. Yet, she is afraid to stand out in the open where she also feels vulnerable. She steps around the corner of her house to be out of view when, suddenly, she's caught in the bright flashlights of two unfamiliar police officers, guns drawn, as they approach her from the shadows.

Scenario 2: After a long day at the office, Mrs. Sally Jones returns home after dark. Approaching her front door, she notices that it is ajar. Looking just past the door she notices the city police squad car in her driveway. Two officers that she has known for years, Officer Bill George and Sergeant Karen Smith are talking to each other — there are two angry looking men already in the back seat of the squad car. As she approaches the officers, Sgt. Smith calls out, "Hi Mrs. Jones, we were on patrol in the neighborhood and saw one of these characters around the corner. Things didn't add up and he eventually led us to his partner who was already working on your front door. These guys will never learn — we know everybody in the neighborhood and it's real easy to see who's out of place."

These scenarios illustrate the difference between the traditional police practice of call-based policing and the more modern approach known as community-oriented policing. In the first scenario, the officers were just doing their job, as impersonal as it may sound. Unfamiliar with the residents of the neighborhood, they were forced to treat everyone as a suspect until proven otherwise. Mrs. Jones not only faced a burglary that night but also probably had the scare of her life looking down the barrels of two guns pointed in her direction. Scenario 2 illustrates true community-oriented policing. The two officers on patrol recognized that someone looked out of place and did a little investigating on their own — not waiting for a call. By the time Mrs. Jones arrived home, the situation was under control.

These idealized scenarios were created for illustrative purposes only, but they do indicate the type of change in policing philosophy that is working its way through police departments across the country. Community-oriented policing places officer and the citizens that they protect into much closer contact on a routine basis. Both sides become much more familiar with each other before problems occur and can work together more effectively when the need arises. Implemented correctly, community-oriented policing can reduce stress for the officers and citizens alike, plus allow the officers to cover more ground in terms of handling the problems that are of greatest concern to the neighborhoods where they work.

The primary focus of this chapter is to describe a mechanism for increasing police/community relations that works in concert with the community-oriented policing programs that a department may currently have in progress. Based on a study of the relationships between three Southwestern Ohio city police departments and their communities, it is proposed that online virtual communities, preferably hosted at city government or police department Web sites, would provide a unique forum for police and citizens to stay in touch with each other, to express and discuss mutual concerns and to implement programs of benefit to the communities. Based on the data collected from surveys conducted in each city, a model for the design of a highly interactive police Web site is proposed. The probability of using the Web site in each unique city environment to create a virtual community for citizens and police officers is assessed.

BACKGROUND
Brief Overview of Community-Oriented Policing

Effective community-oriented policing programs are multifaceted. They rely on a mindset change on the part of the police officers, but also on the part of the citizens in the neighborhood. Community-oriented policing also requires a change in technology, as police officers may need to work on more sophisticated crime prevention techniques. Most importantly, however, community-oriented policing requires a change in the communications patterns that the police officers use with the citizens in their communities. This innovative policing technique is based on clear and open lines of communication with all neighborhood residents. The police officer must be able to sense when something just isn't right, and that requires solid, ongoing communications with residents. Residents need better communications, too. They will not be able to assist the police in keeping the neighborhood safe if they lack information on what has been happening down the block or on the other side of town. Working behind the scenes, but still every bit as critical to the success of these programs, is a solid database and knowledge management effort designed to supply all parties with the information that they require.

It is no longer sufficient for police officers across the country to cruise the streets in squad cars and apprehend criminals when called. Conscious of the number of high technology tools now available and a general trend on the United States toward maximizing satisfaction with all products and services, citizens in small and large cities alike are requiring more from their police departments. In a recent article for a sales and marketing journal, Betsy Cummings (2001) points out that police departments are essentially being asked to enroll in Marketing 101 in order to better sell their services to their constituencies. Cummings quotes officials in the New York Police Department as saying that determining what programs will "sell' to city residents and improve the image of the department is no different than a business looking at its marketing strategy to determine what products and services should be on the shelf. Increasingly, one of those products offered by police departments is a city-personalized version of community-oriented policing.

In a somewhat surprising discovery, the widespread presence of 911 services across the country has been linked to a need for more community-oriented policing approaches. As observed by Fred Siegel (1999), the computerized call tracking of 911 calls to police, and the resulting tendency of departments to track their success based on the speed of responding to those 911 calls caused many departments to lose focus on non-emergency police work over time. The end result was actually a greater disconnect for many city residents who did not experience emergencies but had to deal with mundane issues such as minor thefts, vandalism, etc. These crimes, known as "broken window" crimes in New York City, for example, were largely ignored in favor of stressing a department's statistics in handling/clearing the 911 calls coming in each day. Community-oriented policing in many regards takes an opposite view of success — stressing instead the need to work with city residents to eliminate the more minor "broken window" crimes so that more serious offenses have no room to take root. Whether or not Siegel's analysis is correct, the trend back toward community-oriented policing indicates that residents expect the minor crimes to be dealt with as efficiently as the major emergencies. This situation represents a clear need for an organizational culture shift for many police departments — a shift that more and more departments are prepared to make.

Continuing an examination of newer technologies and their positive or negative effects on the effectiveness of police, many technologies are universally believed to help officers stay in closer contact with the people that they protect and serve. Perhaps the best-known example is the trend to equip squad cars with personal computers or mobile computer terminals so that officers may handle more policing duties without needing to return to the station. Christina Couret (1999) terms the addition of computers to squad cars as a "silent partnership of police officers and technology" that dramatically increases the officers' effectiveness. These Internet-based technologies allow officers to complete reports online while in the field. The officers remain visible within the community and able to interact with residents for a higher percentage of their shift hours. Data transmission is also faster, more accurate and more confidential than speaking over a radio channel with a dispatcher who may actually be handling a more distracting workload than is the officer in the field (Greenemeier, 2002). Reading Greenemeier's account of recent technology additions to squad cars in Sacramento, California, it is clear that officers are rapidly moving to a state of working in virtual offices that roll throughout their communities.

Police departments that have taken advantage of the latest available technologies in terms of communications gear, weaponry, vehicles and other law enforcement equipment are generally well-versed in handling major crimes and emergency situations within their communities. What may not immediately be obvious is that these same departments are also positioned well to move forward with community-oriented policing efforts. Community-oriented policing takes time — time to sit down with residents to understand their concerns and to draw up action plans that could help improve the quality of life in community neighborhoods. Only those departments that are experienced and efficient at handling the major crimes committed within their jurisdictions are likely to have the time, and also the patience, that it takes to pursue a significant community-oriented policing agenda. According to Lumb (1999), however, shifts toward community oriented policing, even under the most ideal circumstances, will be temporary unless the department's overall leadership strategy changes along with the changes in available technologies. Specific training in how to interact with the citizenry in a more proactive, informational way is needed from the Chief of Police's office right down to the individual officer on the beat.

Specific Examples of Community-Oriented Policing

Although the concept of community-oriented policing has been in existence since the 1960s, little formal evidence of studies designed to ease its implementation or enhance its effectiveness through customer satisfaction measurements are observed in the literature prior to the early- to mid-1990s. In one of the earliest published studies, officers of the Merriam Police Department (a suburb of Kansas City, Missouri) developed a brief survey questionnaire that they used in conjunction with personal visits to meet with business owners in the community (Sissom, 1996). The officers' goal was to build a better working relationship with community business leaders across a broad spectrum of the city's economic base.

Prior to implementing the project, police and community leaders agreed that officers knew a small percentage of the business owners well, but were virtually unconnected from the remainder within the community. The business owners that were known to the officers exhibited either or both of two characteristics. First, these business owners may have been repeat crime victims, either due to running a relatively high-risk business or due to their location within a high-crime region of the city. Second, these business owners may have owned businesses that would typically be frequented by the officers for personal reasons, such as meal breaks while on patrol, or similar reasons. In total, the percentage of business owners that the officers knew well was lower than what the department felt was necessary to gauge the true needs of the community (Sissom, 1996).

Results of the Merriam survey project were reviewed personally by the police chief and used to establish a training program to enhance officers' understanding of community-oriented policing principles. Regular contacts with all businesses were instituted as part of the officers' daily patrol duties, and a mechanism was set up to track these contacts on an ongoing basis. The survey process was revised and updated to be used on a recurring basis to give an indication of how the operational changes were affecting community/police relations (Sissom, 1996).

The Merriam study was relatively unique because it focused exclusively on businesses and business owners as partners for improving community-oriented policing. No mention of individual citizens is made in the report, leaving the reader to ponder how the non-business concerns of community residents were to be factored into any strategies for improving overall community relations. More common is a fully integrated approach that focuses attention on a wide sampling of citizens within the community, some of whom may own businesses and some of whom may live but not work in the community.

Newer studies, such as those described by Hugh Culbertson (2000), focus on identifying the issues that tend to divide police officers from their communities and prevent the successful implementation of community-oriented policing initiatives. Culbertson notes a variety of turning points in community/police relations, including the 1995 criminal trial of O. J. Simpson and the early 1990s videotaped beating of Rodney King. He stresses that the failure of police departments to understand and address the divisive issues in their communities can thwart any efforts to implement change in a department's operating procedures.

Unfortunately, police officers are customarily trained in a manner that at best is indifferent to the development of positive community relations and at worst is likely to run counter-current to that goal (Culbertson, 2000). Examples include a training focus on catching criminals and suppressing violence through forceful, often paramilitary, means and the use of a "code of silence" that serves to defend other officers even in times of clear mistakes made in the line of duty (Culbertson, 2000, p. 16). No number of positive initiatives made to build community relationships can circumvent the images left in the eyes of the public when a police department appears to be preprogrammed to suppress criminal acts in a manner that is not supported by the community at large.

Implementing the fundamental change in police operating procedures that is needed to support community-oriented policing in more than a token sense thus becomes a delicate balancing act. Officers must be prepared for any and all conceivable threats to the safety and security of their community, while keeping the obvious trappings of such preparation out of sight as much as possible. On the other hand, officers must treat citizens and business owners as if they are all part of the same team, or partnership, while remaining vigilant for any signs of criminal activity that could undermine the quality of life within the community (Vincent, 1999; Woods, 1999). This "dual role" is difficult to achieve in practice and requires the utmost in careful planning to execute well, yet it exemplifies the true essence of a modern community-oriented police force.

The planning required to implement an effective community-oriented policing approach exposes officers to the inner-workings of the neighborhoods that they protect and serve. Many problems that these officers will be asked to solve are not exclusively within the sphere of influence of the police. As such, the thought processes used and action plans derived by the officers may appear to be comparatively "un-police-like" as compared to traditional crime-fighting activities. In an intriguing and very recent study, William Rohe, Richard Adams & Thomas Arcury (2001) investigated many of the community-oriented policing efforts underway in two North Carolina cities, Asheville and Greensboro. In each case, these researchers identified common themes between the approaches in use by the police and those in use by the cities' planning commissions. The analogy makes sense from the point of view that the police officers are problem solvers within the community, as are the communities' city planners. Although the two city government functions may seem to be very much separate, collaboration between the departments is suggested as a means of increasing the effectiveness of community-oriented policing efforts. The authors' rationale focuses on the tool kit carried by the city planners. Planners are known for their skills in community problem identification, collecting and working with large volumes of data and developing alternative strategies for addressing situations. These are precisely the skills that police departments are trying to build in their officers as they move toward more routine interaction with the general public. Community-oriented policing also looks at building long-term relationships, as opposed to exclusively solving immediate problems. Again, according to Rohe, Adams & Arcury (2001), this approach is very common in city planning departments, where the designs of city infrastructures, such as utilities and roadways, will be in use over very long periods of time. These authors use the term "cross-training" to explain how city planners can help police departments that are just getting started with new community-oriented approaches. Police officers new to the community-oriented approach learn how to move from an action-oriented, immediate problem-solving mode to one of putting solutions in place for the good of the community — solutions that will stand the tests of time.

Whether or not a partnership with city planners is the correct approach to take for all community-oriented policing efforts, the idea of police departments partnering with other city agencies to address issues of importance to the community makes good common sense. Shared knowledge of a city, its residents and its problems can help officers increase their effectiveness at the individual neighborhood level where community-oriented policing is most effective. Citizens concurrently are finding that they can no longer rely on local newspaper accounts or the nightly news to keep them informed of what is going on within their communities. Partnering with the police in an effort to reduce crime and improve the quality of life continues to increase as a viable proposition in many communities. As any and all better forms of communication between the officers on the street and the citizens that they protect are put in, the end result should be to help alleviate these concerns and increase the effectiveness and the efficiency of the policing process.

While the majority of community-oriented approaches to police services originate within the departments themselves, there are external driving forces (such as the aforementioned interactions with city planners) that contribute to the development of these programs and must be viewed in a larger context. For example, the role of city governments as a whole in overseeing the actions of police departments in virtually all communities cannot be ignored. Key findings of a recent study on reinventing city governments include the need to expose all departments under the supervision of the city manager, including the police, to periodic review by outside, third party evaluators. Beyond a general review, specific customer satisfaction studies are recommended for any department that interfaces directly with the public — again including the city's police department (Kearney, Feldman & Scavo, 2000). The results of carefully-executed surveys are suggested as important evaluative tools for city managers to use not only in assessing the resource needs of police departments, but also in monitoring whether or not the departments are operating in a manner that is consistent with community expectations.

City managers, mayors, and other government officials who may be in a position to oversee police departments are more likely to use the results of customer satisfaction studies as part of an ongoing planning process than they are to originate the placement of the studies in the first place. One approach popular in city governments today, for example, uses what is termed the "whole system approach" for including multiple stakeholders within a community in the planning and development process for all city services (Oleari, 2000). When using this approach, a city manager will involve the department under study, professional city planners, politicians and members of the public at large. The goal is to develop a mechanism of sustainable change that will allow the city department (in this case, the police) to move forward in implementing long-term goals that are consistent with community needs at the present time and in the future (Oleari, 2000). In contrast to more conventional planning approaches, in which a draft plan is presented in a public forum for scrutiny and comment, the "whole system approach" places sufficient citizen representation on the planning committee itself to eliminate the need for broad public scrutiny at a later date. The public is again invited to participate when the plan is rolled out, often by monitoring the progress of "action teams" that are charged with implementing the proposed change (Oleari, 2000).

In concluding this brief overview of the forces driving community-oriented policing approaches, it is essential to note that not all parties view the new "shared responsibilities" model of protecting the community as being a positive change. John Worrall & Ricky Gutierrez, for example, observe that empowering employees at various levels, and in various city agencies, to work together in solving problems that are traditionally within the jurisdiction of the police can lead to confusing issues of liability should anything go wrong (Worrall & Gutierrez, 1999). Community-oriented policing efforts tend to increase the discretionary powers of individual officers (and others who may be supporting them) as they move forward with new initiatives. As the clear line of command and control over all possible situations transfers from the police administration and its hierarchy to the individual "cop on the beat" it may be necessary to re-evaluate how cities view their responsibilities to protect and serve their citizens. These authors do not advocate eliminating community-oriented policing by any means. Rather, they take the position that this transfer of authority to individuals lower in the organization, combined with the notion of shared responsibility across multiple city departments, may require different training for individual officers than what was traditionally required in a call-oriented, highly structured police department.

RESEARCH IN SUPPORT OF COMMUNITY-ORIENTED POLICING

Surveys Conducted in Southwestern Ohio

The primary research presented in this chapter was originally conducted to assess city residents' satisfaction with four separate governmental agencies in three Southwestern Ohio communities. *Table 1* lists the studies conducted and their specific purposes.

Table 1: Locations and original purposes of studies conducted

City	Agency	Study Type	Date Conducted
Middletown, Ohio	Police Dept.	Customer Satisfaction	Spring, 2000
Middletown, Ohio	Water Services	Customer Satisfaction	Spring, 2001
Oxford, Ohio	Police Dept.	Customer Satisfaction	Spring, 2001
Trenton, Ohio	Police Dept.	Customer Satisfaction	Spring, 2001

Each of the four surveys was conducted using a mail questionnaire format. Questionnaires were developed jointly with the Chiefs of Police and other high-ranking police officials or with individuals at the Division Director level in the case of the Middletown Water Services Division. Input from the Oxford Citizens' Advisory Board was also used in formulating the questionnaire employed in that city.

All four surveys focused on issues of general concern to the residents of the communities, with special emphasis on the quality of the services provided by the local police or water departments. The questionnaire designs included a number of quantitative ranking questions to provide the best possible statistical assessment of the agencies' performances along with a selection of qualitative questions designed to broaden or "flesh out" the understanding of the issues revealed. Each survey also included a generous selection of demographics questions in order to look for differences of opinion across different age, income, neighborhood or other differentiators. With the exception of the earliest study conducted (that of the Middletown, Ohio Police Department), all surveys also included a selection of questions designed to evaluate respondents' access to and use of the Internet. Had that information been collected in the Middletown Police Department survey, it would not have been necessary to include the Middletown Water Services Division survey in the present analysis. Fortunately, the number of surveys sent out and the distribution of the surveys across the city of Middletown was the same for each of the two city agency surveys. Although not a perfect match, in that a year had elapsed between the police and water surveys, it is not unreasonable to combine the Internet usage data from the water survey with the other data from the police survey when analyzing citizens' opinions in the City of Middletown. The Oxford and Trenton data sets are "cleaner," in that all questions were asked at one time.

The sample size for each survey was approximately 2,000 city residents. Although the surveys are similar in terms of number and scope of questions, they are not identical. The Trenton Police Department survey and the Middletown Police Department survey were the simplest of the group. The Middletown Water Services Department survey was more complex, while the Oxford Police Department survey touched on the greatest number of issues.

Data Analysis and Presentation

All survey respondents returned their completed questionnaires to Miami University, Middletown, where the quantitative and qualitative data analyses were handled by the author and a small group of undergraduate Marketing students. This same team prepared the final reports for the clients. All quantitative data analysis was performed using SumQuest survey software, a package that allows the rapid entry and analysis of multiple questionnaires plus statistical analysis and graphical presentation of results.

Investigation of Internet Usage Trends and Potential Interest in Police Web Sites

The original research conducted for each client included a brief assessment of the Internet usage data collected, but in no case did it explore the possibilities of encouraging the use of police department Web sites to drive virtual communities for community-oriented policing. For the purpose of investigating this potential link, the data concerned with Internet usage were re-examined and compared across all three cities. Trends observed, with the possible implications for Web site usage and virtual communities, are discussed here.

RESULTS AND DISCUSSION

Current Web Site Activity

Of the three cities studied for this report, two have well-developed police department Web sites while the third has begun to construct a Web site as a direct result of the data collected in the present research. The most sophisticated current site is that of Middletown, Ohio, where the Chief of Police is Bill Becker. Chief Becker and his staff have developed a multi-functional Web site that gives a well-rounded view of the department, including the various sub-branches under the Chief and many helpful tips for citizens. Although there is no virtual community operating in conjunction with the Middletown PD site, the site is welcoming to visitors and could likely be adapted to provide a community service of this type without major overhauls.

The city of Oxford, Ohio, also has a police department Web page that is easily accessed from the main City of Oxford government page. The Chief of Police at Oxford is currently Steve Schwein who, unlike long-time Chief Becker in Middletown, has held his position for only a few years. Oxford's site is much simpler that Middletown's, although it, too, strives to provide a welcoming presence for visitors. At the Web site, there are some relevant statistics regarding how Oxford's department stacks up versus others in the local area and some links to career information and the department's vision and mission materials. There is relatively little information on the department itself, or on how citizens might better interact with the police, again demonstrating no obvious link to a virtual community.

The City of Trenton, Ohio, is currently building a police department Web site, beginning with contact numbers and self-generated profiles of the department's officers. The Chief of Police at Trenton is Rodney Hale, who has held his position for less than one year. Trenton's city government Web site in general is less sophisticated than those of the other two cities and is more designed to expose browsers to what the city has to offer, rather than to the inner workings of the various city departments. Nevertheless, the Trenton site is well-designed and could easily be configured to offer interactive capabilities with the police or other departments. (As used in this context, the term "interactive" is meant to convey the idea of a Web site that offers visitors the opportunity to offer input to something seen on the site and/or request information from the site rather than simply to view the site in a static mode.) Adaptation of such a web site to a virtual community would likely be relatively straightforward.

Data collected from all three Ohio cities showed a widespread range of Internet-readiness among the citizens. City of Middletown residents only demonstrated a 40.1% connectivity rate, while City of Oxford residents were much more likely to be connected with a rate of 81.4% among those residents surveyed. City of Trenton residents fell in between with 61.7% connected to the Internet.

Regardless of the percentage of a city's residents that are connected to the Internet, it is clear that those residents will not demonstrate an interest in the city government's Web site unless it offers something specifically of interest. For example, in an unrelated question, City of Middletown residents were asked to evaluate the likelihood that they would be willing to pay bills over the Internet — such as the monthly water and sewer bills that each homeowner and many renters receive. A very low percentage, on the order of seven percent, indicated that they would even consider using the Internet for paying their utility bills. While this may seem disappointing to many that tout the use of the Internet for conducting routine business, it is nevertheless indicative of the sentiment of Middletown residents. Oxford residents, despite their very high connectivity rate, do not frequently visit either the city government site (28.0% of those with Internet access) or the police site (26.1% of those accessing the overall government Web site).

Developing a Web site that is inviting to residents because it contains information that they are seeking, or because it allows them to conduct the type of business that they want to conduct, would be predicted to increase the probability of success. In the Trenton survey, additional questions were added to determine what features residents already made use of on their city government Web site and what features would be most desired if a specific police department Web site were to be implemented. Results obtained on these two questions are shown in *Figures 1* and *2*.

The results obtained from the Trenton survey are somewhat surprising, given the low level of interest in police Web sites at Middletown and Oxford. Digging deeper into the demographic data of the three cities provides a plausible

Figure 1: City of Trenton data — Purpose for accessing city government Web site

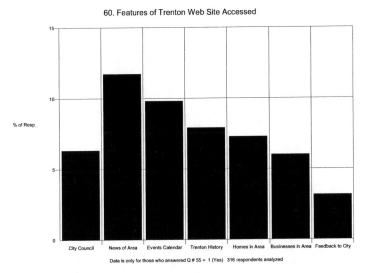

Percentages
City Council - 6.3%, News - 11.7%, Events - 9.8%, History - 7.9%,
Homes - 7.3%, Businesses - 6.0%, Feedback - 3.2%

Figure 2: City of Trenton data — Features desired in a Trenton PD Web site

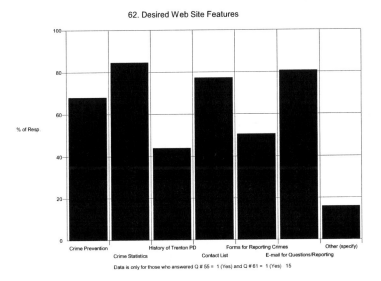

Percentages
Crime Prevention - 68.0%, Crime Statistics - 84.7%, History of PD - 44.0%,
Contact List - 77.3%, Forms to Report Crime - 50.7%,
E-mail for Reporting Crime - 80.7%, Other - 16.0%

Table 2: Overall qualitative assessment of demographic data, all three cities

	Middletown	Oxford	Trenton
Age of Residents	Oldest	Close to Middletown	Younger
Internet Access	Lowest	Highest	Middle
Length of Residency	Very Long	Very Long	Relatively Short
Explanation	Low Internet access rate and set police expectations make Web site use unlikely.	High Internet access rate (college town), but older population accustomed to police services a certain way.	Medium Internet access rate but younger, mobile population willing to try new approaches.

explanation. *Table 2* provides an assessment of each city, based on an overall analysis of the demographic data.

FUTURE TRENDS
Future Police Web Site Usage

From an examination of the research data collected in each of the three cities, it is likely that the City of Trenton may be the best candidate for the development of a new, interactive police Web site. If successful, this site could lead to the roll out of an online virtual community for the police department and local citizens to use as an information resource and mode of communication. With Trenton's acceptable Internet connection rate and the younger, more mobile population living in that city, it is plausible that receptivity to new forms of community-oriented policing may be good or better. Although a discussion of other data obtained from the Trenton survey is beyond the scope of this chapter, there are additional attributes expressed by city residents that make them seem less set in their ways than the residents of Middletown and Oxford.

It is not surprising that Middletown looks like an unlikely candidate for the development of an interactive police Web site and virtual community. Middletown residents have comparatively little familiarity with the Internet and seem relatively set in their ways of doing business. Additionally, they have enjoyed a very well respected, stable police department under the leadership of Chief Becker for a number of years. The impetus for change simply is not evident.

It is surprising, however, to conclude that there would be a relatively low probability of success for the City of Oxford. College communities tend to be more vocal in debating issues and raising concerns than do many other cities of smaller size, and one might predict that this could lead to a very high usage of a virtual community associated with the police department. Such communities may also be more liberal in their politics, but the effect of this parameter on the desirability of an interactive police department Web site is not under study at the present time. Additionally, the survey in Oxford, as conducted, surveyed predominantly permanent residents of the city as opposed to students on campus. The older residents of the surrounding city, despite claiming to have a very high rate of Internet access, did not demonstrate a high interest in city government Web sites and thus may be difficult to convince to try something new.

Creating an Interactive Web Site and Virtual Community

Considering the data obtained from the surveys of Middletown, Oxford and Trenton, Ohio, it is clear that an information resources management professional attempting to set up and operate an interactive police Web site could face a challenging road ahead. Even before work on an actual Web site begins, the developer and/or host must determine three things. According to an interview with Howard Rheingold, as reported by Rodney Moore, every developer must know how the site will be marketed, what the developer wants to get from the site in return for visits by potential members and what technologies will be required in order for the site to function properly (Moore, 2001). Failure to define each of these parameters at the outset will, in the best of cases, seriously slow down development efforts. In the worst of cases, it could prevent the site from gaining acceptance at all, with little to no traffic.

As noted by John Hagel & Arthur Armstrong in *Net Gain: Expanding Markets Through Virtual Communities*, there is "nothing more uninviting to passing Web traffic than a community without members" (1997, p. 134). This is the Internet equivalent of the old adage about giving a party and having no one come. Yet, this appears to be exactly what could happen if one were to begin building a new police Web site for either Middletown or Oxford. There is limited usage of the existing sites, but certainly not enough to be able to predict immediate success of any new launching. Trenton is a different story. With the right publicity, a new police Web site could get off the ground relatively quickly. Trenton residents were not bashful about indicating the types of information that they are seeking and this would give the site developer an excellent place to start.

Virtual communities take on a variety of forms, but it is likely that one of use to a police department would place a premium on running lively discussion forums on topics of community interest. A helpful guide for those who may be just starting to post messages in a discussion forum is presented by Rachel Gordon

(2000). Gordon lists many hints for success, but she also observes one feature of discussion forums that may be of critical importance to the police. One of her examples explores the frustration that many people feel when they cannot get a straight answer out of a technical help line. When these people turn to a discussion forum, it is often true that they can find someone who has had the same exact problem that they are now experiencing. Answers usually come forward in layman's terms and the value of the discussion forum is confirmed. For the police, such interactions can be an invaluable check on their credibility within the community. Officers providing information to a forum are likely to receive corrections and highly potent feedback on anything that seems unusual to the readership. Often cloaked under an amusing pen name, anonymous readers would be predicted to challenge the police when necessary. Police officers known for honest, straightforward interactions within the virtual community would help build the department's reputation.

There has been a significant discussion in the literature regarding the future of virtual or online communities. A number of authors prefer to think that virtual communities are beginning to take a back seat to B2B interactions and will soon lose favor as being unprofitable (Schwartz, 2000; Weir, 2000; Rheingold, 1999). Other authors argue that remaining profitable, or reaching profitability, is not necessarily the ultimate goal for all communities (Brewer, 2000; Wood, 2000). The position taken by the latter authors states that interactions between key groups of people though virtual communities are a desirable goal to aid in the transfer of critical information and the general upgrading of skills within a special interest or professional group. Such efforts do not necessarily generate a profit for an online merchant and thus may be overlooked by many Internet specialists. Yet, this is exactly the type of interaction that may be most desirable for police departments entering the world of virtual communities. If Web sites can be hosted and maintained along with other city government Web sites there will not normally be a burdensome cost involved. Community members, including the police officers, should be able to interact for the good of the community under this type of scenario — to attempt to write off virtual communities such as this because of a lack of traditional profits is to miss the point of their existence.

It is likely that the trend toward community-oriented policing will continue and even be enhanced in future years due to continual improvements in technology that allow police departments to gather better data on what is expected of them by their constituencies. Traditional mail surveys, online survey questionnaires and Web site usage statistics can all contribute significant pieces of information that will allow police departments to align themselves with community needs and wants. At the same time, improvements in technology that make it easier for police officers to transmit and receive critical information while on patrol will make it easier for officers to spend the personal time necessary to get to know the citizens that they protect and serve. The common theme throughout is one of knowing what raw data and interpreted information is needed — and designing approaches to gather it in a timely manner. Police-sponsored virtual communities can be a productive link in this information chain.

CONCLUSIONS

The use of interactive Web sites and virtual communities should be capable of assisting police departments as they move forward with community-oriented policing initiatives. The opportunity to use the technologies of the Internet to provide an alternative means of interacting with community citizens on an informal basis should not be dismissed lightly. The price of entry appears to be to generate Web site content that potential virtual community members will feel is worthwhile, and then to engage these individuals in discussion groups and other site features that will keep returning on a regular basis.

The information generated from the city surveys conducted in Middletown, Oxford and Trenton, Ohio, proved extremely enlightening about the pros and cons of attempting to start up a virtual community concerned with local police work. While it would be easy to say that such an effort would only be worthwhile in Trenton, that answer may be too simplistic. It is possible that the right mix of offerings and ease of access could generate sufficient interest in either of the other two cities to warrant pursuing a Web site at some point in time.

Generalizing these conclusions, it is clear that much work remains to be done to optimize the effective use of Internet technologies as information gathering mechanisms for police departments. With much of today's focus centered around technologies that enhance police voice and data communications rather than interactions with the citizenry, progress in this latter area may not always be top of mind for resource-limited police departments. Nevertheless, efforts to engage citizens through police-sponsored virtual communities could prove to be a significant step forward in improving community-oriented policing programs.

REFERENCES

Brewer, C. (2000, October). Community is the fly paper of your site. *Computer User, 18* (12), 49.

Couret, C. (1999, August). Police and technology. *The American City & County, 114* (9), 31-32+.

Culbertson, H. M. (2000, Spring). A key step in police-community relations: identifying the divisive issues. *Public Relations Quarterly, 45* (1), 13-17.

Cummings, B. (2001, April). NYPD meets marketing 101. *Sales and Marketing Management, 153* (4), 14.

Gordon, R. S. (2000, January/February). Online discussion forums. *Link-up, 17* (1).

Greenemeier, L. (2002, April). Sacramento cops take e-tools on the beat. *Information Week, 886,* 60.

Hagel, J., III., & Armstrong, A. G. (1997). *Net Gain.* Boston, Massachusetts: HBR Press.

Kearney, R. C., Feldman, B. M., & Scavo, C. P. F. (2000, November). Reinventing government: city manager attitudes and actions. *Public Administration Review, 60* (6), [24 pages].

Lumb, R. C. (1999). Understanding police organizational transition to community policing. Carolinas Institute for Community Policing. Retrieved from http://www.cicp.org/article3.htm.

Moore, R. (2001, April 2). Focus on virtual communities. *B to B, 86* (7), 14.

Oleari, K. (2000, December). Making your job easier: using whole system approaches to involve the community in sustainable planning and development. *Public Management, 82* (12), 4-12.

Rheingold, H. (1999, Fall). Virtual community; another metaphor. *Whole Earth, 98,* 18.

Rohe, W. M., Adams, R. E., & Arcury, T. A. (2001, Winter). Community policing and planning. *Journal of the American Planning Association, 67* (1), 78-90.

Schwartz, M. (2000, April 10). Do communities pay? *Computerworld,* p. 50.

Siegel, F. (1999, Winter). Two tales of policing. *Public Interest, 134,* 117-121.

Sissom, K. (1996, December). Community-oriented policing means business. *FBI Law Enforcement Bulletin, 65* (12), 10-14.

Vincent, E. (1999, Fall). How citizens' voices are heard in Jacksonville. *Sheriff Times, 1* (10), [3 pages].

Weir, J. (2000, August 24). Investing care in the community. *New Media Age,* p. 11.

Wood, J. M. (2000, August). The virtues of our virtual community. *Instructor, 110* (1), 80.

Woods, D. D., Jr. (1999, Fall). Supervising officers in the community policing age. *Sheriff Times, 1* (10), [3 pages].

Worrall, J. L., & Gutierrez, R. S. (1999, Spring). Potential consequences of community-oriented policing for civil liability: Is there a dark side to employee empowerment? *Review of Public Personnel Administration, 19* (2), 61-70.

About the Authors

Gerald Grant is an assistant professor of Information Systems at the Eric Sprott School of Business, Carleton University in Ottawa, Canada. He is a coordinator of the Information Systems Area and serves as chair of the Enterprise Systems/e-Business Committee in the school. He previously taught at McGill University, Montreal, Canada, and in the Department of Computer Science and Information Systems at Brunel University, Uxbridge, UK. He also served as vice-principal for Financial Administration at Solusi University, Bulawayo, Zimbabwe. Dr. Grant obtained his Ph.D. in Information Systems from the London School of Economics and Political Science, University of London, UK. He has consulted for the Commonwealth Secretariat in the UK and the COMNET-IT Foundation in Malta on projects related to e-business and e-government strategies, institutional networking and IT capability building, national and sectoral IT strategies. He served as a program coordinator for the Commonwealth-sponsored "Regional Initiative for Informatics Strategies." He serves on the advisory board of the Ottawa Manufacturers Network. He is editor of the book, *Managing Telecommunications and Networking Technologies in the 21st Century: Issues and Trends*, published in March 2001 by Idea Group Publishing.

* * * * *

I. Androwich is a professor of Community and Administrative Nursing at the Marcella Niehoff School of Nursing, Loyola University, Chicago, USA. She has an A.D. from Morton College, a B.S.N. Magna Cum Laud from Loyola, a M.S. in Public Health Nursing from the University of Illinois and a Ph.D. in Public Health from the University of Illinois. She is a fellow in the American Academy of Nursing.

Susan A. Baim is an assistant professor of Business Technology (BTE) on the Miami University, Middletown campus, USA. She joined the faculty in August 1999, teaching Marketing, Internet Marketing, Economics, Online Economics, Finance and Management courses in the University's two-year BTE program. She earned her MBA in Marketing Management from the University of St. Thomas in Minneapolis/St. Paul, Minnesota in 1998, and is currently studying for her Ph.D. in E-Business through Capella University, also in Minneapolis. She was named a Service Learning Ambassador at Miami University in 2000. She has a strong interest in distance education programs and how they may be applied to two-year academic programs. She and her students in the BTE program are also known for their customer satisfaction survey work for police departments and other governmental agencies in Southwestern Ohio.

Joachim Berlak finished his Master of Science in Mechanical Engineering from the Technische Universtitaet Muenchen, Germany, in 1999. He was the recipient of the first price for his master thesis on supply chain management by the German Gesellschaft fuer Produktionsmanagement (GfPM) in 2000. In the same year, he became a research assistant at the Institute for Machine Tools and Industrial Management (*iwb*) and manager of the research project CHANGESYS from the Bavarian Network for Software Engineering (FORSOFT). He has published papers at several conferences, like the OESSEO2001, OOPLSA2001, IRMA2002, ICSTM2002, ICSE2002, and in international journals, like the *Journal for Production Planning and Control* or the *Journal for Business Process Management*.

Edward W. N. Bernroider is assistant professor at the Vienna University of Economics and Business Administration, Institute of Information Processing in Austria. He holds a Master of Science degree in applied informatics from the University of Salzburg and a Ph.D. in business administration from the Vienna University of Economics and B.A., where he teaches in the undergraduate and MBA programs. His current research and industry projects focus on the international software industry, ERP systems and the evaluation of IT costs and benefits.

Andrew S. Borchers, DBA, serves as an associate professor of Information Systems at Kettering University (formerly, GMI Engineering and Management Institute) in Flint, Michigan, USA. Prior to entering full-time academic life, Andy spent 21 years working as an IT professional and manager for General Motors and Electronic Data Systems. His professional and academic interests are broad and include data management, e-commerce, networking and IT management topics. Andy holds academic degrees from Kettering, Vanderbilt and Nova Southeastern.

Andreas Borell is a master student at the School of Economics, Department of Informatics, Lund University, Sweden. He is a former employee of the dot.com world working for an old world enterprise. He has been jointly published in international conferences as well as books.

Farhad Daneshgar is a senior lecturer of Information Systems at the University of New South Wales, Australia. Prior to joining academia in 1994, he was an IT consultant in the building and telecommunications industries. He received his Ph.D. in Computer Science from the University of Technology, Sydney, and his current research interests include data mining, design of collaborative support systems and collaboration patterns in organizational processes. More recently he has been playing an important role in the design and commercialization of a new generation of Internet server appliance for SMEs that is based on virtually infinite word length processor.

Bernhard Deifel is scientist and the chair for Software and Systems Engineering at the Institut fuer Informatik of the Technische Universtitaet Muenchen (Germany) since 1996. Until 1995, he studied informatics at the University of Passau. Afterwards, he worked on concepts for rapid prototyping of embedded systems within BMW. He currently works within interdisciplinary research projects on Software Engineering in close cooperation with industry companies. His main focus is Requirements Engineering and Software Architectures. In Summer, 2001, he finished his Ph.D. on Requirements Engineering of complex commercial off-the-shelf software.

K. C. Desouza is a doctoral candidate and research associate at the Center for Research in Information Management at the University of Illinois at Chicago, USA. He has over a dozen papers published or forthcoming in journals such as Communications of the ACM, Competitive Intelligence Review, Business Horizons, International Journal of Healthcare Technology Management, and in various conference proceedings. His recent book, *Managing Knowledge with Artificial Intelligence,* was published by Quorum Books. He has a B.Sc. with distinctions in Accounting, and Information & Decision Sciences from the University of Illinois at Chicago, and an MBA with distinction in Information Management from the Stuart Graduate School of Business, Illinois Institute of Technology.

Aryya Gangopadhyay is an assistant professor of Information Systems at the University of Maryland, Baltimore County (UMBC), USA. He has a Ph.D. in Computer Information Systems from Rutgers University. His research interests include electronic commerce, data warehousing and mining, and geographic information systems. He has co-authored and edited three books, many book chapters, numerous papers in journals, such as *AI in Engineering, Decision Support Systems, Quarterly Journal of Electronic Commerce, IEEE Computer, IEEE Transactions on Knowledge and Data Engineering, Journal of Management Information Systems,* as well as presented papers in many national and international conferences. He can be reached at gangopad@ umbc.edu.

Narasimhaiah Gorla is an associate professor of Information Systems at Wayne State University, USA. He obtained his Ph.D. from University of Iowa, Iowa City. He obtained his MBA from Indian Institute of Management, Calcutta. He has over 28 years of experience in Information Systems – nine years in industry and 19 years in academia. His research interests include database/data warehouse design, data mining, software metrics, IS outsourcing, etc.

Paul Hawking is a senior lecturer in Information Systems at Victoria University, Melbourne, Australia. He has contributed to the *Journal of ERP Implementation and Management, Management Research News* and contributed many conference papers on IS theory and practice. He is responsible for managing the university's strategic alliance with SAP and is coordinator of the university's ERP Research Group. Dr. Hawking is the immediate past Chairperson of the SAP Australian User Group.

Jonas Hedman is a Ph.D. candidate at the School of Economics, Department of Informatics, Lund Universitym Sweden. He has been responsible for the development of their e-business management program and SAP university alliance program. He has been published in international conferences, accepted for publication in European Journal of Information Systems, recently co-published a book entitled *IT and Business Models: Concepts and Theories*, and has been an invited guest speaker at SAP University Alliance Congress.

Bonn-Oh Kim is an associate professor in the Department of Management and Director of the Center for Electronic Commerce and Information Systems at the Seattle University, USA. He holds Ph.D. and MBA degrees from the University of Minnesota and the University of Washington, respectively. His research interests include strategic and technical issues in corporate information systems.

Stefan Koch is an assistant professor of Information Business at the Vienna University of Economics and Business Administration, Austria. He received a MBA in Management Information Systems from Vienna University and Vienna Technical University, and a Ph.D. from Vienna University of Economics and Business Administration. Currently he is involved in the undergraduate and graduate teaching programs, especially in software project management and

ERP packages. His research interests include cost estimation for software projects, the open source development model, software process improvement, the evaluation of benefits from information systems and ERP systems.

M. R. Kraft has a diploma from the George F. Geisinger School of Nursing at the Geisinger Medical Center in Danville, Pennsylvania. Her Baccalaureate in Nursing is from the Frances Payne Bolton School of Nursing at Case Western Reserve University in Cleveland, Ohio. Her Master of Science is from the School of Nursing at Northern Illinois University in DeKalb, Illinois. She has a Ph.D. in Nursing from Loyola University, Chicago. Her areas of clinical practice include rehabilitation, geriatrics, spinal cord injury, and informatics. She is currently the Clinical Coordinator of the Decision Support System at the Edward Hines Jr. Veterans' Administration Hospital, USA.

Ted E. Lee is an assistant professor of MIS at The University of Memphis, USA. He received a M.S. in Computer Science from the Pennsylvania State University, and a Ph.D. in MIS from University of Nebraska. His research interests include knowledge engineering/management, database systems, and data warehousing/mining.

Ernest L. Nichols, Jr., is the director of the Center for Supply Chain Management in the FedEx Technology Institute and Associate Professor of Supply Chain and Operations Management at The University of Memphis, USA. Dr. Nichols research interests include a range of integrated supply chain management issues.

Robert Otondo, Ph.D., is an assistant professor of MIS at The University of Memphis, USA. He earned his Ph.D. from Arizona State University. Dr. Otondo's research interests include knowledge management, system dynamics, and computer-mediated communication.

Pattarawan Prasarnphanich is a doctoral candidate in the Management Information Systems Department at The University of Memphis. She received her MBA from Virginia Commonwealth University. Her research interests include organizational learning, team learning, electronic commerce, and information technology diffusion.

Frederic Rowohl is an external doctoral student at the Institute of Information Management, University of St. Gallen, Switzerland. He received his diploma in business economics from the University of St. Gallen in 2000. During his studies he worked as a junior assistant in the research project "Data Warehouse Strategy" at the Institute of Information Management, University of St. Gallen.

He is working at Bayer AG, Leverkusen, Germany. His research interests are in customer relationship management (CRM) and in enterprise application integration (EAI).

Joachim Schelp manages the research projects "Application Integration Management" and "Relationship Management Architecture" at the Institute of Information Management, University of St. Gallen, Switzerland. He is also working on his postdoctoral thesis ("Habilitation"). He holds a diploma in economics from the University of Bochum, Germany. He received his Ph.D. in economics, with a specialization in information management from the University of Bochum, Germany. His current research interests include strategic management of information technology, information technology architecture and infrastructure, relationship management, and the interfaces between business models, processes, and information systems.

Roel W. Schuring, Ph.D., is associate professor in the Management of Healthcare Organizations at the University of Twente, Enschede, The Netherlands since 2000. His particular research interest lies in the effective organization of healthcare processes and in the effective use of new technologies in these processes. He has a background in operations management. Various healthcare organizations cooperate in the research project of his team on both subjects. He did previous research projects on continuous improvement, autonomous work groups, innovation diffusion and organizational change.

Iftikhar U. Sikder is a doctoral candidate at the University of Maryland, Baltimore County, USA. His research interests include spatial database, probabilistic reasoning and machine learning. He has published in the *Information Resources Management Journal* and *International Journal of Aerospace Survey and Earth Sciences*. He has co-authored several book chapters. He can be reached at isikde1@umbc.edu.

Ton A. M. Spil, Ph.D., is assistant professor at the department of Technology & Management at the University of Twente, Enschede, The Netherlands. He is teaching in the area of Business Information Systems, mainly in project-based education. In 1988, he finished his master's in Computer Science and started his own company consulting big firms on strategic information systems planning. In 1996, he finished his Ph.D. thesis on the effectiveness of these plans, and after that he specialized in the application area healthcare and professional organizations. Since 2000, he has led various e-health research projects and he has been a track chair on HICSS.

Andrew Stein is a lecturer in the School of Information Systems in the Faculty of Business and Law at Victoria University, Melbourne, Australia. He has contributed to the *International Journal of Management, Journal of Information Management, Journal of ERP Implementation and Management, Management Research News* and contributed many conference papers on IS theory and practice. His research interests include enterprise systems, e-procurement applications, e-marketplace business models and reverse auction systems. He is a member of the university's ERP Research Group and the Australian SAP user group.

Aareni Uruthirapathy until recently worked as a policy analyst with the Department of Finance, Government of Canada. She previously taught Economics and Statistics at Methodist College, Sri Lanka. Aareni holds an MBA from Carlton University (Ottawa), as well as a B.Com from University of Colombo (Sri Lanka). Her area of concentration for the MBA program was Information Systems and Organizational Behavior. She intends to pursue a Ph.D. in the same area.

Index

New Titles from IGP!

Text Databases and Document Management: Theory and Practice
Amita Goyal Chin
Virginia Commonwealth University, USA

Text Database and Document Management: Theory and Practice brings insight to the multifaceted and inter-related challenges of the effectively utilized textual data and provides a focal point for researchers and professionals helping to create solutions for textual data management.

ISBN 1-878289-93-4(s/c); eISBN 1-930708-98-X • US$69.95; 256 pages • Copyright © 2001

Developing Quality Complex Database Systems: Practices, Techniques and Technologies
Shirley Becker
Florida Institute of Technology, USA

Developing Quality Complex Database Systems: Practices, Techniques and Technologies provides opportunities for improving today's database systems using innovative development practices, tools, and techniques. It shares innovative and groundbreaking database concepts from database professionals.

ISBN 1-878289-88-8 (s/c); eISBN 1-930708-82-3 • US$74.95; 374 pages • Copyright © 2001

IDEA GROUP PUBLISHING

Hershey • London • Melbourne • Singapore • Beijing

701 E. Chocolate Avenue, Hershey, PA 17033-1240 USA
Tel: (800) 345-4332 • Fax: (717)533-8661 • cust@idea-group.com